The Counseling Dictionary

CONCISE DEFINITIONS OF FREQUENTLY USED TERMS

THIRD EDITION

SAMUEL T. GLADDING

Wake Forest University

PEARSON

Boston   Columbus   Indianapolis   New York   San Francisco   Upper Saddle River
Amsterdam   Cape Town   Dubai   London   Madrid   Milan   Munich   Paris   Montreal   Toronto
Delhi   Mexico City   Sao Paulo   Sydney   Hong Kong   Seoul   Singapore   Taipei   Tokyo

Vice President and Editor in Chief: Jeffery W. Johnston
Senior Acquisitions Editor: Meredith D. Fossel
Editorial Assistant: Nancy Holstein
Senior Marketing Manager: Christopher D. Barry
Senior Managing Editor: Pamela D. Bennett
Senior Production Editor: Mary M. Irvin
Project Manager: Susan Hannahs

Senior Art Director: Jayne Conte
Cover Design: Suzanne Behnke
Cover Art: SuperStock
Full-Service Project Management and Composition: Sudip Sinha, Aptara®, Inc.
Text and Cover Printer/Bindery: R.R. Donnelley & Sons
Text Font: Garamond

Credits and acknowledgments borrowed from other sources and reproduced, with permission, in this textbook appear on appropriate page within text.

Every effort has been made to provide accurate and current Internet information in this book. However, the Internet and information posted on it are constantly changing, so it is inevitable that some of the Internet addresses listed in this textbook will change.

Library of Congress Cataloging-in-Publication Data
Gladding, Samuel T.
  The counseling dictionary : concise definitions of frequently used terms / Samuel T. Gladding. — 3rd ed.
    p. cm.
  Includes bibliographical references and index.
  ISBN-13: 978-0-13-705042-0 (alk. paper)
  ISBN-10: 0-13-705042-9 (alk. paper)
  1. Counseling—Dictionaries. 2. Psychotherapy—Dictionaries. I. Title.
  BF637.C6G5332 2010
  361'.0603—dc22

                                2010006021

10 9   V056 16 15 14

www.pearsonhighered.com

ISBN 10:   0-13-705042-9
ISBN 13: 978-0-13-705042-0

*To my graduate students in counseling at Fairfield University,
the University of Alabama at Birmingham (UAB),
and Wake Forest University
Who have taught me to be precise and concise with my words
and inspired me to be a better counselor.*

Preface

Behind every book there is a story, and this dictionary is no exception. The story is simple. Some years ago, one of my students asked me if I could give her a concise definition of a word often used in counseling. I thought I could provide a definition, but I told her I would consult the glossary of a leading book in the field to make sure the definition was concise. To my surprise, that book did not have a glossary. "No problem," I thought. "I'll go to another leading book in the field." That book had a glossary but did not include the word I needed. "Well, surely another major book in the field will have what I want," I thought. However, I was wrong again!

Not one to give up easily, I decided I would find a dictionary of counseling terms. Surely, going to an authoritative source would solve my problem and save me time. Well, I was incorrect once more. I found a lot of dictionaries for a number of professions, but when it came to counseling, I could locate only three. One had been published in the 1960s, one in the early 1980s, and the most recent one, published in the 1990s, contained fewer than 300 terms—but not the one I wanted. Wow! The task that I expected would be simple had turned out to be anything but that.

Thus the idea of my writing a dictionary of counseling was born. The purpose of this book is threefold. First, it is aimed at students and new professionals who are entering or have entered the profession of counseling and wish to better learn the language that goes with it. Second, this dictionary is intended to serve professors and practicing counselors as a quick reference source for commonly used counseling terms and historical contributors to the field. Finally, the dictionary is meant to be a resource to help laypersons discern what counselors and other helping professionals mean when they use specific words or refer to someone who influenced the development of counseling.

It is my hope that you will enjoy as well as benefit from this reference. If so, your frustration in finding concise descriptors of counseling terms may be alleviated. More important, your understanding of counseling and related mental health fields may be enhanced.

New to This Edition

More than 400 new terms have been added to this edition of *The Counseling Dictionary,* thus providing basic information on more than 3,000 words, names, and abbreviations often used or referred to in the profession of counseling. Moreover, new examples have been provided to help you as a reader better understand the definitions given. Words that are defined elsewhere in the dictionary are *italicized* when included in the definition of another term. Thus, if a reader does not understand an italicized word in a definition, it is easy to find an explanation of that word within the confines of the text. This dictionary also contains updated URLs of organizations and associations that can enrich your understanding in select areas of counseling.

Another new feature of this edition is that more names of prominent professionals who have influenced the development of counseling have been included. They are now found in Appendix A. Many of these names are of historical figures, but there are more names of contemporary counselors who have made and are still making contributions to the field. Because of the political sensitivity to being included or excluded from a work of this nature, I have purposefully tried to limit the number of my contemporaries. Thus, with a few rare exceptions, no one still living who is referred to in these pages is under 60 years of age, and a great many of the ones who are included are retired.

Another feature new to the third edition of *The Counseling Dictionary* is the inclusion of a list of self-help organizations in the United States, found in Appendix B. Often, professionals wish to make referrals or find information about such groups and run into difficulties securing the information they need, even when searching the Internet. The list in Appendix B describes these groups from "A," Adult Children of Alcoholics, to "W," Workaholics Anonymous.

Finally, I have updated in Appendix C highlights of key events in counseling and the American Counseling Association from the 1890s to 2010.

Acknowledgments

In writing this dictionary, I am indebted to my teachers, colleagues, students, and clients, both past and present. They are too numerous to name individually. However, some have been especially helpful in recent years. Anita Hughes, my assistant, read the initial drafts of this text and offered invaluable input and suggestions. Also providing me with excellent preliminary feedback were my colleagues in the Department of Counseling at Wake Forest University—Donna Henderson, Pamela Karr, John Anderson, and Debbie Newsome—and my graduate students, Mike Ryan, Paige Bentley, Dan Barnhart, Anne McMullan, and Katie Anne Burt. Outside reviewers for the first editions of this dictionary included Scott E. Gillig, Barry University; Jerry A. Mobley, Fort Valley State University; Jeannette Seaberry, University of Nebraska, Omaha; H. Lori Schnieders, Vanderbilt University; and Stephen R. Wester, University of Wisconsin–Milwaukee. I am also thankful to the reviewers of this more recent manuscript for their insights and helpful comments: Diana Gibb, George Mason University; Barbara O'Rourke, The University of Iowa; and Cynthia L. Trumbo, University of Louisville. Furthermore, I am indebted to my wife, Claire, and our children, Ben, Nate, and Tim. They made many interesting and constructive comments about this text. They allowed me as well to use our home computer in between their community correspondence, schoolwork assignments, instant messaging, e-mails, and blogging activities. Finally, I appreciate the fine professionals at Pearson, with whom I have been associated since the mid-1980s. My editor, Meredith Fossel, in particular has been encouraging and supportive. Mary Irvin, senior project manager, has also been wonderful to work with. Who could ask for more?

SAMUEL T. GLADDING

About the Author

Samuel T. Gladding is chair of and a professor in the Department of Counseling at Wake Forest University in Winston-Salem, North Carolina, where he has also served as the associate provost and assistant to the president. He has been a practicing counselor in both public and private agencies. His leadership in the field of counseling includes service as president of the American Counseling Association (ACA), the Association for Counselor Education and Supervision (ACES), the Association for Specialists in Group Work (ASGW), the American Association of State Counseling Boards (AASCB), and Chi Sigma Iota (counseling academic and professional honor society international).

Dr. Gladding is the former editor of the *Journal for Specialists in Group Work* and the author of over 30 books and 100 professional refereed publications. In 1999, he was cited as being in the top 1% of contributors to the *Journal of Counseling and Development* for 1978–1993. Some of his most recent books include *Counseling: A Comprehensive Profession* (6th ed.), *Groups: A Counseling Specialty* (5th ed.), *Family Therapy: History, Theory, & Practice* (5th ed.), *Counseling as an Art: The Creative Arts in Counseling* (3rd ed.), *Clinical Mental Health Counseling in Community and Agency Settings* (3rd ed., with Deborah W. Newsome), and *Becoming a Counselor: The Light, the Bright, and the Serious* (2nd ed.).

Gladding's previous academic appointments have been at the University of Alabama at Birmingham (UAB) and Fairfield University (Connecticut). He also worked as director of children's services in a mental health center and in a counseling private practice group. He received his degrees from Wake Forest (B.A., M.A. Ed.), Yale (M.A.R.), and the University of North Carolina–Greensboro (Ph.D.) and is a National Certified Counselor (NCC), a Certified Clinical Mental Health Counselor (CCMHC), and a Licensed Professional Counselor (North Carolina). Gladding is a member of the North Carolina Board of Licensed Professional Counselors and a trustee and chair of the American Counseling Association Foundation (ACAF). He is also a Fellow in the Association for Specialists in Group Work and the American Counseling Association.

Dr. Gladding is married to the former Claire Tillson and the father of three children—Ben, Nate, and Tim. Outside of counseling, he enjoys swimming, poetry, and humor.

Contents

Dictionary   1

Appendix A   Prominent Names
              in the Counseling
              Profession   167

Appendix B   Self-Help
              Organizations   181

Appendix C   Marker Events
              in the History
              of Counseling
              and the American
              Counseling
              Association   193

a

AA See *Alcoholics Anonymous*.

AABT See *Association for Advancement of Behavior Therapy*.

AACC See *American Association of Christian Counselors*.

AACD See *American Association for Counseling and Development*.

AACE See *Association for Assessment in Counseling and Education*.

AADA See *Association for Adult Development and Aging*.

AAMFT See *American Association for Marriage and Family Therapy*.

AAPC See *American Association of Pastoral Counselors*.

AARP See *American Association of Retired Persons*.

AASCB See *American Association of State Counseling Boards*.

AASECT See *American Association of Sex Educators, Counselors, and Therapists*.

AAT See *animal assisted therapy*.

AATA See *American Art Therapy Association*.

AB research design A simple time series *experimental research* design method in which a *baseline* (A) is established before an *intervention* strategy (B) is introduced.

ABAB research design A more complex and involved *experimental research* design than an AB simple time series *experiment*. In this *method*, a *baseline* (A) is established, followed by an *intervention* (B), which is then discontinued after a time, followed by a second baseline (A) and intervention (B). The ABAB research design is used to confirm that the *treatment* intervention (B) really had an effect on the *baseline behavior*.

abandonment **1.** The act of leaving a child alone, which is considered a form of child abuse. **2.** When a counselor terminates a client without informing the client of this fact.

A-B-C theory of personality Albert Ellis's *rational emotive behavior therapy (REBT) method* of conceptualizing the origin of human *feelings* and their resulting *behaviors*. In this model, A stands for an *objective* event or experience, B stands for a person's *thought*(s) or belief(s) about A, and C represents feeling(s) or *emotion*(s) resulting from the *thought*(s) in B. In this model, the thinking/belief aspect around an event is crucial in regard to the effective *outcome*. For example, if a person thinks s/he will be rejected when asking another person for a date, s/he may avoid asking the other person out.

ABCs of REBT

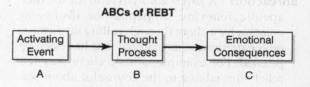

| Activating Event | Thought Process | Emotional Consequences |
| A | B | C |

A-B-C-D-E-F paradigm Albert Ellis's *rational emotive behavior therapy (REBT) method* of correcting illogical or *irrational thinking* and promoting and maintaining *change*. In this model, the A, B, and C are the same as in the *A-B-C theory of personality*. D is the counselor disputing any *irrational thoughts* or beliefs of the *client*. E refers to the presumed *consequences* of the counselor's *interventions*, that is, the client gaining a different *perception* of an event. F represents new *feelings* the client has in regard to the event or *situation* in A. To change a negative or nonproductive feeling, individuals need to think differently, such as in either a neutral or positive way. For example, if the individual thinks going to the dentist is "horrible," s/he may be encouraged to think of the experience as "just a checkup" or as a "preventive measure" to avoid greater pain later from a toothache. See also *rational emotive behavior therapy (REBT)*.

ability test   A *test* that measures the extent to which a person is presently functioning in a particular area, such as math. An ability test provides an estimate of what the person is capable of performing in regard to a certain task.

ableism   A type of discrimination that excludes people who have mental, emotional, behavioral, or physical disabilities.

abnormal   Functioning that is divergent or *maladaptive* from what is considered normal among a *population*, especially if the *behavior* is persistent. Abnormal is a culturally sensitive concept because what is considered appropriate in one society may not be seen as such in another. For example, looking people in the eye when speaking to them may be considered essential in some societies and inappropriate in others.

abreaction   A *psychoanalysis* term for the therapeutic relieving of painful or distressing *emotion* by a client through calling into awareness experiences or material that has been repressed. For example, a male client may feel relief after talking to the counselor about sexual fantasies he had about his sister when they were both adolescents.

absolutism   A term in Jean Piaget's *stage*s of *moral development* for the concern that children, beginning at about age 5, have about right and wrong and the *rules* of life. At this stage, children have absolute faith in the rules their parents have given them. For example, "never talk to a stranger."

abstract   **1.** A brief formal summary at the beginning of a *research* study or theoretical paper. **2.** The ability to understand symbolic concepts.

abstract reasoning   The ability to manipulate thoughts that include dealing with *situation*s that have not yet occurred, to use logical thought *process*es, and to develop symbolic *meaning*. For example, abstract reasoning has developed when persons can imagine what will happen if they make certain *choices* in life, such as following particular career paths.

absurdity   A statement that is half truthful and even silly if followed to its conclusion. For example, "I'll simply fall apart if my son acts that way again." *Counselors* sometimes work with individuals and families by using absurdities and exaggerating *client* statements to help them recognize realities. The use of absurdities is a favorite *method* of many *REBT* therapists.

abuse   **1.** All forms of *maltreatment* or improper *behavior* of one person or group by another (or on oneself), whether physical, sexual, behavioral, cognitive, economic, or emotional. **2.** The misuse of *substances*, such as alcohol or drugs, to the detriment of a person's physical, mental, spiritual, and moral health and well-being.

ACA   See *American Counseling Association*.

ACAF   See *American Counseling Association Foundation*.

ACC   See *Association for Creativity in Counseling*.

ACCA   See *American College Counseling Association*.

accent   Highlighting the last few words of a *client*'s statement. For example, if a client says, "The *situation* I'm in now is driving me crazy," the counselor might reply, "Driving you crazy?"

acceptance   **1.** Also known as *unconditional positive regard;* a deep and genuine caring for the *client* as a person; a prizing of the person just for being. Carl Rogers stated that acceptance is one of the three *necessary and sufficient conditions of counseling*. The other two are *congruence (genuineness)* and *empathy*. **2.** A simple acknowledgment by the counselor of the client's previous statement with a *response* such as "Yes" or "Uh-huh" that encourages the client to continue. See also *minimal encouragers*. **3.** Acknowledging what is happening in a counseling session as opposed to evaluating it. **4.** The final stage in *Elizabeth Kübler-Ross*'s five stages of *grief*. This stage is one of peace, almost devoid of *feeling*.

accommodation   **1.** The ability of a person or group to modify cultural ways to fit in better

with a new *environment* or another group.
2. The *process* in which a *counselor* joins with
a *client* to achieve a therapeutic alliance based
on the nature of the client. To accommodate,
counselors make personal adjustments, such as
modifying their speech patterns or *behavior*s.
3. Jean Piaget's term for the way children alter
their *thinking* when new experiences cannot
be incorporated through assimilation into their
intellectual frame*work;* for example, when a
child realizes that all women are not his or her
"mother." The opposite of *assimilation*.

accountability Documenting effectiveness
through the use of measured means such as
outcome research or *feedback*. To be responsible to their *clients* and the *profession, counselors* must be able to document that the
procedures and *method*s they use are effective, such as informing clients that the
treatment being used has been found to be
effective in 80% of similar kinds of cases.

accreditation An approval *process,* usually involving an academic program of study, in
which members of an outside agency authorized by a *profession,* such as *counseling,* in-
spect and certify that program training
standards as well as *practicum* and *internship*
site requirements are being met at or above a
minimum level. In counseling, approved programs of study are accredited by the *Council
for Accreditation of Counseling and Related
Educational Programs (CACREP).*

acculturation **1.** The ways people learn the
customs, beliefs, *behavior*s, and traditions of a
culture. **2.** The degree to which individuals
from *minority cultures* identify with or con-
form to the attitudes, *lifestyle*s, and *values* of
the *majority culture*. For example, a member
of a minority culture may act, dress, and speak
like persons from a majority culture in an attempt to fit in.

acculturation stress The psychological, so-
matic, and social difficulties that may accompany the acculturation process by a member
of a minority group.

ACEG See *Association for Counselors and Educators in Government.*

ACES See *Association for Counselor Education
and Supervision.*

ACGPA See *American Council of Guidance
and Personnel Associations.*

achievement The degree of success, accomplishment, attainment, or competence of a
person in a particular area. For example, an
individual may *score* at the 90th percentile on
a *standardized test*.

achievement test An instrument that measures an individual's degree of competence or
learning in regard to a given *subject* or skill
(e.g., the *National Counselor Examination*).

acid An abbreviated name for *lysergic acid
diethylamide (LSD)*.

ACoAs See *Adult Children of Alcoholics.*

ACPA See *American College Personnel Association.*

acquired culture Learned habits picked up
from others outside one's own *culture,* such
as shaking hands instead of bowing when
greeting someone.

**acquired immunodeficiency syndrome
(AIDS)** The most advanced phase of the
human immunodeficiency virus (HIV). AIDS
breaks down the body's immunization *system*
and is fatal. Both HIV infection and AIDS are
considered to be chronic illnesses and are
managed with both pharmaceutical therapies
(pharmacy *drug*s) and complementary (alternative) therapies. See also *human immunodeficiency virus (HIV)*.

acrophobia An exaggerated fear of being in
high places or being up in the air.

ACT See *American College Testing, Inc.*

acting "as if" An *Adlerian counseling technique* in which *client*s are instructed to act "as
if" they were the person they wanted to be, the
ideal person they envision. For instance, a person may act as if s/he is brave even if scared.

acting out **1.** A *psychoanalytic* term for the
direct or indirect *enactment* of *unconscious*
tensions or wishes by a *client* in the form of

disruptive or irrational *behavior*s. For example, a person may take a step backward every time the individual approaches a door. **2.** A term for the disruptive and inappropriate behavior(s) of children, such as a child running around a classroom when other children are seated as requested.

action   1. When a *client* translates *insight*s gained in *counseling* into a *change* in *behavior.* For example, a client may come to realize s/he can obtain more of what s/he desires in life by using the *assertiveness skills* learned in *counseling*. **2.** Slang for the act of gambling, placing a bet.

action bias   The tendency of a *client* to become mired in a *problem situation* because of the client's preference for reacting and following rather than acting and initiating. For example, instead of telling someone before the fact that s/he is upset with the way s/he is usually treated, the person may wait until s/he has been treated that way again and then complain.

action exercises   Sensory awareness *method*s or *guided imagery* used in the *warm-up* phase of a group session or a *psychodrama* to help members discover common themes within the group as well as to focus more on individual concerns.

action phase   1. When *client*s in *counseling* put *insight*s into action. **2.** The second part of a *psychodrama process* that involves the *enactment* of a *protagonist's* concerns. For example, the protagonist may tell someone how s/he feels about him or her rather than bottling up the *emotion.*

action research   *Research* that is *experience-near* and that focuses on resolving practical relevant *problem*s that *counselor*s routinely encounter, such as evaluating the effects of a psychoeducational program or *treatment* on *client*s. This type of research may not be as tightly controlled or as easily generalized as other types of research.

action stage   The *working stage* of individual, group, or family *counseling* in which *client*s focus on changing their *behavior*s. For example, clients may work on asking for what they want instead of being passive.

action therapy   A term for the *treatment* procedures that are based on direct alterations of *behavior,* such as *behavior modification.*

active imagination   A Jungian *technique* of analysis in which individuals actively focus on experiences or images such as in dreams or fantasies and report *change*s in these images or experiences as they concentrate on them.

active mastery   A concept from the *microcounseling supervision model (MSM)* that is defined as the ability to produce specific and intentional results from chosen *counseling* skills.

active listening   Attending to *verbal* and *nonverbal* aspects of a *client's* communication without judging or evaluating to encourage *trust,* client *self-disclosure,* and *exploration* within the counseling *relationship.* Hearing what is being implied as well as what is explicitly stated. For example, when a client says, "It's not the same for me anymore," s/he may be implying s/he is discouraged.

activity   1. Movement or *behavior,* including mental *process*es, on the part of a person. **2.** In *transactional analysis,* an activity is a way of structuring time that deals with external reality (e.g., *work*).

activity group guidance (AGG)   *Group guidance* that involves activities that are developmental in nature, for example, *learning* proper etiquette. AGG typically includes coordinated *guidance* topics.

activity theory of aging   The idea that adults who are older should remain as involved in life-satisfying activities as long as they desire. The opposite of the *disengagement theory of aging.*

actors   Individuals (also known as *auxiliaries*) who play the parts of important people or objects in a *psychodrama* play. With prompting from the *protagonist,* actors play the protagonist's *double,* an *antagonist,* or even a piece of furniture. In the same psychodrama, an auxiliary can play more than one part, such as being the protagonist's best friend and worst enemy.

actualizing tendency An innate tendency or *motivation* in human beings toward growth and the fulfilling of their potential—an important concept in the *person-centered counseling* theory of Carl Rogers and in *humanistic* approaches to *counseling*. See also *self-actualization*.

acute The relatively rapid or sudden onset of a condition, such as a *school phobia*, that is generally of brief duration (i.e., less than 6 months).

ADA See *Americans with Disabilities Act*.

adaptation See *adaptive behavior*.

adaptive behavior Also known as adaptation and adjustment; a *response* intended to deal positively with *changes* in one's *environment*, for example, working harder instead of complaining at certain times of the day when the workload picks up.

adaptive child A term in *transactional analysis theory* for the part of the *child ego state* that learns to adapt to the expectations of others to gain acceptance and approval, for example, being courteous to adults.

ADD See *Attention Deficit Disorder*.

addiction Psychological or physiological dependence on a *substance* (e.g., *alcohol*, tobacco, *cocaine*) or preoccupation on an activity (e.g., gambling, sex) to function. Addiction is characterized by increased *tolerance* to the *drug* or *behavior* and *withdrawal symptoms* when the substance or activity is unavailable.

addiction counseling *Counseling* that focuses on working with *clients* who have *addictions*.

adding cognitive constructions The *verbal* component of *structural family therapy* consisting of advice, information, pragmatic fictions, and *paradox*.

additive responses Empathetic *verbal responses* counselors give that add to a *client*'s understanding of a *situation*. For example, "and that frustrates you." Additive responses clarify *thoughts* and *feelings* as well as provide a fresh perspective of *meaning*.

ADHD See *Attention Deficit Hyperactivity Disorder*.

Adjective Checklist A pencil-and-paper *personality test* generally used with adults. The test contains 300 adjectives and measures 37 dimensions of *personality*. It is not timed but usually takes from 15 to 20 minutes.

adjourning The final *stage* in *group development*, when *counseling* comes to an end. Adjourning is also referred to as *mourning* and *termination*.

adjustment The degree of harmony between people and their *environments*, for example, being able to speak the predominant language spoken. Successful adjustment results in *adaptive behavior*; unsuccessful adjustment results in behavior that is *maladaptive*.

adjustment disorders A *DSM* category of *diagnosis* for people who are responding to either negative *stressors* (e.g., *divorce*) or positive stressors (e.g., marriage). Appropriate modifiers, such as "with depressed *mood*" or "with *anxiety*," must accompany the diagnosis. Impairment of persons under this category should have occurred within 3 months of the stressor(s). The diagnosis itself, which is considered among the mildest in the *DSM* classification, is time limited and must be *changed* after 6 months. Most individuals appropriately diagnosed with adjustment disorders respond well to *counseling*.

adjustment test A *personality test* that measures the ability of a person to function well in society and achieve personal *needs*.

Adlerian counseling An approach to *counseling* devised by Alfred Adler. It includes an emphasis on the family *constellation* (especially *birth order*), *fictions* (subjective *evaluations* about oneself or the environment), and an analysis of a *client*'s *lifestyle*. *Treatment* involves both the promotion of *insight* and reeducation with accompanying behavioral *changes*. See also *individual psychology*.

administrative (regulatory) law Specialized regulations passed by authorized government agencies that pertain to certain specialty areas, such as the *profession* of *counseling*.

a

administrative model   A model of providing student activities in which professionals in college administration (i.e., admissions, *records, food, health,* and *financial aid*) are put in charge of offering services.

adolescence   A term originated by G. Stanley Hall at the beginning of the 20th century for the age span between *childhood* and *adulthood* beginning at *puberty*. Adolescence is characterized as a period of transitions, a time of unevenness and *paradoxes* marked by physical, emotional, moral, and intellectual *change*. The basic challenge of adolescence according to Erik Erikson is to develop a *self-identity*. Failure to do so leads to *role confusion* and an *identity crisis*.

Adolescent Family Life Act (AFLA)   The first federal program devoted exclusively to addressing concerns about adolescent pregnancy. AFLA programs promote abstinence as a *primary prevention*.

ADTA   See *American Dance Therapy Association*.

Adult Children of Alcoholics (ACoAs)   Adults who, as children, spent part or all of their *childhood* in a stressful *family environment* in which one or more *caregivers* abused *alcohol*. Many ACoAs have special issues to resolve through *counseling*, such as establishing *trust* and establishing a clear *identity*. Many ACoAs suffer from similar emotional disorders, including *depression, anxiety,* low *self-esteem,* and *anger*.

adult ego state   A term in *transactional analysis* for the *objective* part of the *personality* that functions rationally in a planned and organized way. The *adult ego state* receives and *process*es materials from the *parent ego state* and the *child ego states* as well as the *environment* and makes decisions based on available information.

adulthood   A somewhat nebulous term implying that a person has reached physical, mental, social, and emotional maturity. Adulthood encompasses a wide *range* of ages, from 18 years and up. It is usually broken down into early, middle, and late periods. According to Erik Erikson, the challenge of *young adulthood* is to achieve *intimacy* (i.e., a sharing of *self* in a close *relationship* with others). A failure to do so leads to *isolation*. The challenge of *middle adulthood* is to become *generative* (i.e., to create and become productive through one's *career, family,* or *leisure* time). A failure to achieve *generativity* leads to *stagnation*. Finally, according to Erikson, the task of late adulthood is to achieve a sense of *integrity* (i.e., acceptance of life in all its multiple dimensions). The opposite of such an accomplishment is *despair*.

advance beneficiary notice (ABN)   A written notice that a physician must give a *Medicare patient* before materials or services are provided.

advanced empathy   A *process* in which the *counselor* gets at *feelings* and *meanings* in the *client*'s life that are hidden or beyond the immediate awareness of the client. Advanced empathy goes beyond what has been stated to what is implied. Sometimes advanced empathy is expressed in the identification of and/or *linking* of *themes* in the client's life, such as *anxiety*. See also *primary empathy*.

adverse   A negative or unwanted condition or side effect.

advice   A suggestion or recommendation. For example, "I think you should take the *job* and move."

advice giving   Instructing or providing someone with information or recommendations about what to do in a particular *situation*. Advice was one of the main *techniqu*es of E. G. Williamson and his *directive counseling approach* of the 1930s. Advice giving was challenged as a technique by Carl Rogers because of its tendency to promote *client dependency* and interfere with the client's growth. Advice is used sparingly in most counseling approaches today. It is employed mainly in *crisis* situations in which it either prevents clients from engaging in destructive acts or gives clients something beneficial to do when they are not able to generate constructive plans of action because of being overwhelmed by *trauma*. Advice giving, if not used judiciously, prevents clients from struggling with their own *thoughts*, *feelings*, and *behaviors*.

advocacy Actively working for, supporting, or espousing a cause or person(s) (e.g., lobbying, writing, petitioning, speaking, or politicking). Advocacy occurs on many levels (e.g., local, state, national). *Counselors* advocate for the welfare of their *clients* and the *profession* of *counseling*.

advocacy counseling Counseling that includes *outreach*, *empowerment*, and *social action*.

Advocates for Youth A national organization that champions efforts to help young people make informed and responsible decisions about their reproductive and sexual health (www.advocatesforyouth.org).

affect Pertaining to *emotion, feeling, mood,* a person's overt emotional state. Affect is a primary emphasis of some *counseling* approaches.

affect blocks Rollo May and Irvin Yalom's term for places where a *client* gets emotionally stuck, for example, not being able to get over his/her anger. Affect blocks are like roadblocks in the journey of life.

affect disorder Also known as *mood disorder;* a *disorder* associated with inappropriate expression of *emotion* (e.g., *depression*).

affective-oriented counseling Theories in *counseling,* such as *Gestalt therapy,* that focus on making an impact on *clients'* *emotions* to bring about *change.* The *objective* is to arouse, handle, and/or modify emotional *responses* in clients.

affiliation A positive emotional *relationship* with someone (e.g., it might include smiling and talking) but without attachment.

affirmation When a *counselor* affirms the correctness of information or encourages a *client's* efforts at self-determination. For example, the counselor might state, "That's helpful new information" or "You seem to be gaining more control."

AFLA See *Adolescent Family Life Act.*

African Americans People in the United States whose ancestors came from Africa. African Americans constituted approximately 13% of the total *population* of the United States in 2010.

AFTA See *American Family Therapy Association.*

aftercare Any *follow-up* or continued care services given to *clients* after their release from *counseling.* For example, individuals released from *mental health* facilities are often seen in aftercare groups periodically.

age discrimination The unfair *treatment* of individuals based on their age.

age norms *Scores* or *values* on *tests* that represent the typical or average *performance* of individuals at certain chronological *ages,* for example, age 12.

ageism The untrue assumption that *chronological age* is the primary determinant of human characteristics. People who practice ageism *stereotype* and discriminate against older people.

aggression Any behavior—verbal, physical, relational—directed at an individual or group with the intention of causing harm.

aging A biological and psychological *phenomenon* composed of physiological *changes* as well as a mental *process* of considering oneself older. See also *gerontology.*

AGLBIC See *Association for Gay, Lesbian, and Bisexual Issues in Counseling.*

agoraphobia An exaggerated and irrational fear of being in an unfamiliar place or of leaving one's home.

AGPA See *American Group Psychotherapy Association.*

aha reaction A sudden *insight* into one's *situation* or *environment;* it may be accompanied by the exclamation of the word "aha."

AHEAD The *Association for Humanistic Education and Development.* The name has been modified to include the word *"counseling"* before "association." See *Counseling Association for Humanistic Education and Development (C-AHEAD).*

a

ahistorical counseling　*Theories* or *techniques* of *counseling* that focus on the present and not the past.

AIDS　See *Acquired Immune Deficiency Syndrome.*

Al-Anon　A voluntary *mutual-help group* organization founded in 1951. It is comprised of relatives of alcohol abusers who meet regularly to discuss common *problems*. The Al-Anon World Service Office is located at 1600 Corporate Landing Parkway, Virginia Beach, VA 23454 (http://www.al-anon.alateen.org/).

Albert Ellis Institute　Formerly known as the *Institute for Rational-Emotive Therapy;* a not-for-profit educational organization founded in 1968 to promote *rational emotive behavior therapy (REBT)*. The institute is located at 45 E. 65th Street, New York, NY 10021 (800-323-4738; http://www.REBT.org/).

alcohol　Also known as ethyl alcohol (ethanol); a clear liquid with a bitter taste that acts as a *depressant,* to which someone can become physically addicted. Alcohol is the most widely used *drug* in the United States. When abused, it can detrimentally affect almost every organ in the body. *Withdrawal symptoms* are often severe. See also *alcoholism; delirium tremens.*

Alcoholics Anonymous (AA)　An organization that helps *alcohol* abusers gain and maintain control of their lives by remaining sober. Established in the late 1930s, there is a dependence within the AA program on a higher power outside oneself. Much of the work of Alcoholics Anonymous is carried out in *self-help groups*. AA's address is P.O. Box 459, Grand Central Station, New York, NY 10163 (212-870-3400; http://www.aa.org/). See also *self-help groups.*

alcoholism　The chronic abuse of and compulsive increased use and *tolerance* of *alcohol*. Alcoholism is considered a progressive disease in which the *client* becomes physically and psychologically dependent on drinking alcohol.

alexia　The loss of ability to understand written words and/or sentences.

alienation　*Feelings* of being estranged or cut off from a *group;* a term often used for the separation of persons from their cultural groups.

alignments　The ways *family* members join together or oppose one another in carrying out a family activity; for instance, siblings may band together against their parents.

alloplastic approach　An *adjustment* to a culturally different *environment* through confronting obstacles in the environment and changing them. The opposite of the *autoplastic approach*.

all-or-nothing thinking　A type of *cognitive distortion* characterized by assuming that things are either absolutely perfect or absolutely terrible.

alpha error　See *Type I error.*

alter ego　A *psychodrama* term for another version of oneself, usually the opposite of oneself.

alternate form　A different but comparable form of a *standardized test,* such as *achievement tests* or *aptitude tests*. If a person is tested twice, the second test can consist of the alternate form of the first test.

alternative hypothesis　A possible *outcome* in *research* not covered by the *null hypothesis*.

alternative narratives　A *process* in *narrative therapy* of exploring strengths, special abilities, and aspirations to construct a positive story with good *outcomes* rather than a *problem*-saturated story.

altruism　Being concerned for others rather than oneself; sharing experiences and *thoughts* with others; *helping* others by giving of one's *self* unselfishly; working for the common good.

Alzheimer's disease　An organic mental disease, occurring mostly in older people, characterized by disorientation, forgetfulness, confusion, and *mood* swings.

ambivalence　When an individual experiences two opposite *feelings* at the same time, for example, wanting help and being afraid to ask for it.

AMCD   See *Association for Multicultural Counseling and Development.*

American Art Therapy Association (AATA)   The primary association for promoting the visual arts therapies in the United States. AATA is located at 1202 Allanson Road, Mundelein, IL 60060 (847-949-6064; http://www.arttherapy.org/). See also *art therapy.*

American Association for Counseling and Development (AACD)   The name of the *American Counseling Association (ACA)* from 1984 to 1992.

American Association for Marriage and Family Therapy (AAMFT)   The oldest and largest association for couple and *family counseling* in the United States, established in 1942. AAMFT is located at 1133 NW 15th Street, Suite 300, Washington, DC 20005 (202-452-0109; http://www.aamft.org).

American Association of Christian Counselors (AACC)   An interdisciplinary association of professional helpers, religious leaders, and lay counselors "committed to integrating biblical truth with practical counseling principles." AACC's address is P.O. Box 739, Forest, VA 24551 (800-526-8673; http://www.aacc.net).

American Association of Pastoral Counselors (AAPC)   An association that represents and sets professional standards for pastoral *counselors* and *pastoral counseling* centers in the United States. Founded in 1963, AAPC is nonsectarian in nature and practice. AAPC is located at 9504-A Lee Highway, Fairfax, VA 22031-2303 (703-385-6967; http://www.aapc.org).

American Association of Retired Persons (AARP)   A leading *advocacy group* for people ages 50 and above, AARP seeks to influence social and political activities that affect the aging and aged. The address is 601 E. Street NW, Washington, DC 20049 (http://www.aarp.org/).

American Association of Sexuality Educators, Counselors, and Therapists (AASECT)   A multidisciplinary organization dedicated to informing the public about and promoting healthy expressions of human sexuality and setting standards for *counseling* professionals who treat sexual dysfunction. AASECT's address is P.O. Box 1960, Ashland, VA 23005-1960 (804-752-0026; http://www.aasect.org).

American Association of State Counseling Boards (AASCB)   An association of state counseling boards whose members meet regularly to coordinate efforts at uniformity and discuss issues pertaining to the regulation of counseling (http://www.aascb.org/).

American College Counseling Association (ACCA)   A division of the *American Counseling Association (ACA)* that fosters student development in higher education (http://www.collegecounseling.org/).

American College Personnel Association (ACPA)   An association of professionals employed in the field of student affairs. ACPA is located at 1 Dupont Circle, Suite 300, Washington, DC 20036 (202-835-2272; http://www.myacpa.org).

American College Testing, Inc. (ACT)   An independent, nonprofit organization that provides educational services to students and their parents, to high schools and colleges, to *professional associations* and government agencies, and to business and industry. ACT is best known for its college admissions testing program. The address is P.O. Box 168, 2201 North Dodge Street, Iowa City, IA 52243-0168 (319-337-1028; http://www.act.org/).

American Council of Guidance and Personnel Associations (ACGPA)   A loose confederation of organizations that was concerned with educational and vocational *guidance* as well as other personnel activities. ACGPA operated from 1935 to 1952 and was a forerunner of the *American Counseling Association* (ACA).

American Counseling Association (ACA)   The largest professional *counseling* association in the world, founded in 1952. ACA is located at 5999 Stevenson Avenue, Alexandria, VA 22304 (800-347-6647; 703-823-9800; http://www.counseling.org/).

American Counseling Association Code of Ethics   The American Counseling Association has a *code of ethics* that each member of the association is expected to follow. The first code was initiated by Donald Super in 1961. Since that time the code has been revised five times: 1974, 1981, 1988, 1995, and 2005. See *Code of Ethics.*

American Counseling Association Foundation (ACAF)   A foundation that focuses on preserving and enhancing the *counseling profession* through work in advocacy, *research,* and professional standards. ACAF is located at 5999 Stevenson Avenue, Alexandria, VA 22304 (703-823-9800; http://www.acafoundation.org/).

American Dance Therapy Association (ADTA)   The primary association in the United States working to establish and maintain high standards of professional education and competence in the field of *dance/movement therapy.* ADTA is located at 2000 Century Plaza, Suite 108, 10632 Little Patuxent Parkway, Columbia, MD 21044 (410-9974040; http://www.ADTA .org). See also *dance/movement therapy.*

American Family Therapy Academy (AFTA)   An association that was formed in 1977 by Murray Bowen and is identified as an academy of about 1,000 advanced professionals interested in the exchange of ideas in the field of *family therapy.* AFTA is located at 1608 20th Street, NW, 4th Floor, Washington, DC 20009 (202-483-8001; http://www.afta.org/).

American Group Psychotherapy Association (AGPA)   A psychoanalytically oriented organization established by Samuel R. Slavson in 1943. AGPA is located at 25 East 21st Street, 6th Floor, New York, NY 10010 (212-477-2677; http://www.groupsinc.org/).

American Mental Health Counselors Association (AMHCA)   A division of the *American Counseling Association (ACA)* that represents and advocates for *mental health counselors* in many behavioral health settings. AMHCA is located at 801 N. Fairfax Street, Suite 304, Alexandria, VA 22314 (800-326-2642; http:// www.amhca.org/).

American Music Therapy Association (AMTA)   Founded in 1998, AMTA's purpose is the progressive development of the therapeutic use of music in *rehabilitation,* special education, and community settings. Predecessors of the American Music Therapy Association include the *National Association for Music Therapy* founded in 1950 and the *American Association for Music Therapy* founded in 1971. AMTA's address is 8455 Colesville Road, Suite 1000, Silver Spring, MD 20910 (301-589-3300; http://www .musictherapy.org/). See also *music therapy.*

American Personnel and Guidance Association (APGA)   Formed in 1952 as an interest group from the *American Council of Guidance and Personnel Associations (ACGPA),* APGA operated from 1952 to 1984 as an evolving professional *counseling* association. APGA later was renamed the *American Association for Counseling and Development (AACD)* (1984–1992) and the *American Counseling Association (ACA)* (1992 to present).

American Psychiatric Association (APA)   An association of medical specialists that includes physicians who specialize in the *diagnosis* and *treatment* of mental and emotional illnesses and *substance* use *disorder*s. APA is located at 1000 Wilson Boulevard, Suite 1825, Arlington, Va. 22209-3901 (703-907-7300; http://www .psych.org).

American Psychoanalytic Association (APA)   A professional organization of *psychoanalysts* located throughout the United States and a regional association of the *International Psychoanalytical Association.* APA is located at 309 E. 49th Street, New York, NY 10017 (212-752-0450; http://www.apsa.org).

American Psychological Association (APA)   Founded in 1892, the American Psychological Association is the largest professional group for *psychologists* in the world. APA's address is 750 First Street, NE, Washington, DC 20002 (202-336-5500; http://www.apa.org).

American Red Cross   Founded in 1881 by Clara Barton, the American Red Cross is the premier emergency response organization in the United States. Its aim is the prevention and relieving of suffering. It provides assistance in five areas: community services that help the needy; support and comfort for military members and their families; the collection, processing, and distribution of lifesaving blood and blood products; educational programs that promote health and safety; and international relief and development programs. The American Red Cross National Headquarters is 2025 E Street, NW, Washington, DC 2000 (202-303-5000; http://www.redcross.org).

American Rehabilitation Counseling Association (ARCA) A division of the *American Counseling Association (ACA)* that is devoted to enhancing the development of people with disabilities and promoting excellence in *rehabilitation counseling* (http://www.arcaweb.org/).

American School Counselor Association (ASCA) A division of the *American Counseling Association (ACA)* that promotes excellence in professional *school counseling* and the development of all students. ASCA's address is 801 North Fairfax Street, Suite 310, Alexandria, VA 22314 (800-306-4722 [4SCA]; http://www.schoolcounselor.org/). See also *school counseling*.

American Society of Group Psychotherapy and Psychodrama (ASGPP) A professional *group* association established by Jacob L. Moreno in 1942. ASGPP is located at 301 North Harrison Street, Suite 508, Princeton, NJ 08540 (609-452-1339; http://www.asgpp.org/). See also *psychodrama*.

Americans with Disabilities Act (ADA) A *law* enacted by Congress in 1990 that heightened awareness of the *need*s of the millions of people in the United States with disabilities. The ADA increased national efforts in providing multiple services for those with mental, behavioral, and physical disabilities. This act extended to people with a *disability* the same protection and guarantees given to minorities in the Civil Rights Act of 1964.

AMHCA See *American Mental Health Counselors Association*.

amnesia The *loss* of memory, either total or partial.

amphetamines A class of *stimulant* drugs that temporarily energize, increase mental alertness, produce a sense of euphoria, ward off sleep, and reduce fatigue. Amphetamines are also known as *uppers, speed, beans*, and *bennies*. Amphetamines are addictive and can cause *anxiety,* restlessness, headaches, rapid heartbeat, and difficulty breathing.

amplify To emphasize statements made by the *protagonist* in a *psychodrama*. Examples include verbalizing *nonverbal* communications, *questioning* one's *self,* interpreting statements for what is being said and not said, contradicting *feelings*, self-observing, and *denial*.

AMTA See *American Music Therapy Association*.

anal stage The second *stage* of Freud's stages of *psychosexual development*. In this stage, children (between the ages of 18 months and 3 years) obtain erotic pleasure from withholding and eliminating feces. Toilet training is a major experience during this time, and children's personalities are influenced by the ways in which their parents respond to them as they master this task.

analogies test A type of *test* that requires respondents to complete sentences that compare different *situation*s or things with each other. For example, a rose is to a bush, as a leaf is to a _____. *Miller's Analogy Test* is the best known of this type of test.

analysis **1.** An abbreviated term for *psychoanalysis*. **2.** An *evaluation* of a concern in *counseling* such as to do an analysis of a *client*'s *problem*. **3.** The *interpretation* of *data* through the use of statistical *test*s. **4.** The first step in E. G. Williamson's *directive counseling* approach. It involves the collection of data on a client.

analysis of variance (ANOVA) An *inferential statistics* procedure used to *test* the *null hypothesis* that the *means* of two or more *populations* are equal to each other. Often, these groups represent *performance* on a *dependent variable* as a result of *treatment* by one or more *independent variables*. ANOVA can be used to *test* the significance of mean differences among several groups simultaneously.

analyst   A practitioner of *psychoanalysis*.

analytical psychology   Carl Jung's approach to *therapy* that begins with an *exploration* of a *client*'s *conscious* state and proceeds to explore and interpret a client's *unconscious* mind, for example, dreams, fantasies.

androcentricism   The practice of placing the masculine view, or men, at the center of one's view of the world, culture, and history.

androgyny   The coexistence and display of what are considered male and female characteristics in the same person. The flexible *integration* in a person of traditional masculine and feminine characteristics, for example, strong and gentle.

anecdotal record   An informal notation about a person, *group, family,* or *situation* in which a standard record reporting form is not used.

angel dust   See *phencyclidine hydrochloride*.

anger   **1.** A strong feeling of annoyance, displeasure, antagonism, irritation, or rage. **2.** The second stage in the grief process as outlined by Elizabeth Kübler-Ross.

angst   A German word meaning anxiety or psychic pain.

anima   A Jungian *archetype* term for the feminine component of the male *personality*.

animal assisted therapy (AAT)   The integration of qualified animals, most commonly dogs and horses, into counseling sessions as therapeutic agents. Many clients, especially children, relate positively to animals and make significant progress in their presence. Boris Levinson is credited with discovering the therapeutic effects of animal assisted therapy.

animus   A Jungian *archetype* for the masculine component of the female *personality*.

anomie   A state of normlessness or the elimination or reduction of *values,* mores, and *norms,* and codes of conduct. Anomie usually occurs in rapidly changing societies that are subject to much *stress*.

anonymity   Protecting participants in a study from risk of harm by ensuring that their identities or any identifying information about them is not revealed.

anorexia nervosa   An *eating disorder* that primarily affects young women; it involves an avoidance of food and severe weight loss based on a distorted *perception* of one's *self* as being fat or overweight. Physical harm such as malnutrition or even death results from untreated anorexia.

ANOVA   See *analysis of variance*.

Antabuse   The trade name for the *drug* disulfiram. Antabuse causes nausea when introduced into the bloodstream of someone who has consumed *alcohol*. It is used in recovery programs to discourage drinking in recovering alcohol abusers.

antecedent   An event that precedes a *behavior* and is thought to influence it.

antecedent-response-consequence (A-R-C) model of behaviorism   A behavioral model that proposes *behavior* is functionally related to its *antecedent* and *consequent* events. Behaviors become more frequent or are suppressed, depending on what precedes or follows them.

anticathexes   A Freudian term for the control or restraint exercised by the *ego* over the *id* to keep id impulses out of *consciousness*.

antidepressant   A drug such as Zoloft, Imipramine, or Prozac or an herb such as St.-John's-wort that helps to reduce or eliminate depression and improve a person's mood. Antidepressant medications contain selective serotonin reuptake inhibitors.

antideterministic   A *humanistic* approach that proposes that each person is able to *change* and become responsible for his or her own life. This view is the opposite of the *psychoanalytic* view that *psychosexual* influences determine people's *behavior*s.

antisocial personality disorder   A *disorder* characterized by irresponsible *behavior*, low *tolerance* for *frustration*, frequent *conflict*s, lack of remorse or acknowledged responsibility for one's actions, and a low level of *socialization*. Someone with this disorder is sometimes referred to as a *psychopath* or *sociopath*.

antiwork group See "*BA*" (basic assumption) activity.

anxiety Mental and physical nervousness and uneasiness, often resulting in increased tension, usually associated with pressure to please, fear of failure, or fear of the unknown. Anxiety may be connected with concrete events or be free floating and not attached to any one particular thing.

anxiety disorders *Disorders* characterized by a chronic state of tension, uneasiness, worry, and fear that is reoccurring and has no known source or cause. The *DSM* classifies *phobia*s, *compulsive disorder, panic disorders, posttraumatic stress disorder,* and acute and general anxiety disorders in this category.

anxiolytics Anti-*anxiety* drugs.

ANWC See *Association for Non-White Concerns*.

APA See *American Psychiatric Association; American Psychoanalytic Association; American Psychological Association.*

apathy Indifference, a lack of emotion, a common symptom of depression.

APGA See *American Personnel and Guidance Association.*

applied behavior analysis The use of *reinforcement, punishment, extinction, stimulus control,* and other procedures derived from laboratory *research* to human interactions in a pragmatic way.

applied research *Research* conducted for the purpose of applying or testing a *theory* and evaluating its usefulness in solving specific *client* or *system problem*s. It is the opposite of *basic research*.

appraisal Assessing or evaluating an individual, group, family, or situation.

approach reaction The tendency of an individual to move toward a *situation* or issue regardless of whether it is positive or negative. An approach reaction is a positive sign; people who display it tend to work through difficulties.

approach-approach conflict When a person must choose between two equally attractive options, for example, getting married or taking an exciting *job* in a new exotic location.

approach-avoidance conflict When a person must choose between an option that is attractive and one that is not, for example, eating a dessert or going to the dentist.

appropriateness **1.** *Behavior* or conduct that is at an expected age or *stage* level. **2.** When *factor*s extraneous to the purpose and nature of a *test,* such as testing conditions, have no influence on a *client*'s performance or *response* to the test.

approval Support, usually given in a *verbal* way by a *counselor,* of a *client*'s *behavior* or action.

APT See *Association for Play Therapy*.

aptitude Specific capacities and abilities required of an individual to learn or adequately perform a *job* or task; the potential for acquiring a skill.

aptitude test A type of ability test, a standardized *measurement* device used to assess the readiness of someone to learn and become proficient in a given area in the future. The *Armed Services Vocational Aptitude Battery (ASVAB),* the *General Aptitude Test Battery (GATB),* and the *Miller Analogies Test* are examples of aptitude tests.

Arab Americans Individuals whose ancestry is from one of the 22 countries in the Arab Middle East that make up the League of Arab States. Arab Americans are a diverse group of at least 3 million individuals who are Christian and Muslim, foreign and native born. Mental health concerns may be reported as physical ailments, and a medical model, where the *counselor* is the expert, may prove most effective.

arbitrary inferences Conclusions people make about situations without knowing facts.

A-R-C model of behaviorism See antecedent-*response-consequence* (A-R-C) model of *behaviorism.*

ARCA See *American Rehabilitation Counseling Association.*

archetypes A Jungian concept that refers to the inherited primordial images of the *collective* *unconscious* that have accumulated over generations of human experience. Major archetypes are the *anima* and *animus*. Other archetypes include the Great Mother, the Wise Old Man, the Trickster, the Divine Child, rebirth, wholeness, and God. Archetypes that influence the development of the *personality* include the *persona*, the *shadow*, the *animus*, the *anima*, and the *self*.

arithmetic mean   The sum of a set of *scores* divided by the number of scores. See also *mean*.

Armed Service Vocational Aptitude Battery (ASVAB)   A multiple *aptitude test* first developed in 1966 and revised periodically since. The ASVAB measures aptitude for general academic areas and for military and civilian *work*. The test is used in Grade 11 and higher.

Army Alpha and Army Beta tests   Two of the earliest *intelligence tests* created in the United States. These tests were used to screen recruits during World War I. The Alpha test was given to recruits who were literate; the Beta test was given to inductees who were illiterate.

art therapy   The systematic use of art media, images, and creative art *process*es as a primary or adjunct means to bring about therapeutic *change*. To conduct art therapy, *counselors* must receive specialized training in this area. See also *American Art Therapy Association (AATA)*.

artistic people   Individuals, according to Holland's career typology, who enjoy working in creative environments that require imagination, originality, and independence (e.g., drama, music, writing, art, dance, crafts). See *RIASEC*.

as if   See *acting "as if."*

ASCA   See *American School Counselor Association*.

ASERVIC   See *Association for Spiritual, Ethical, and Religious Values in Counseling*.

ASGPP   See *American Society of Group Psychotherapy and Psychodrama*.

ASGW   See *Association for Specialists in Group Work*.

Asian American/Pacific Islander   A resident of the United States whose background and

identity are with peoples of Asia and the Pacific Islands (e.g., the Chinese, Japanese, Filipinos, Vietnamese, Koreans, Samoans, Thais, and Indians). There is tremendous heterogeneity within this *population*. It is the third largest ethnic *minority* group in the United States.

asking the question   An *Adlerian counseling intervention* in which *client*s are asked the question, "What would be different if you were well?" The question is often asked during the initial *interview* in Adlerian counseling.

asocial behavior   *Behavior* that is indifferent to people or social *norms* and *values*.

aspirational ethics   The highest level of conduct toward which a *counselor* may aspire. Counselors are guided by aspirational ethics when they make choices in accordance with higher principles behind the literal meaning of ethical codes.

assertiveness   Asking for what one wants in a timely and appropriate manner. Assertiveness is in contrast to either passive or aggressive *behavior*s.

assertiveness training   Training designed to help either aggressive or passive people learn how to ask for what they want or *need* in a timely and appropriate manner. The major tenet of assertiveness training is that people should be free to express their *thought*s and *feelings* appropriately without undue *anxiety* or anger. Assertiveness training involves *counterconditioning* through *role playing* and *modeling* as well as instruction.

assessment   Collecting *data*, such as those found through administering *tests* or *inventories*, and evaluating the data and/or utilizing behavioral observations to gain information and make decisions about the *diagnosis, treatment*, and possible *outcome* of a *counseling situation*.

assimilation   **1.** The process of becoming part of the *culture* in which one lives by adopting the *values* and *norms* of the majority *population*. **2.** In Jean Piaget's *theory*, the incorporation of an experience in one's *environment* into an already existing *thought* structure. It is the opposite of *accommodation*.

Association for Adult Development and Aging (AADA) A division of the *American Counseling Association (ACA)* that addresses concerns in *counseling* and *development* across the human *life span* (http://www.aadaweb.org/).

Association for Assessment in Counseling and Education (AACE) A division of the *American Counseling Association* (ACA). As an organization of counseling professionals, AACE provides leadership, training, and *research* in the creation, development, production, and use of assessment and diagnostic *techniques* (http://www.theaaceonline.com/). When it was chartered in 1965, AACE was known as the *Association for Measurement and Evaluation in Guidance*.

Association for Behavioral and Cognitive Therapies (ABCT) A professional, interdisciplinary organization that is concerned with the application of behavioral and cognitive sciences in understanding and enhancing human *behavior*. ABCT is located at 305 Seventh Avenue, 16th Floor, New York, NY 10001-6008 (212-647-1890; http://www.abct.org/).

Association for Counselor Education and Supervision (ACES) A division of the *American Counseling Association* (ACA) composed primarily of counselor educators. ACES emphasizes the *need* for quality education and *supervision* of counselors in all *work* settings (http://www.acesonline.net/). ACES was one of four groups that founded the *American Personnel and Guidance Association* in 1952. Its original name was the *National Association of Guidance and Counselor Trainers*.

Association for Counselors and Educators in Government (ACEG) A division of the *American Counseling Association* (ACA) that attends to counseling and educational concerns of professionals in local, state, and federal government and military-related agencies (http://www.dantes.doded.mil/dantes_web/organizations/aceg/index.htm).

Association for Creativity in Counseling (ACC) A division of the *American Counseling Association* (ACA) that promotes creativity and the use of the *creative arts* in *counseling* (http://www.creativecounselor.org/).

Association for Gay, Lesbian, and Bisexual Issues in Counseling (AGLBIC) A division of the *American Counseling Association* (ACA) that educates and promotes sensitivity among counselors on issues related to *gay, lesbian,* and *bisexual client*s (http://www.aglbic.org/).

Association for Humanistic Education and Development (AHEAD) See *Counseling Association for Humanistic Education and Development (C-AHEAD)*.

Association for Humanistic Psychology An international, multidisciplinary association of professionals who share humanistic values and are dedicated to people's growth and positive actions (http://www.ahpweb.org/).

Association for Measurement and Evaluation in Guidance The original name for the *Association for Assessment in Counseling and Education (AACE)*.

Association for Multicultural Counseling and Development (AMCD) A division of the *American Counseling Association* (ACA) that emphasizes leadership, *research,* training, and development of *multicultural counseling* professionals. AMCD focuses on racial and ethnic issues in *counseling* (http://www.amcdaca.org/).

Association for Non-White Concern (ANWC) The forerunner of the *Association for Multicultural Counseling and Development*. ANWC was founded in 1972.

Association for Play Therapy (APT) An international organization dedicated to the advancement of *play therapy*. APT is interdisciplinary and eclectic in orientation. It defines play therapy as "a distinct group of *intervention*s that use play as an integral component of the therapeutic *process*." APT's address is 2100 North Winery Avenue, Suite 104, Fresno, CA 93703-2884 (209-252-2APT; http://atpt.org/).

Association for Religious and Values Issues in Counseling (ARVIC)   The original name for what is now known as the *Association for Spiritual, Ethical and Religious Values in Counseling* (ASERVIC).

Association for Specialists in Group Work (ASGW)   A division of the *American Counseling Association* (ACA) that specializes in research and facilitating the practice surrounding *counseling, psychotherapy, educational,* and *task groups* (http://www.asgw.org/).

Association for Spiritual, Ethical, and Religious Values in Counseling (ASERVIC)   A division of the *American Counseling Association (ACA)* that is devoted to professionals who believe that spiritual, ethical, religious, and other human *values* are essential to the full development of persons and *counseling* (http://www.aservic.org/).

assurance   A statement or action on the part of a *counselor* that enhances *client* confidence and removes uncertainties (e.g., "I think you can overcome this problem in time and with work").

ASVAB   See *Armed Services Vocational Aptitude Battery.*

asynchronous counseling   *Internet counseling* where there is a time lapse in communication between the *counselor* and the *client,* for example, e-mail and bulletin board counseling.

at-risk   People most likely to develop *problems* because of their background environments, genetics, and/or present *behaviors.* At-risk individuals often have not finished school or leave school without the necessary skills to be successful. Internal *factors* (e.g., a negative attitude) and external *variables* (e.g., poverty) play a part in making some people more at-risk than others. Being at-risk is charted along on a continuum with minimal to high *probability.*

attachment   The emotional bonds between people that develop because of dependence and attraction, especially important in early life, as in child/parent *relationships.*

attachment theory   A *theory* that describes the *processes* infants go through in developing close emotional bonds and dependence on one or more adult *caregivers.*

attack on the leader   When members of the *group* become hostile or rebellious in regard to a leader's authority or his or her conducting of the group. Underlying reasons for such attacks are *subgrouping,* fear of *intimacy,* and extragroup socializing.

attending skills   Being with and communicating to a *client* a sincere acceptance of him or her. Physically attending *behaviors* such as smiling, leaning forward, making eye contact, gesturing, and nodding one's head are effective *nonverbal* ways of conveying to clients that the *counselor* is interested in and open to them. *Active listening* and the use of *minimal encouragers,* such as "Hmm" and "Yes," are other ways of attending. Attending skills *processes* can be summed up in the mnemonic device called *SOLER.* See also *SOLER.*

attention deficit disorder (ADD)   A *disorder* that includes specific *symptoms* of inattention. A related malady, *attention deficit hyperactivity disorder (ADHD),* includes an additional list of symptoms of hyperactivity/impulsivity. Individuals with forms of ADD and ADHD may know what to do but do not consistently do what they know because of their inability to efficiently stop and think prior to responding, regardless of the setting or task. Characteristics of the disorder have been demonstrated to arise in early *childhood* for most individuals. ADD and ADHD are treated and managed through medication and *behavior therapy.*

attention deficit hyperactivity disorder (ADHD)   See *attention deficit disorder.*

attentiveness   The amount of *verbal* and *nonverbal behavior* shown to a *client* by a *counselor* to establish and continue *rapport* and show care. Attentiveness behaviors include *probing, restating, summarizing,* making eye contact, smiling, and leaning forward.

attitude   A relatively stable and enduring *predisposition* to respond positively or negatively to a person, object, *situation,* institution, or event. An attitude carries a strong emotional component; when generalized, it becomes a *stereotype*. Attitudes emerge from cultural, familial, and personal sources.

attractiveness **1.** The physical and/or psychological similarity between a *client* and *counselor* and the appeal of that to either or both. **2.** A multidimensional concept referring to group members positively identifying with others in the *group*.

attribution bias Faulty *cognitive* skills or reasoning that *adversely* affect an individual's reactions to people and situations, such as all women are weak or salesmen cannot be trusted.

attribution theory A theory that tries to explain internal and external factors that influence why people act in particular ways.

attrition The loss of participants during the course of a research study.

atypical Uncommon *behaviors, feelings, symptoms*, and *thoughts*.

audience A term used for others who may be present during a *psychodrama*.

authentic happiness The title of a book and a movement started by Martin Seligman to use *positive psychology* to help people realize their potential for fulfillment in life (http://www.authentichappiness.org/).

authenticity The ability to be transparent, real, and genuine; to be the same inwardly as one is outwardly.

authoritarian A person or *environment* characterized by a lack of democracy and a structure of *power* that is punitive for those who do not comply with requirements handed down.

authoritarian leaders Leaders who envision themselves as experts and retain all decision-making *power*. These leaders interpret, give advice, and generally direct the movement of others much like a parent controls the actions of a child. They are often charismatic and manipulative. They feed off obedience and expect conformity.

autism A developmental *disorder* that begins prior to 30 months of age. Major characteristics include a lack of responsiveness to people, severe language impairment, and strong *resistance* to *change* in routine or the *environment*.

autodrama See *monodrama*.

autohypnosis Self-*hypnosis*.

automatic thoughts **1.** A term used by Aaron Beck to explain the large number of *thoughts* that go through people's minds so fast that they are often unaware of them and unable to stop them. **2.** Personal beliefs and ideas, specific to a *stimulus,* that are unexamined and *dysfunctional* (e.g., seeing a person that one has not met before and thinking that he or she is boring).

autonomic nervous system That part of the *peripheral nervous system* that controls breathing, heart rate, and sweating.

autonomy **1.** Respecting freedom of *choice,* the promotion of self-determination, or the *power* to choose one's own direction in life. **2.** A *stage* in life development between ages 1 and 2, as defined by Erik Erikson. The focus of the stage is on acquiring self-mastery. It is the opposite of *shame*.

autophobia Fear of being alone.

autoplastic approach An adjustment to a culturally different *environment*—usually the dominant one—through changing oneself. It is the opposite of the *alloplastic approach*.

auxiliary A person in *counseling* who assists a *counselor* or a *client* in an *enactment,* such as in *family counseling* or *psychodrama,* or who functions like a counselor in a *group*.

auxiliary ego A person in a *psychodrama* group selected by the *protagonist* to represent inanimate objects, people, or pets—real or imagined, dead or alive.

Avanta Network An association that carries on the interdisciplinary work of training *counselors* in Virginia Satir's *method*s. The network is located at 2104 SW 152nd Street #2, Burien, WA 98166 (206-241-7566; http://www.avanta.net/).

average A *descriptive statistic* and *research* term for *measures of the central tendency* of a

a
b

group of numbers. An average is expressed in three different ways: *median, mean,* and *mode.*

aversive therapy   Behaviorally based unpleasant *interventions,* such as *overcorrection* and *punishment,* that are intended to suppress or eliminate negative or undesirable *behaviors* so positive behaviors can be taught. Aversive therapy is used only as a last resort and with *informed consent.*

avoidance reaction   The tendency of people to withdraw from or avoid a *situation* or issue that might be threatening or adversarial. An avoidance reaction is a negative sign because individuals who display it tend to eschew *problems* and issues and refuse to work through them.

avoidance-avoidance conflict   When a person tries to escape two equally unpleasant *choices,* for example, having to pay a large fine or having to go to jail.

avoiding conflict   **1.** A style of coping in which a person is free from the *stress* that comes with *conflict* because he or she minimizes or denies conflict and/or does not directly address it. For example, people may say that others only slightly disagree with them politically, when the differences are between going to war or waging peace. **2.** The silencing of members who expose a group's shortcomings or disagree with what the majority of a *group* thinks.

awareness   **1.** An ongoing *process* in *counseling* of recognizing and being cognizant and *conscious* of what one is thinking as well as what one is doing, *feeling,* and sensing. **2.** A *Gestalt therapy* term for a total organism *response.*

awfulizing   When a *client* irrationally believes that an inconvenience or disappointment is awful, terrible, and a major catastrophe. Albert Ellis theorizes that many individuals awfulize to the point of making themselves and others miserable.

Axes of the DSM   The *DSM* suggests making a *diagnosis* using a five axes *system.* Axis I includes clinical syndromes and other conditions that may be a focus of clinical attention. It is usually thought of as the axis on which a *client's presenting problem* and principal diagnosis appear. Axis II contains diagnostic information only on *personality disorders* and mental limitations. Axis III contains information about general medical conditions (e.g., chronic pain) of the client. Axis IV contains information on *psychosocial* and environmental *problems* that may affect the *diagnosis, treatment,* and *prognosis* of *mental disorders* (e.g., a lack of friends, inadequate housing). Axis V gives a global assessment of functioning (GAF) for the client on a scale from 0 to 100 (higher numbers on the scale indicate a better level of functioning). The assessment can be in *relationship* to the past or the present. When all the axes are combined, the result might look like the following: Axis I—305.00, *alcohol abuse,* moderate; Axis II—317.00, mild *mental retardation;* Axis III—chronic pain; Axis IV—divorced, unemployed, no friends; Axis V—GAF = 30 (present). See also *multiaxial assessment.*

AYP   Adequate Yearly Progress.

b

"BA"   (basic assumption) Activity A classification devised by Wilfred Bion for the emotional pattern of an *antiwork group* (as opposed to a "W" [*work group*]). BA groups can be broken down further into three subpatterns: BA dependency (in which members are overdependent on the *group leader*); BA pairing (in which members are more interested in being with each other than in working on a goal); and BA fight-flight (in which members become preoccupied with either engaging in or avoiding hostile *conflict*).

band-aiding The premature insertion of and misuse of support; a *process* of preventing *client*s from fully expressing their emotional pain by overly assuring them everything will work out. For example, a *counselor* might assure clients that the pain they feel now will be gone after a few months.

bar graph A *graph* that depicts *data* through the use of parallel strips drawn from a common base.

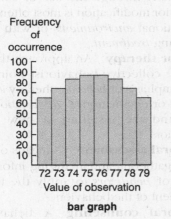

Frequency of occurrence

bar graph

barbiturates *Drugs* that act as *sedatives* and are prescribed by physicians to *facilitate* sleep or to control convulsions. Barbiturates are also popularly known as *downers, yellow jackets, red birds,* and *rainbows.* As a street drug, barbiturates produce a euphoric *mood* that can shift suddenly to one of sadness.

barbs An abbreviated name for *barbiturates*.

bargaining The third stage in Elizabeth Kübler-Ross's five-stage grief process where a person and/or their family may try to make promises with God for a reversal of a diagnosis or a miracle cure.

Barnum effect A description of someone's *personality* that appears to be genuine but which is written in such a vague way that it could apply to anyone.

bartering The practice of exchanging *counseling* and *psychotherapy* for goods or other services. Bartering has the potential for *conflict*s between *counselors* and *client*s and is at times ethically inappropriate.

basal age The highest year level on an *intelligence test,* such as the *Stanford-Binet,* at which a person passes all *subtests.* It is the opposite of *ceiling age.*

baseline A *research* term for the recording of the occurrence of targeted *behavior*s before an *intervention* is made. A baseline is usually a pretreatment procedure instituted so that the effectiveness of a *counseling* intervention can be measured. For example, a baseline might be how many times a child hits another child in a half-hour period of free play.

basic encounter See *encounter.*

basic encounter group Also known as an *encounter group, personal growth group,* or *sensitivity group;* an approach to *group work* first established by Carl Rogers. A basic encounter group focuses on individuals' awareness of their own emotional experiences and the *behavior*s of others. Emphasis is placed on the awareness of and *exploration* of *intrapsychic* and *interpersonal* issues, with a special focus on personal development.

BASIC ID An acronym for the fundamental concepts in Arnold Lazarus's *multimodal therapy.* The concepts are *behavior, affect,* sensation, imagery, *cognition, interpersonal* relations, and *drugs.*

basic mastery A concept from the *microcounseling supervision model (MSM)* that is defined as the ability to demonstrate chosen *counseling skills* during the counseling interview.

basic mistakes An *Adlerian counseling* concept for the myths, *irrational belief*s, and self-defeating *perception*s that are a part of a person's *lifestyle.* Basic mistakes include *overgeneralization,* false or impossible *goals* of security, misperceptions of life demands, *denial* of one's self-worth, and faulty *values.*

basic needs   The lower *need*s on Abraham Maslow's *hierarchy of needs*. At the base of the hierarchy are physiological needs followed by safety needs, belongingness and love needs, esteem needs, and *self-actualization*. See *hierarchy of needs*.

basic psychological needs   Inner resources important to survival that are universal in nature and include the need for relatedness, competence, and autonomy.

basic research   *Research* conducted for the purpose of *theory* development or refinement, such as research conducted on the effectiveness of Adlerian theory. It is the opposite of *applied research*.

BATHE technique   An assessment method that focuses on five specific areas that lay the groundwork for working collaboratively with a client: background, *affect*, trouble, handling, and *empathy*.

batterer   A person who is physically abusive, a perpetrator of *abuse*.

battery   **1.** A group of several tests used to evaluate an individual or group of persons. See also *test battery*. **2.** *Abuse* that involves physical force, such as hitting someone.

battle for initiative   A *process* by which a *counselor* gets a *client* to become motivated to make *changes* through stressing the need and urgency for doing so. Clients must "win" the battle for initiative if *counseling* is to be effective.

battle for structure   The struggle to establish the parameters under which *counseling* is conducted (e.g., time limits, frequency of sessions). *Counselors* must "win" the battle for structure if counseling is to be effective.

BDI   See *Beck Depression Inventory*.

Beck Depression Inventory (BDI)   A 21-*item* self-report measure of *depression*. The BDI is easily administered, scored, and interpreted, with high *reliability* and *validity* components. The Internet address is http://www.beckinstitute.org/.

becoming   Gordon Allport's term for the human tendency to move toward growth and *self-actualization*. This term is often used in *humanistic/existential counseling*.

before-after design   An *experimental design* in which both the *experimental group* and *control group* are given a *pretest* and then an *posttest* to assess what kind of effect the *intervention* in the *experiment* made.

behavior   Any movement or *response* (i.e., action or reaction) by an individual or *group* to external or internal stimuli.

behavior modification   A general term for behavioral *method*s used in altering *behavior*s, especially through the use of *conditioning*. Behavior modification is most often applied in educational *environment*s or with *client*s undergoing *treatment*.

behavior therapy   An approach that focuses on the collective behaviorist point of view. The emphasis of *behavior* therapy is on the removal or elimination of *dysfunctional* behaviors and the instilling of new functional behaviors.

behavioral assessment   A means of systematically gathering and analyzing information on a set of *behaviors* to apply the findings to treatment of the behaviors.

behavioral counseling   A behavioral approach to *counseling* based on *learning* principles. The approach focuses on dealing with *client*s' *behavior*s directly to produce *change*.

behavioral determinist   A *counselor* or *helping professional* who emphasizes *learning* as the primary determinant of human actions. B. F. Skinner is a prime example of a behavioral determinist.

behavioral family counseling   A school of *family therapy* that is primarily nonsystemic and that stresses the importance of *learning*. Behavioral family counseling emphasizes the importance of *family rules* and skill training and the belief that *behavior*s are determined by *consequences* rather than *antecedents*. The *goals* of behavioral family counseling are specific. Work is usually limited to three main areas: *behavioral parent education,* behavioral *marriage counseling,* and *treatment* of sexual dysfunctioning.

behavioral groups Either *interpersonal* or transactional groups, depending on the purposes of the leader and members. *Interpersonal groups* are highly didactic and involve specified *goals* that usually center on self-improvement. *Transactional groups* are more *heterogeneous* and focus on broader, yet specific, *goals.*

behavioral objective A specific behavioral *outcome* that is observable and that is agreed on beforehand to be the target of an *intervention,* for example, walking or talking in a particular way.

behavioral parent education An approach associated with direct *change* and manipulation. Parents are trained to be *change agents* and to record and reinforce certain prosocial and adaptive *behavior*s in their children.

behavioral rehearsal Procedures that involve practicing a desired *behavior* until it is learned and performed the way one wishes, for example, asking for directions. The *process* consists of gradually *shaping* a behavior and getting corrective *feedback.*

behaviorism A school of *thought* that began in the United States with the work of John B. Watson. Behaviorism emphasizes the *role* of environmental stimuli and the importance of *reward* in the *learning* and *conditioning* of *behavior.*

behaviorist A *clinician* who ascribes to the tenets of *behavior therapy* and who usually emphasizes overt *behavior techniques* and *processes,* such as changing of *maladaptive* actions, over other *techniques* and processes.

becoming An *existential* and developmental term for growth, especially that which is psychological.

being A *humanistic* and *existential* term for the individual's concept of *self.*

being-in-the-world An *existential* term derived from the German word *Dasein,* which refers to examining oneself, others, and one's

relationship with the world, thus attaining higher levels of *consciousness.*

bell-shaped curve A curve obtained by plotting the frequency of a *normal distribution.*

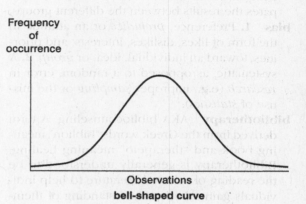

bell-shaped curve

belonging An innate *need* or drive in human life to associate with others and be gregarious. Belonging leads individuals to seek out *relationship*s and involvement with fellow human beings.

Bender Gestalt Test An evaluative *test,* officially named the *Bender Visual Motor Gestalt Test,* in which *client*s are asked to copy on a blank sheet of paper nine cards containing abstract designs. The test was designed to measure visual–motor *integration* and function in children ages 5 to 11. Aspects of personality, such as impulsivity, *anxiety,* and *aggression* are also revealed in the test.

Bender Visual Motor Gestalt Test See *Bender Gestalt Test.*

beneficence An ethical principle that stresses promoting the good of others.

bennies A lay term for *amphetamines.*

benzodiazepines A group of prescriptive *drugs* that are widely used in the *treatment* of *anxiety* and *insomnia;* they include diazepam (Valium), chlordiazepoxide (Librium), and triazolam (Halcion). Benzodiazepines can be *addictive.* They often are used as street drugs to treat the adverse effects of *cocaine, heroin,* and *alcohol.*

bereavement   See *grief.*

beta error   See *Type II error.*

between-groups design   A research design that uses a separate sample of participants for each treatment condition and then statistically compares the results between the different groups.

bias   **1.** Preference, *prejudice* or an attitude in the form of likes, dislikes, interests, and priorities, toward an individual, idea, or *group.* **2.** A systematic, as opposed to a random, error in *research* (e.g., improper *sampling* or the misuse of *statistics*).

bibliotherapy   AKA bibliocounseling. A term derived from the Greek words "biblion" meaning book and "therapeio" meaning healing. Bibliotherapy is generally understood to be the reading of selected literature to help individuals gain a better understanding of themselves and others as well as to produce at times a healing or helpful *catharsis.* See also *scriptotherapy.*

Big Book   A guidebook used in *Alcoholics Anonymous* full of stories of individuals fighting *alcohol addiction.*

Big Five   A model of *personality* that classifies personality traits along five bipolar dimensions: openness, conscientiousness, extraversion, agreeableness, and neuroticism (*OCEAN*).

Big Four feeling words   Four common words *counselors* often use: anger, sadness, fear, and joy.

bigotry   Blindly held beliefs of intolerance against people or ideas.

bimodal distribution   A *frequency distribution* in which two *values* occur at the same frequency.

binge drinking   The consumption of five or more drinks of *alcohol* for men or four or more drinks of alcohol for women at one sitting.

binge eating   The consumption of excessive amounts of food over a relatively brief period of time with a lack of self-control over the volume of food eaten.

binuclear family   A post-*divorce family* structure in which ex-spouses reside in separate but interrelated households. The two interrelated family households comprise one family *system.*

bioecological model   A model of human development that focuses on the settings in which *development* occurs and on the interaction of individuals within and across those settings. The model integrates the various components that contribute to developmental outcomes, including the individual, the environment, and the processes of interaction that affect the individual in that environment.

biofeedback   A behavioral *therapy process* that involves the training of individuals to control or *change* automatic *responses* (e.g., heart rate, blood pressure, and brain wave activity) once thought to be involuntary. In biofeedback therapy, mechanical instruments provide information about a *client*'s physiological processes. The *client* then controls these processes through *self-monitoring,* even though he or she may be unsure how these processes are being modified.

biographic inventory   A *questionnaire* used to obtain information about a person's background and experiences.

bipolar disorder   Formerly known as *manic-depressive illness;* a *disorder* (with several variations) characterized by *maladaptive mood* swings that vary from being *manic* (e.g., hyperactive, euphoric) to being *depressed* (e.g., low in *self-esteem,* sad).

biopsychosocial model (BPS)   An approach to medicine and *mental health* that recognizes the interrelated and integrated roles played by biology, psychology, and social/cultural factors in the maintenance of *wellness* and the understanding of illness.

biracial/multiracial   Individuals who identify themselves as being from two or more racial groups.

birth order   **1.** The *position* a child occupies in a *family.* **2.** Five *ordinal positions* are emphasized in *Adlerian counseling:* firstborns, children born second, middle children, youngest children, and the only child. Adler believed birth order was a determinant of *personality* and that individuals with the same birth order had more in common (in regard to experiences and approaches to life) than siblings.

birth trauma   **1.** The shock of birth described by Otto Rank as being the basis for all other human anxieties. **2.** Physical damage occurring to a child at birth.

bisexual   **1.** A person who is sexually attracted to both males and females. **2.** Having characteristics of both sexes.

Black   A term sometimes used in the United States to describe descendants whose ancestry was African. See also *African American.*

black box warning labels   An attached warning put on medications that emphasizes the adverse side effects of the medicine, such as the increased risk of suicidal ideation among young people who take *antidepressants.*

blackout   A term used for a loss of memory due to physical or emotional factors.

blamer   A person, according to Virginia Satir, who attempts to place blame on others and not take responsibility for what he or she is doing.

blended family   See *stepfamily.*

blind self   One of the four quadrants in the *Johari Awareness Model.* The blind self is known to others but not known to *self.*

blocking   **1.** The *suppression* of painful *feelings* and *thoughts* by a *client.* **2.** In *group counseling* or *family counseling,* the *technique* of protecting vulnerable members in which the leader intervenes to stop counterproductive *behavior.* This *intervention* can be done verbally or nonverbally through hand signals or other behaviors.

blocking role   An antigroup member *role.* Individuals who take this role act as aggressors, dominators, recognition seekers, and self-righteous moralists.

body dysmorphic disorder   A *somatoform disorder* characterized by an imagined defect in a person's appearance and a preoccupation with that flaw.

body language   *Nonverbal communication* (e.g., hand tapping) associated with body posture and movement. Body language is emphasized in many *counseling* approaches, such as *Gestalt therapy.*

Bogust v. Iverson   A 1960 case ruling that a *counselor* with a doctoral degree could not be held liable for the *suicide* of one of his *clients* because counselors were "mere teachers" who received training in a department of education. It was not until 1971 in an *Iowa Law Review Note* that counselors were legally recognized as professionals who provided personal as well as vocational and educational counseling.

bonding   **1.** An emotional and physical *process* that occurs between a mother and a child early in the baby's life that brings them close together. A failure to bond may lead to *neglect* or *abuse.* **2.** *Cohesion* within a group.

borderline personality   A *personality disorder* characterized by impulsive, unpredictable, and often self-destructive *behavior*s, intense *mood* swings, chronic boredom, manipulation of others for short-term gain, uncontrollable anger, and *maladaptive* patterns of relating to others.

Boston's Civic Service House (CSH)   An organization and physical facility set up in 1901 to meet food, shelter, clothing, education and employment *need*s of immigrants. It was at the CHS that Frank Parsons started the vocational bureau in 1908, which was the beginning of *counseling.*

Boston Vocational Bureau   The agency set up by Frank Parsons in 1908 to offer *career* services to youth who needed to choose a *vocation.* The place where *career counseling* began.

boundaries   **1.** The physical and psychological *factor*s that separate people from one another and organize them. **2.** The parameters under which *counselors* operate their sessions, such as starting and ending on time.

Bowen family therapy   A therapeutic approach that focuses on differentiation of one's *thought*s from one's *emotion*s and oneself from others. *Technique*s in this approach focus on ways to differentiate oneself from one's *extended family* of origin. In the *process,* there is an attempt to create an individuated person with a healthy *self-concept* who will not experience undue *anxiety* when *relationship*s become stressful. Ways of achieving this goal include assessment of *self* and *family* through a *genogram* and a focus on *cognitive* processes, such as asking *content*-based questions of one's family (e.g., "how many siblings did you have?"). The therapeutic interaction takes place with both spouses together or with an individual.

brainstorming A way to stimulate *divergent thinking.* It requires an initial generating of ideas in a nonjudgmental manner within a *group.* The premise of this approach is that *creativity* is often held back because of the critical *evaluation* of ideas and actions.

Brief Symptom Inventory (BSI) A *checklist* often used during intake sessions in mental health settings.

brief counseling/therapy An approach to working with *client*s that generally requires 10 sessions or less. However, brief therapy has to do more with the clarity about what needs to be *changed* rather than time. A central principle of brief therapy is that one evaluates which *solutions* have so far been attempted (without success) and then tries new and different solutions to the *problem.*

broadband assessment instruments *Tests* that measure a wide range of *characteristics, behaviors,* and *symptoms* and that are usually used for initial diagnostic purposes (e.g., the *MMPI*).

bruxism Grinding one's teeth, usually when asleep.

bubblegummers An informal term that refers to middle-school children between the ages of 10 and 14.

bubbles An informal term for the flaws found in all *research method*s.

Buckley Amendment See *Family Educational Rights and Privacy Act (FERPA).*

bulimia An *eating disorder* characterized by periods of binge eating followed by purging.

bullying The act of trying to control and maintain power over someone by doing such things as calling them names, saying or writing nasty things about them, leaving them out of activities, not talking to them, threatening them, making them feel uncomfortable or scared, taking or damaging their things, hitting or kicking them, or making them do things they do not want to do.

burnout A gradually intensifying pattern of physical, psychological, and behavioral *response*s to a continual flow of *stressors* in which a person becomes physically and emotionally exhausted. Burnout is characterized by apathy, fatigue, anger, and *conflict.*

Buros Institute of Mental Measurements An institute set up by Oscar and Lucella Buros at the University of Nebraska–Lincoln to continue their work in advancing the field of *measurement.* The Buros Institute encourages improved *test* development and measurement *research.* The institute publishes important works in the measurement field, including the *Mental Measurement Yearbook* and *Tests in Print (TIP)* (published by the University of Nebraska Press, 312 North 14th Street, P.O. Box 880484, Lincoln, NE 68588-0484; http://www.unl.edu/buros).

C

C group A type of Adlerian *parent education group.* Each component of the group—collaboration, *consultation, clarification, confrontation,* concern, *confidentiality,* and commitment—begins with the letter c. The group is primarily *psychoeducational.* It emphasizes developmental and preventive aspects of parenting.

CA See *chronological age.*

CACGS See *computer-assisted career guidance systems.*

CACREP See *Council for Accreditation of Counseling and Related Educational Programs.*

caffeine A mild *stimulant* that dissipates drowsiness or fatigue, speeds up one's heart rate, raises blood pressure, and irritates the stomach. Caffeine is found primarily in coffee, tea, cola beverages, and chocolate. Caffeine can be *addictive.*

C-AHEAD See *Counseling Association for Humanistic Education and Development.*

California Achievement Test (CAT) A *battery* of *tests* used to evaluate children's academic *achievement* in grades 2 through 12. The CAT is a widely used *achievement test* in the schools.

California Psychological Inventory (CPI) A pencil-and-paper personality *inventory* for ages 12 through 70 designed to *diagnose* and understand *interpersonal behavior,* such as sociability, *tolerance,* and responsibility, within normal *populations.* The *CPI* is sometimes called the sane person's *MMPI.*

camera check A *rational self-analysis technique* in which the *client* is asked to envision a *situation* the way a camera would. The idea behind the technique is to objectify events so that they do not become contaminated with emotional *content* and can thus be handled cognitively.

cannabis A controversial *stimulant* in the United States that can be smoked, eaten, or drunk. Cannabis is known by many names (e.g., *hashish, pot, grass, dope,* and *marijuana*).

capacity The ability to make rational decisions.

capitation A form of payment in health care where the provider is paid on a per-member basis.

capping The *process* of easing out of emotional interaction and into *cognitive reflection,* especially useful during *termination* of *counseling.* For instance, the *counselor* might say at the end of a session or at the end of counseling: "We've looked at a lot of issues during our session(s) including your *relationship* with your mother, spouse, and children. You've had quite a bit to say about each."

card sort A semistructured *assessment method* of sorting out or prioritizing the interests, skills, *needs, values,* or any predetermined array of ideas for a *client.* This method is used in both *career counseling* settings and in personal counseling sessions. See *Q-Sort.*

care A genuine concern for and interest in others and their well-being.

career The activities and *positions,* both remunerated and nonremunerated, involved in *work*-related *roles* and *leisure* over the course of one's life.

career adjustment The ability to adapt to a *work* environment.

career assessment The broad process of gathering information on careers in a systematic way using multiple methods such as interviewing, formal testing, and *self-assessment.*

career change group A type of *group* for adults, usually in *midlife,* that is both psychoeducational and psychotherapeutic in nature.

career construction theory A *theory* originated by Mark Savickas that views *work* as a context for human development. The theory is integrative dealing with *personality* types, developmental tasks, and life themes. *Counselors* using this theory encourage people to design their lives to achieve success and enjoy satisfaction by engaging in work activities that matter to them and to their communities. *Clients* engage in autobiographical reasoning to narrate what matters to them and how they might manifest it in work activities that are meaningful and matter.

career counseling Counseling that focuses on matters dealing with *work* and *career choices,* especially the *relationships* between the *needs* of *clients* and their vocational development over the *life span.* Career counseling is one of the foundation stones of the counseling profession.

career decision making A dynamic and lifelong process where a person makes choices about entering or continuing in a career based on knowledge about self, values, interests, culture, temperament, financial needs, physical requirements, and other factors relevant to personal and professional satisfaction within a *work* environment.

career development   The *process* of choosing, entering, adjusting to, and advancing in an *occupation*. It is a lifelong process that interacts dynamically with other life *roles*.

career-development assessment and counseling (C-DAC) model   A model based on Donald Super's *theory* of *career development* that views a *client* as an individual in a constantly changing *environment*. It assesses career maturity and identifies *values* placed on *work* and occupational careers using a *battery* of *tests* and *interest inventories*. Clients high in career salience and ready for career decision-making activities work with a *counselor* to objectify their interests, abilities, and values. They then take the final step of subjectively assessing life themes and patterns they can identify. The C-DAC model is employed over the *life span* and incorporates culturally based *variables* such as work-*role* importance and values.

career fair   A *career guidance* activity, often found in educational settings, in which practitioners in a number of fields are invited to explain their *job* responsibilities, backgrounds, and the necessary requirements needed to be employed in their line of *work*.

career guidance   All activities that seek to disseminate information about present or future *vocations* in such a way that individuals become more knowledgeable about and aware of who they are in *relationship* to the world of *work*. *Guidance* activities can take the form of *career fairs*, library assignments, outside *interviews*, computer-assisted information experiences, *career shadowing*, didactic lectures, and experiential *exercises* such as *role playing*.

career information   Information related to the world of *work* that can be useful in the

process of *career development*, including educational, occupational, and *psychosocial* information related to working (e.g., availability of training, the nature of *work*, and status of workers in different *occupations*).

career maturity   AKA *vocational maturity*. A concept created by Donald Super to describe the degree to which a person achieves developmental tasks expected by society relative to the person's peers.

Career Occupational Preference System (COPS)   A career *interest inventory* composed of three parts designed to measure interests and present a *profile* in 14 areas.

career planning   Gathering and interpreting occupational information related to a future *career* a person might wish to pursue.

career problems   Difficulties that include but are not limited to career indecision and undecidedness, unsatisfactory *work performance*, *stress* and adjustment, *incongruence* of the person and *work environment*, and inadequate or unsatisfactory *integration* of life *roles* (e.g., parent, friend, citizen).

career salience   The level of importance people place on the role of their careers and *work* in relationship to other life roles.

career shadowing   Also known as *shadowing*; a *career guidance* activity in which an individual follows a worker around on his or her daily routine to learn more about a given *profession*.

career typology   *John Holland's* view that people have a preference because of their personalities and genetic inheritance for working in certain environments that are congruent with their interests: *realistic, investigative, artistic, social, enterprising,* or *conventional*. See *RIASEC*.

caregiver   **1.** A person who provides for the physical, emotional, and social *needs* of another who is dependent and who cannot provide for his or her own needs. **2.** A term sometimes used to describe a professional helper such as a *counselor*.

caring The ability to show genuine concern for someone or for a *group*.

caring days A behavioral marital procedure devised by Richard Stuart in which one or both marital partners act as if they *care* about their spouse regardless of the other's action(s). This *technique* embodies the idea of a *positive risk*.

Carl D. Perkins Vocational Act Federal legislation that amended the *Vocational Education Act* of 1963 and mandated that *career guidance* and *career counseling* must be made accessible to all segments of the *population*.

case A client's file or record.

case conference A clinical conference with other *helping professionals* for the purpose of presenting circumstances surrounding a *client* and reviewing *treatment* and recommending *interventions*.

case law The type of *law* determined by decisions of courts at all levels from state to federal.

caseload All the *clients* a *counselor* is currently *helping*.

case management A coordinated set of professional activities focused on *client* needs. Activities revolve around cost-effective treatment and quality deliverance of services.

case manager A *mental health professional* who works with *clients*, providers, and insurers to coordinate all services needed for the well-being of a person, *group*, or *family*.

case notes Notes written (in each session) by a *counselor* that document a *client*'s progress toward stated *goals*.

case rate A preestablished fee paid to a provider for an entire course of *treatment* for one case.

case study An attempt to understand one unit, such as a person, group, or program, through an intense and systematic investigation of that unit longitudinally. Some case studies rely on a self-report *research* format; others involve *natural observation*, in which the study extends over a period of time.

CASS *Counseling and Student Services Clearinghouse*. See *Educational Resources Information Center/Counseling and Student Services Clearinghouse (ERIC/CASS)*.

castration anxiety/complex During the *Oedipal complex*, the fear a boy has that his father will castrate him in retaliation for the boy's wish to possess his mother.

CAT See *California Achievement Test*.

catastrophizing A cognitive *distortion* in which a negative event becomes exaggerated so that it becomes more important than it actually is. For example, if a person makes a mistake at *work*, the person may think he or she is going to be fired. Albert Ellis popularized this term in his *rational emotive behavior therapy (REBT)*.

catatonia A *mental disorder* in which a person appears in a stupor with a lack of movement seemingly detached from reality and his or her *environment*. A person with catatonia may occasionally become excited and uncontrollable.

catching oneself An *Adlerian counseling* term for when *clients* learn to become aware of self-destructive *behaviors* or *thoughts*.

catchment areas Geographical areas of 75,000 to 250,000 people established under the *Community Mental Health Centers Act* of 1963. Centers were to provide quality services to people in their catchment areas.

catharsis The release of pent-up or repressed *emotions* such as anger or joy that once expressed provide the *client* relief. Catharsis is sometimes used as a synonym for *abreaction*.

cathexis A *psychoanalytic* term for emotional attachment to an idea, person, or object.

CCMHC See *Certified Clinical Mental Health Counselor*.

C-DAC model See *career-development assessment and counseling model*.

ceiling The upper limit of a particular ability as measured by a *test* or examination.

ceiling age The year level on a *test*, such as the *Stanford-Binet*, at which a person fails all *subtests*. It is the opposite of *basal age*.

Center for Play Therapy A center at the University of North Texas, established by Garry L. Landreth. Its mission is to encourage the unique development and emotional growth of children through the *process* of *play therapy.* The center's address is P.O. Box 311337, Denton, TX 76203-1337 (940-565-3864; http://cpt.unt.edu/).

centering skills The *process* of getting "in touch" and then "in tune" with parts and then all of oneself.

Centers for Medicare and Medicaid Services (CMS) The government body that administers and maintains the various federal *health care* programs.

central nervous system One of two systems within the nervous system, which contains the brain and spinal cord and is responsible for control of all major systems of the body.

centration A narrow topical focus on one aspect of a situation while neglecting others; a characteristic of Piaget's preoperational stage (ages 2–7).

centrifugal **1.** Directed away from a center. **2.** A tendency to move away or disengage from a *family,* either physically or emotionally (i.e., family disengagement). At points in the *family life cycle,* centrifugal movement is considered appropriate, such as during *adolescence,* when teens are attracted more toward their *peer*s than their parents.

centripetal **1.** Directed toward a center. **2.** A tendency to move toward *family* closeness. At points in the *family life cycle,* centripetal movement is considered appropriate and healthy, such as after the birth of a baby.

certification The *process* by which an agency, government, or association officially grants recognition to an individual for having met certain professional qualifications that have been developed by the *profession.* Certification in *counseling* is voluntary at the national level (e.g., the *National Board for Certified Counselors [NBCC]*), but it is mandatory for *school counselor positions* at the state level.

Certified Clinical Mental Health Counselor (CCMHC) A specialized *certification* in *mental health counseling* that is obtained after

a professional becomes a *national certified counselor (NCC).*

Certified Employee Assistance Professional (CEAP) A professional *EAP* provider certified by the Employee Assistance Professional Association (www.eapassn.org).

Certified Rehabilitation Counselor (CRC) A *counselor* certified by the *Commission of Rehabilitation Counselor Certification (CRCC).* Counselors must complete *CORE*-accredited programs and specific courses and satisfy experience requirements.

CEU See *continuing education units.*

chain A *group* arrangement in which people are positioned or seated along a line, often according to their rank. Communication is passed from the person at one end of the configuration to the person at the other end through those in between the two. The chain is a popular way to run some group organizations, such as the armed forces. Disadvantages of the chain include the indirectness of communication, the lack of direct contact with others, and the *frustration* of relaying messages through others.

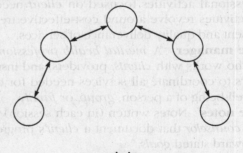

chain

chaining Specific behavioral *response* sequences used in *shaping behavior.* For example, a chaining sequence to help a shy person become more outgoing might initially start with teaching the person to look at another person in the eye and then chain appropriate facial expressions, such as smiling, with the first behavior and then chain appropriate *verbal* expression, such as saying "hello," with the first two behaviors.

CHAMPUS See *Civilian Health and Medical Program of the Uniformed Services.*

change **1.** A *process,* whether gradual or dramatic, that involves shifts in how a person behaves, thinks, or feels. Change is at the heart of *counseling.* **2.** A modification in a document or in the wording that describes a person or a process, such as an adjustment in the way a person is diagnosed or the way counseling is delivered.

change agent A *counselor* or other *helping professional* who attempts to improve conditions for *client*s through actions that foster *changes* in society.

changing questions to statements A *Gestalt therapy* procedure that requires a person who raises a question to make it into an "I" statement. For example, "Don't you think you should act differently?" would be *changed* to "I think you should act differently."

character disorder A behavioral disorder characterized by immaturity and the general inability to cope with the challenges of adult life. Persons with character disorders are frequently in trouble in society either through self-imposed means, such as alcohol *abuse,* or through breaking *law*s.

characteristic A defining quality or feature that makes somebody or something recognizable.

charting A procedure that involves asking *client*s to keep an accurate record of problematic *behavior*s. The idea is to get clients to establish a *baseline* from which *intervention*s can be made and to show clients how the *changes* they are making work.

checklist A list of adjectives, phrases, or other descriptors of *behavior*s. Individuals are asked to check the presence or absence of each *item* and sometimes the degree (e.g., always, often, sometimes, seldom, never) to which it is present or displayed in their lives.

chemotherapy The use of prescriptive *drugs* or chemicals in the *treatment* of physical or *mental disorder*s.

Chi Sigma Iota (CSI) The international honor society for counselors-in-training, counselor educators, and professional *counselors.* CSI's mission is to promote scholarship, *research,* professionalism, leadership, and excellence in *counseling* and to recognize high attainment in the pursuit of academic and clinical excellence in the field of counseling. The society's address is: School of Education, UNCG, P.O. Box 26171, Greensboro, NC 27402-6171 (336-334-4035; http://www.csi-net.org/).

chi square test A *nonparametric statistics test* used to determine whether two *variables* are statistically independent, that is, whether a set of observed frequencies differ significantly from a set of hypothesized expected frequencies by chance alone.

Chicano A term sometimes used to describe a citizen of the United States who is of Mexican birth or heritage; a Mexican American.

child An individual who has not yet reached maturity. A term usually used to designate a person between birth and puberty (i.e., age 12).

Child Abuse Prevention and Treatment Act A federal law originally passed in 1974 that provides funding for preventing and investigating child *abuse.*

child custody evaluator A *counselor* who acts on behalf of a court to determine what is in the best interest of a *child* in a custody arrangement.

child ego state A *transactional analysis* concept describing one of three *ego states* in persons. The child ego is divided into two parts: the *adaptive child,* who conforms to the *rules* and wishes of the *parent ego state* within the *self* and others, and the *free child* (or *natural child*), who reacts more spontaneously and intuitively and takes care of his or her *needs* without regard for others.

childhood The period in the human *life cycle* from birth to puberty (i.e., around age 12). Childhood is often divided into two periods: *early childhood* (up to age 6) and *middle childhood* (age 6 up to *puberty*). This time of life is characterized by rapid physical, cognitive, and social growth.

choice 1. A decision-making *process* about *behavior*s over which individuals have some control (e.g., whether to use *drugs*). Much of life involves *learning* how to make good choices. The concept of *guidance* revolves around *helping* individuals learn to make choices. **2.** Picking between two alternatives such as answers on a *test* (e.g., a forced choice test).

choice theory A *theory* that underlies William Glasser's *reality therapy*. In choice theory, the idea is that people have mental images of their *need*s and behave accordingly; thus, individuals are ultimately self-determining (i.e., they choose). Individuals can choose to be miserable or mentally disturbed. They may also choose to determine the course of their lives in positive ways and to give up trying to control others.

Choosing a Vocation A book written by Frank Parsons and published a year after his death in 1909. It outlines Parsons' systematic *method* for obtaining employment and was the forerunner of *trait-and-factor theory*.

choreography A *process* in which *client*s symbolically enact a pattern or a sequence involving a *relationship,* often with *family* members. This process is similar to mime and can be considered the enactment of *sculpting*.

chronic *Problem*s, *situation*s, or conditions that have developed and persisted over an extended period.

chronological age (CA) A person's actual age in years and months.

chunking The process of organizing and grouping information into small, easily remembered units (about 5 to 9; i.e., chunks) so they can be retained in short-term memory. Chunks can range from simple letters or numbers to more complex words or phrases.

cinematherapy An approach to *counseling* using films to evoke *emotion*s, foster *empathy*, and provide *role models* for *client*s.

circle A *group* configuration in which all members have direct access to each other and implied equality in status and *power*. The circle is probably the best way to ensure that group members have an opportunity to express themselves.

circular causality Also known as *nonlinear causality* and *nonlinear thinking*. Circular causality is based on the idea that causality is nonlinear. Actions are a part of a causal chain within a context and within a network of interacting loops, each reciprocally influencing and being influenced by the other. Circular causality is at the heart of *systems theory*. It is the opposite of *linear causality*.

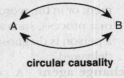

circular causality

circular counseling An unproductive type of *counseling* in which the same ground is covered over and over again.

circular questioning A *Milan family therapy technique* of asking questions that focus attention on *family* connections and highlight differences among family members. This procedure is done through framing every question so that it addresses differences in *perception* about events or *relationship*s by various family members.

Circumplex Model of Marital and Family Systems A model created by David Olson to map family cohesion (i.e., emotional bonding) and family adaptability (i.e., ability to be flexible and change). These two dimensions are curvilinear with couples and families very high or low on both dimensions being dysfunctional.

circumscription When an individual makes a vocational choice by eliminating occupational alternatives that conflict with his or her *self-concept*.

civil law *Law* dealing with acts offensive to individuals. The remedy in most civil law cases is compensation for the *victim*. Most of the law involving *counselor*s pertains to civil law, for example, divorce law.

civil liability Responsibility for acting wrongly toward another or for failing to act when there is a recognized duty to do so.

Civilian Health and Medical Program of the Uniformed Services (CHAMPUS) A federally funded health insurance company that provides benefits for active and retired U.S. military personnel.

clarification A *counselor technique* that attempts to focus on and understand the *content* or intent of a *client*'s statement and at the same time help the client better comprehend what was said.

clarifying the purpose When *group leader*s remind members and the *group* as a whole what behavioral interactions or foci are appropriate in the group and why.

classical conditioning A *theory* developed by Ivan Pavlov; also known as *respondent conditioning*. It is the oldest form of *behaviorism*. In *classical conditioning,* a *stimulus* that was previously neutral is repeatedly paired up with another stimulus (*unconditioned*) that elicits a natural *response* so that it comes to elicit the same response (conditioned). For example, the neutral stimulus of a green Ford van might be paired with the *unconditional stimulus* of food so that every time a person sees the car, his or her mouth waters (a conditioned response).

classism Oppression by upper class persons against low class or poor persons.

classroom guidance See *guidance*.

claustrophobia Extreme fear of closed places such as closets or rooms without windows.

clean claim A claim that meets all the necessary requirements of an insurance carrier; the "cleaner" the claim, the faster the reimbursement.

clear boundaries *Rules* and habits that allow people to enhance their communication and *relationship*s with one another because they allow and encourage *dialogue*.

client A person, *group, family,* or community receiving help from the *counselor*. Analogous words for client are *helpee* or *counselee*. In the *medical model*, a client is known as a *patient*.

client agenda See *goals*.

client-aimed intervention In *rehabilitation counseling* a focus on personal adjustment counseling, vocational counseling, behavioral modification, and skill development in performance of the activities of daily living.

client records See *records*.

client-centered therapy A *theory* developed by Carl Rogers. This name was used between the original name of *nondirective counseling* and the more modern name of *person-centered counseling*. The idea of the approach is that the *client,* not the *counselor,* should direct the counseling *process* in terms of focus.

clinic A place where people can receive needed or requested medical or mental *treatment*. The word "clinic" is often the last word in the names of a *mental health* facility (e.g., mental health clinic).

clinical counseling E. G. Williamson's directive approach to *counseling,* developed in the 1930s. See also *counselor-centered counseling; directive counseling*.

clinical mental health counseling One of the major specialty areas in *counseling* accredited by *CACREP*. In 2009 CACREP merged the specialty of *community counseling* with *mental health counseling* because the distinction between the two had blurred.

clinical psychology A *mental health* treatment branch of *psychology* that focuses on and specializes in working with persons who are experiencing *distress* and *disorder*s.

clinician The general term for a *helping professional* who works with *client*s in a variety of settings.

closed **1.** A term used to signify that a *client* case has been terminated. **2.** The psychological stance of a person in *counseling* who refuses to consider different perspectives or options for his or her life.

closed group A *group* that does not admit new members after its first session. A closed group is usually more cohesive than an *open group*.

closed system   A *system* that is self-contained with impermeable *boundaries,* not open to forces outside it. Closed systems are prone to increased disorder over time.

closed-ended questions   Queries that can be answered in a few words and are generally used to gather information, for example, "How old are you?" or "Do you like music?" See also *open-ended questions; questioning.*

closed panel health care   Where a *managed care organization (MCO)* requires participants to utilize services (e.g., practitioners, facilities, pharmacies, that the MCO has a contract with).

closure   1. A *Gestalt therapy* term for the completion of unfinished experiences by a *client.* Closure helps a person gain *insight* or resolve a *situation.* **2.** The *termination* of a *counseling* case.

cluster suicides   *Suicide* behavior, such as suicidal attempts, that follow or imitate another *suicide.* These suicides occur because those who have already been experiencing despair may begin to see a self-inflicted death as a viable *response* to their *stress* and *feelings* of hopelessness.

CMHC Act   See *Community Mental Health Centers Act*

coaching   1. A *technique* for *helping* individuals, couples, or families make appropriate responses by giving them *verbal* instructions. **2.** A *method* for working with executives to help them become more aware of their strengths, weaknesses, and impact on others. This type of coaching is known as *executive coaching.* **3.** A *method* used for *helping test* takers answer specific types of questions and improve their *test* performance. This type of coaching is sometimes known as *teaching to the test.*

coalition   An alliance found in groups and families in which two persons join together against a third person. There are two types of coalitions: a *stable coalition* and a *detouring coalition.*

COAMFTE   See *Commission on Accreditation for Marriage and Family Therapy Education.*

cocaine   A *drug* derived from the leaves of the coca plant that produces a *feeling* of euphoria, energy, alertness, and heightened sensitivity in users when *snorted* (i.e., taken through the nostrils), injected, or *freebased* (i.e., smoked). Cocaine is also known as *coke* or *snow.* With continuous use, it produces a marked deterioration in the nervous *system* as well as general physical deterioration and *maladaptive disorder*s, such as *hallucinations, paranoia,* and *depression.*

code of ethics   A set of standards and principles that organizations create to provide guidelines for their members to follow in working with the public and each other.

codependent/codependency   A mutually dependent but often emotionally unhealthy *relationship* in which two people meet each others' *need*s and rely on each other to the point of being inseparable. This term is often used in regard to a marriage relationship in which one spouse suffers from alcoholism or is a *substance abuser* and the other (the codependent) is the long-suffering spouse who takes care of the abuser at the expense of taking care of *self.*

codeine   A *narcotic* derived from *opium* or *morphine* used as a cough suppressor. Codeine can become *addictive* if not monitored closely. When sold as a *drug* on the street, codeine is often called *pops* or *school boy.*

cognition   A *thought,* idea, or *conscious* intellectual *process* involved in knowing.

cognitive   Referring to thinking, reasons, and imagining.

cognitive approaches to human relations   Approaches based on the *theory* that how one thinks largely determines how one feels and behaves. Aaron Beck's *theory* is an example of a cognitive approach to human relations.

cognitive assessment   Systematically gathering and analyzing information on an individual's overall cognitive abilities and functioning.

cognitive behavioral theory An approach to *counseling* in which *interventions* make use of both cognitive and behavioral *treatment techniques* that are direct, structured, goal oriented, and time limited in nature. Examples of cognitive behavioral techniques include *cognitive restructuring, shame attacks, stress inoculation,* and *thought stopping.*

cognitive bypass The belief of the *client* that an experience directly causes *feelings,* for example, when a client says: "Because you did not say hello to me, I am depressed." The client is attributing the lack of a greeting by another directly as the cause of despondency.

cognitive constriction An inability to see options for solving *problems,* which leads to *dichotomous thinking.* This type of thinking is common in the critical *stages* of suicidal ideation.

cognitive counseling Approaches to *counseling* that emphasize working with *clients* in modifying their *thought processes* so that they do not *overgeneralize* or distort cognitive messages in a *dysfunctional* way. Aaron Beck's *cognitive therapy* emphasizes modifying thought processes as the primary means of bringing about *change.*

cognitive development The development of *thoughts* and ideas over the *life span.* Jean Piaget has formulated one of the most thorough theories of this *process.*

cognitive disorders A *disorder,* either temporary or permanent, that is organic in nature and involves some form of impairment to the brain (e.g., *delirium, dementia, and amnestic disorders*).

cognitive disputation A *technique* used in Albert Ellis's *rational emotive behavior therapy* and Maxie Maultsby's *rational behavioral therapy* that involves the use of direct questions, logical reasoning, and *persuasion* to dispute irrational thoughts and *irrational beliefs.*

cognitive dissonance Leon Festinger's *theory* that people have a strong *need* or drive toward consistency (i.e., consonance). There-fore, when two ideas are inconsistent at the same time, individuals have a need to resolve them (i.e., make them consistent). They can do so by changing either their actions or beliefs. For example, if a person pays a high fee for *mental health* services but does not think he or she received much for the money, the person will either reevaluate the service upward or quit the therapeutic *process.*

cognitive distortions Pervasive and systematic errors in reasoning that are negative and inaccurate and can result in unhealthy misperceptions of events, for example, exaggerating the negative, minimizing the positive, overgeneralizing, catastrophizing, and personalizing.

cognitive restructuring A cognitive therapeutic *process* for coping with *stress* that involves replacing stress-provoking or irrational *thoughts* with more constructive or rational *thoughts,* thus helping clients recognize and modify their inner dialogue and develop coping self-statements.

cognitive self-care Taking the time to evaluate one's beliefs about self, the *counseling process,* and clients to evaluate and modify irrational self-inducing cognitions and promote positive *mental health.*

cohesiveness The togetherness or closeness of a *group;* "we-ness." Cohesiveness in a group can be increased through friendly interaction, cooperation, increased group status, an outside threat, or democratic (as opposed to authoritarian) leadership.

cohort effect When observed differences between age groups (i.e., cohorts) are due to differences in their generation and experience rather than age.

coke A slang term for *cocaine.*

cold turkey Giving up an *addiction* quickly and abruptly, usually without outside support.

coleader A professional or a professional-in-training who undertakes the responsibility of sharing the leadership of a *group.* The use of coleaders usually occurs when group membership is 12 or more.

collaborative empiricism A *technique* of cognitive *therapy* by Aaron Beck in which *client* and *counselor* treat automatic *thoughts* as hypotheses that can be tested out in behavioral *experiments* and be subjected to logical scrutiny. For example, the automatic thought that when people do not smile, they dislike me or they are unhappy, could be tested through collaborative empiricism.

collective counseling The term used to describe Alfred Adler's form of *group counseling*.

collective unconscious Carl Jung's term for that part of the *unconscious* that is universal in human beings and contains inherited psychic functions, such as *archetypes,* that are passed on genetically from one generation to another (e.g., the *anima* and *animus*). See *personal unconscious*.

College Adjustment Scale An important *assessment* instrument for *college counseling* centers to use in deciding what services and programs they will emphasize. This *test* screens college students for common developmental and psychological *problems* using nine scales that measure psychological distress in the following areas: *anxiety, depression, suicidal ideation, substance abuse, self-esteem problems, interpersonal problems, family problems,* academic problems, and *career problems*.

college counseling *Counseling* that focuses on the *needs* and development issues of both *traditional college students* (ages 18 to 22) and *nontraditional college students* (ages 25 years and higher) enrolled in colleges and universities. See also *American College Counseling Association (ACCA)*.

coming out When a person who is *homosexual* publicly reveals he or she is *gay* or *lesbian*.

commission A term used in connection with *malpractice* for doing something that should not have been done, for example, soliciting a *client* to refer friends to your practice.

Commission on Accreditation for Marriage and Family Therapy Education (COAMFTE) A specialized accrediting body that accredits the master's, doctoral, and postgraduate clinical training programs in *marriage and family therapy* throughout the United States and Canada. Since 1978, the *COAMFTE* has been recognized by the U.S. Department of Education (USDE) as the national accrediting body for the field of *marriage and family therapy*. COAMFTE is located at 1133 NW 15th Street, Suite 300, Washington, DC 20005-2710 (202-452-0109; http://www.aamft.org/about/coamfte/aboutCOAMFTE).

Commission on Accreditation of Rehabilitation Facilities (CARF) an independent, nonprofit accreditor of human service providers in the areas of aging services, behavioral health, child and youth services, DMEPOS, employment and community services, medical rehabilitation, and opioid treatment programs. CARF International offices are located at 4891 East Grant Road, Tucson, AZ 85712 (888-281-6531; http://www.carf.org/).

Commission on Rehabilitation Counselor Certification An independent, not-for-profit organization dedicated to improving the lives of persons with *disabilities*. CRCC is located at 1699 E. Woodfield Road, Suite 300, Schaumburg, IL 60173 (847-944-1325; http://www.crccertification.com/).

commitment **1.** A dedication by a *client* to *counseling* and the *process* of *change*. **2.** An involuntary institutionalization of a person who is mentally disturbed to a *mental health* facility.

common law *Law* derived from tradition and usage. Most common law in the United States is based on British common law.

communication The *verbal* and/or *nonverbal* exchange of information or messages, for example, telling someone how you feel or where you would like to go.

communication stance An experiential and *humanistic family therapy* procedure of Virginia Satir's in which *family* members are asked to exaggerate the physical *positions* of their *roles* such as blaming others for everything that has gone wrong in their lives by pointing a finger at them. The intent of this action is to help them "level." See *leveling*.

communications theory An approach to working with families originated by Virginia Satir. It focuses on the *clarification* of *verbal* and *nonverbal transactions* among *family* members. Much communication *theory* work has been incorporated into *strategic family therapy*.

community counselor A term coined by Judith Lewis and Michael Lewis in the 1970s to describe a *counselor* who can function in multidimensional *roles* regardless of employment setting. These functions are now incorporated under the term *clinical mental health counselor*.

community mental health centers Local centers, located in *population catchment areas*, that provide *mental health* services for those with life transitions, difficulties, and *mental disorders*.

Community Mental Health Centers Act (CMHC Act) A congressional act in 1963 that authorized the establishment of 2,000 *community mental health centers* in the United States. These centers were charged with providing mental health services in five core areas: outpatient, inpatient, consultation and education, partial hospitalization, and emergency/crisis intervention. The CMHC Act opened up opportunities for *counselor* employment outside educational settings.

commuter marriage A *marriage* in which each partner maintains a separate household, usually in a different city, to pursue a *career*. Holidays and weekends are times that individuals in commuter marriages usually spend together.

comparative research studies Studies (also called *correlational studies*) that form a link between *case study methods* and *experimental design* and *quasi-experimental design*. They make directional and quantitative comparisons between sets of *data*. Such studies are nonmanipulative. They simply note similarities in variations among *factors* with no effort to discern cause-and-effect relationships.

compassion A *response* to the perceived suffering of others that requires *listening* intently and acting in a concerned, kind, and empathic way. The origins of compassion come from one's deepest understanding of what life is.

compassion fatigue AKA *secondary traumatization*, the *burnout* and stress-related symptoms experienced by helping professionals after prolonged exposure to clients who have experienced tragedy or *trauma*.

compensation 1. An *Adlerian counseling* term for the act of making up for a deficiency in one area by excelling in a different but related activity. **2.** An amount of money given in payment for services.

competency A person's ability to function adequately in his or her *environment*.

competency test 1. A *test* that assesses an individual's level of knowledge or skill in a particular domain, such as math. **2.** A *test* or tests given to determine if a person who claims or is claimed to be mentally disturbed or deficient is competent to stand trial.

complainants One of three types of *clients* classified by Steve deShazer. These clients are characterized by their expectation that they will find some solution to their *problems* through the *process* of *therapy*. They are given observational and thinking tasks by deShazer to combat *resistance*. See also *customers; visitors*.

complementary relationship A *relationship* in which *family* member *roles* are specifically and even rigidly different from each other, for example, one being dominant and the other submissive. If members fail to fulfill their roles, such as that of a decision maker or a nurturer, other members of the family are adversely affected.

complementary transaction A communicative *process* in *transactional analysis* in which both persons are operating either from the same *ego state* (e.g., child to child, adult to adult) or from complementary ego states (e.g., parent to child, adult to parent). Responses are predictable and appropriate. For example, an adult-to-adult transaction might transpire as follows: *Person 1:* "What time is it?" *Person 2:* "It is 7 o'clock."

compliment A written message used in *brief family therapy* designed to praise a *family* for its strengths and build a *"yes set"* within it. A compliment consists of a positive statement with which all members of a family can agree. For example, the *counselor* might say "Most families would have folded under the pressure you have faced, but yours didn't."

composite score The direct sum or weighted sum of the scores on two or more *tests* or subsections of tests.

compulsion A repetitive *behavior* (usually as the result of an *obsession*), for example, washing one's hands every few minutes.

compulsive disorder A *disorder* that involves repetitive *behavior*s, often performed in a ritualistic manner.

computer or rational analyzer According to Virginia Satir's *theory,* a person who interacts in a *family* primarily on a cognitive or intellectual level.

computer-assisted career guidance systems (CACGS) Computer-based *systems* that offer *career information* and help individuals sort through their *values* and interests or simply find *job* information.

computer-assisted counseling The use of computers and technology to help *clients* in the *counseling process.*

computer-assisted testing *Testing* that is completed by using a computer-based program rather than in a *test* booklet.

computer-based interpretation The use of computers to *score* and interpret *standardized tests*. In this *process,* narrative descriptors about results are usually provided in addition to the *score*s themselves.

computer-based testing The use of computer technology, software programs, or Internet sites for the administration, analysis, and interpretation of testing instruments.

con words Expressions used by *clients,* such as "try" or "maybe," that are not specific to a designated *behavior* or *outcome objective.* Such expressions usually result in *clients* failing to achieve a *goal.*

conclusions *Generalizations* about a *phenomenon* made as a result of *research* or clinical observations.

concrete operations The third phase in Jean Piaget's four *stages* of *cognitive development*. In concrete operations, children (from ages 7 to 11) learn mentally to manipulate objects and apply logic to specific observations. Children master the idea of *conservation* at this phase but cannot think abstractly. They are literal minded.

concreteness The ability to help a *client* turn something that is vaguely understood or defined into something that is clear and understood, for example, a feeling of sadness or joy.

concurrent marriage counseling A session where the married couple is counseled separately.

concurrent validity A type of *validity* that compares a *test* with a criterion available at the time of testing, such as an independent measure of the same construct (e.g., mental well-being). The *MMPI* is a test with concurrent validity. See *criterion-based validity.* Concurrent validity is usually reported in terms of a *correlation coefficient.*

condemning questions Questions that put people down and prevent them from seeing *situations* more honestly and openly, for example: "Don't you think you should feel differently?"

condition of worth When an individual responds in a certain manner because of the expectations of others and the does so to be accepted. Such a response leads to the creation of a *false self* and *incongruence* because the individual is behaving to please others and not self.

conditioned response   A learned *response*. In *classical conditioning,* a learned response comes about because of being paired repeatedly with a *conditioned stimulus.*

conditioned stimulus   A term in *classical conditioning* for when a neutral *stimulus* becomes associated with a positive stimulus and an organism learns to respond to the neutral stimulus in the same way it responds to the positive stimulus. For example, in Pavlov's famous conditioning of dogs, the animals learned to salivate to the sound of a bell after the bell was associated with food.

conditioning   A *process* of *learning* that involves stimuli and *responses* becoming paired through association or training. The two primary types of conditioning are *classical conditioning* and *operant conditioning.*

conduct disorder   Children or adolescents with conduct disorder exhibit a number of behavioral and emotional symptoms, some of which include: aggression to people and animals, such as bullying or cruelty, deliberate destruction of property, deceitfulness, lying, or stealing, and serious violations of rules, such as staying out all night or truancy from school.

confabulation   See *false memory syndrome.*

confidentiality   The professional, ethical, and *legal* obligation of *counselors* that they not disclose *client* information revealed during *counseling* without the client's written *consent.* Confidentiality must be broken when a client is potentially dangerous to *self* or others. See *duty to warn.*

configuration equation prevention model   A primary prevention model by Bloom focused on: (a) increasing individual strengths and decreasing individual limitations; (b) increasing social supports and decreasing social stresses; and (c) enhancing environmental resources and minimizing environmental pressures.

confirmation   A *transactional analysis technique* in which the *counselor* points out to the *client* that a previously modified *behavior* has occurred again. Only when the client has a firmly established *adult ego state* can this *technique* be effective.

confirmation of a family member   A *process* that involves using a *feeling* word to reflect an expressed or unexpressed emotion of a *family* member or using a nonjudgmental description of an individual's *behavior* to acknowledge their presence. For example, in the latter *situation,* a *counselor* might say to a father, "You seem to be very active today."

conflict   **1.** An *intrapersonal* struggle in making a decision between two or more *choices,* for example, staying up late or getting up early. **2.** An *interpersonal* striving by two or more parties to achieve opposite or mutually exclusive *goals.*

confrontation   Verbally challenging *clients* to look at the discrepancies and *incongruence* between their words and actions. For example, "I hear you want to meet new people, yet I understand you watch television at home every night." The purpose of confrontation is to promote awareness of self-contradictions and to foster *change.*

congruence   **1.** A consistency between the way people feel and the way they act. **2.** A key concept, also known as *genuineness,* in the *theory* of Carl Rogers. According to Rogers, congruence is one of the *core conditions* necessary in *counseling* if *treatment* is to be successful. **3.** In Holland's career typology theory, the goodness of fit between *personality* and *environment.*

conjoint family drawing   A procedure in which families are initially given the instructions to "draw a picture as you see yourself as a *family.*" Each member of the family makes such a drawing and then shares through discussion the *perceptions* and *insights* that emerged from doing the activity.

conjoint family therapy   A session in which two or more members of a *family* are counseled together at the same time. Conjoint family therapy was pioneered and promoted by Virginia Satir in the 1960s.

conjoint marriage counseling   A session in which the married couple is counseled together at the same time.

conjoint sexual therapy   A Masters and Johnson's approach where two therapists, a man and a woman, work together as a cotherapy team in treating sexual problems.

conscience   **1.** In *psychoanalysis,* the part of the *superego* that induces *guilt* when persons act against ways they have been taught. **2.** An internal set of *rules* that governs a person's *behavior* (i.e., the moral characteristics of a person).

conscious   A term in *psychoanalysis* for that part of the mind that is attuned to events in the present, to an awareness of the outside world.

consciousness   A total *awareness* of oneself.

consciousness-raising group   A *group* that is set up to help its participants become more aware of the issues they face and the wide variety of *choices* they have within their *environment.*

consent   To give approval or *permission;* to agree. In *counseling,* written consent on the part of the *client* is necessary in some *situations* (e.g., for the transfer of *client records*), and *verbal* consent on the part of the client is necessary in other situations (e.g., when trying a *technique*).

consequences   The results of a *behavior.* In *Adlerian counseling,* consequences are either *natural consequences* or *logical consequences.*

conservation   A Piagetian concept that deals with an understanding that physical properties of objects do not *change,* even when appearances change. For example, children cannot understand that changing the shape of the object that water is poured into does not change the volume of the water. The concept of conservation is typically acquired around the age of 7, when a *child* reaches the *stage* of *concrete operations.*

construct   A *trait* or *behavior,* such as extroversion, that is measured by a *test.*

construct validity   The degree to which a *test* measures an intended *construct* (i.e., that

which it was constructed to measure, such as shyness or dogmatism).

constructional interpretation   A level of *interpretation* that focuses on *thought* patterns and the way *clients* express themselves. See also *interpretation.*

constructivism   A philosophy that proposes that reality is subjective in nature, a *reflection* of observation and experience, not an *objective* entity. Some *counseling* theories, such as *narrative therapy,* are based on constructivism.

consultant   A resource person with special knowledge who assists individuals and *groups* in resolving difficulties they have not been able to resolve on their own.

consultation   A voluntary *relationship* between a professional helper and an individual or *group* that needs help. In such a relationship, the *consultant* provides assistance by *helping* to define and resolve a *problem* or potential problem of the *client.* Consultant relationships are described as triadic (i.e., client, consultant, problem) and are *content* based, goal directed, and *process* oriented.

contact   A term used in *Gestalt therapy* to refer to the sensory and motor immediacy that may be experienced when a *client* meets the *environment* directly.

contagion   The tendency of *group* members to behave in the same way (e.g., feeling sad or happy).

contaminating variables   *Factors* that invalidate an *experimental research* study, such as one group of *clients* being healthier initially than a comparison group.

contamination   **1.** In *transactional analysis,* the intrusion of the *parent ego state* and/or the *child ego state* into the *boundaries* of the *adult ego state.* **2.** In *research, variables* that invalidate an *experimental research* study, such as comparing two unequal groups.

content   The actual ideas and facts discussed in a *counseling* session and/or the words used between *counselors* and *clients.* Content is the material or the "what" of counseling, and is the opposite of *process.*

content analysis The analysis of a *client* session to see what *themes* emerge.

content bias Items in an *assessment* instrument that favor one group over another.

content validity The degree to which a *test* measures intended *content* (i.e., a specific body of knowledge such as math or vocabulary). Content validity is determined judgmentally and not through the use of statistical procedures. Content validity is especially applicable to *achievement tests*.

contingency contract A written *treatment plan* that defines *goals,* procedures, and expected *outcomes,* as well as the identification of *rewards* if the *client* performs the expected *behaviors.* One action is *contingent* (i.e., dependent) on another.

Week 1
(must earn 5 points for a reward)

	make bed	clean room	hang up clothes	pick up toys	Goal
George	✓	✓		✓	Pizza
Will		✓		✓	Baseball game
Ann	✓	✓	✓	✓	Spend-the-night party

contingency contract

continuing education unit (CEU) Credit for participating in professional educational programs that update one's knowledge. CEUs are often required for continuing a *counselor's licensure* and/or *certification.*

continuous development Change that results from small, stable, and predictable shifts or changes in *behavior, cognition,* or *emotional* states. Continuous development is also known as *quantitative growth.*

continuous reinforcement The constant rewarding or *reinforcement* of a *behavior.* Continuous reinforcement is often used to establish a behavior. It is the opposite of *intermittent reinforcement.*

contract A formal agreement between *counselors* and *clients,* often in writing, about what

behavioral *changes* will be made and when; there are built-in *rewards* for behaving in a certain manner.

control group A comparison group that is treated equivalent to the *experimental group,* except that they are not exposed to the *independent variable.* Thus, researchers can determine whether the experimental group would have *changed* significantly without the manipulation of the independent variable.

control theory A complete *system* for explaining how the brain works. Control theory was integrated into *reality therapy* by William Glasser from the late 1980s to the late 1990s, when it was replaced with *choice theory.*

conventional people Individuals, according to Holland's *career* typology, who enjoy working in well-organized environments and are good at following plans in a systematic, orderly way. See *RIASEC.*

conventional stage The second of three major *stages* of Lawrence Kohlberg's stages of *moral development.* The conventional stage contains two levels. At the first level, *morality* is based on what other people think. At the second level, morality is based on what authorities say. According to Kohlberg's *research,* most people do not get past the conventional stage of moral development.

conversion reaction A *defense mechanism* in which *feelings* that a person is unable to express are converted into physiological *symptoms,* such as blindness, loss of feeling, or paralysis.

conversion therapy AKA *reparative therapy,* involves methods intended to convert *bisexual, lesbian,* and *gay* people to *heterosexuality* (i.e., change their sexual orientation).

cooperation Individuals, especially in *groups,* working together for a common purpose or good.

cooperative learning groups *Study groups* established so that assigned tasks can be divided and accomplished; members are responsible for meeting regularly and teaching each other what they have learned.

copayment The amount a *client* owes for services after an insurance company pays its part.

coping skills The skills and *behavior*s people use to adjust to their *environment*s and avoid *stress*. For example, persons may learn techniques on how to control *emotion*s and stay calm.

COPS See *Career Occupational Preference System*.

CORE See *Council on Rehabilitation Education*.

core conditions The necessary *personality* qualities a *counselor* must possess and show for effective *counseling* to take place. These conditions, as outlined by Carl Rogers, are *empathy*, *unconditional positive regard* (i.e., acceptance), and *congruence* (i.e., *genuineness*).

core mechanisms of group leadership The essential conditions necessary in a *group* for it to properly function. For example, for a group to run well, it must contain the following five leader behaviors: *emotional stimulation, caring, meaning attribution, feedback,* and *executive function*.

correctional counseling *Counseling* that is conducted in correctional or prison settings and often referred to as *offender counseling*.

correlation The statistical *relationship* between two *variables,* for example, a *score* on an *ability test* and the relationship of that score to an actual skill. Correlation does not deal with cause and effect but with dependence.

correlation coefficient A numerical index of the *relationship* between two *variables,* ranging from +1.00 (perfect positive relationship) to −1.00 (perfect negative relationship). An index of .00 indicates an absence of a relationship.

correlational research *Research* that examines the *correlation* between two *variables,* for example, height and leadership. Neither variable is said to cause a change in the other.

correlational studies See *comparative research studies*.

Council for Accreditation of Counseling and Related Educational Programs (CACREP) Founded in 1981, *CACREP* is an independent accrediting agency for *counselor education* programs at the master's and doctoral levels. CACREP-accredited programs are in *school counseling, clinical mental health counseling, addiction counseling, career counseling, student affairs and college counseling, counselor education and supervision, and marriage, couple and family counseling*. CACREP is located at 1001 North Fairfax Street, Suite 510, Alexandria, VA 22314 (703) 535-5990; http://www.cacrep.org/template/index.cfm

Council of Guidance and Personnel Associations A forerunner (1934 to 1951) of what became the *American Personnel and Guidance Association (APGA)*. This group included the Alliance for Guidance of Rural Youth, the *American College Personnel Association*, the National Association of Deans of Women, the National Association of Guidance Supervisors and Counselor Trainers, and the *National Vocational Guidance Association*.

Council on Rehabilitation Education (CORE) The accrediting agency of institutions of higher education that offer *rehabilitation counseling*. CORE's address is P.O. Box 1788, Champaign, IL 61824-1788 (217-333-6688; http://www.core-rehab.org/).

counselee Another name for a *client*.

counseling "The application of mental health, psychological or human development principles, through cognitive, affective, behavioral or systemic interventions, strategies that address *wellness, personal growth,* or *career development,* as well as *pathology*" (*American Counseling Association,* www.counseling.org/).

Counseling and Human Development A monograph on current issues in *counseling* published nine times a year by Love Publishing Company, 9101 East Kenyon Avenue, Suite 2200, Denver, CO 80237 (303-221-7333, http://www.lovepublishing.com).

Counseling and Student Services Clearinghouse (CASS) See *Educational Resources Information Center/Counseling and Student Services Clearinghouse (ERIC/CASS)*.

Counseling Association for Humanistic Education and Development (C-AHEAD) A division of the *American Counseling Association (ACA)* that advocates positive attitudes toward *self* and others through diversified *learning* and developmental *processes*. Until 1999, C-AHEAD was known as the *Association for Humanistic Education and Development (AHEAD)*, (http://www.c-ahead.com/).

counseling groups *Groups* that focus on each person's *behavior* and growth or *change* within the group in regard to a particular *problem* or concern. These groups are also sometimes known as *interpersonal problem-solving groups*.

Counseling Psychologist See *The Counseling Psychologist*.

counseling psychology A psychological specialty also referred to as *Division 17* (i.e., society of counseling psychology) of the *American Psychological Association (APA*; see their brochure at http://www.apa.org/about/division/div17.html). Its aim is to *facilitate* personal and *interpersonal* functioning across the *life span* and to focus on emotional, social, vocational, educational, health-related, developmental, and organizational concerns. Counseling psychology encompasses a broad *range* of practices that help people improve their well-being, alleviate *distress* and maladjustment, resolve crises, and increase their ability to live more highly functioning lives. See *Division 17 of the American Psychological Association*.

counseling skills Basic proficiencies needed to help someone achieve a desired state of being in life. Abilities such as *attending, responding, reflecting, paraphrasing, confronting, summarizing,* and *interpreting* are among those that must be mastered.

counseling specialty A narrowly focused entity in *counseling* (e.g., *career counseling, rehabilitation counseling*) requiring advanced knowledge and experience and often *certification* or *licensure*.

Counseling Today The monthly magazine of the *American Counseling Association (ACA)*.

counselling The international way of spelling what professionals in the United States refer to as *counseling*.

counselor A *helping professional* who has obtained at least a master's in *counseling*, who has passed competency *tests* on a general and/or specific level in the field of *counseling*, and who is educationally equipped to help others prevent, solve, or cope with life problems. Counselors who are licensed by states are often referred to as *licensed professional counselors* (LPC).

counselor education **1.** The degree title often conferred on a person who earns a doctorate in *counseling*. **2.** The name often given a department where counseling is taught at either the master's or doctoral level.

counselor educator A professor who teaches and/or researches *counseling*.

Counselor in a Changing World A landmark book in the history of *counseling*, written by Gilbert Wrenn and published in 1962. The book proposed a blueprint for *school counseling* and for *school counselors* and broached the subject of *multicultural counseling* in an influential way.

Counselor Preparation A national comprehensive study, published every 3 years, of programs, faculties, and trends in the field of *counseling*. New editions are published by the *National Board for Certified Counselors;* this landmark text was initiated and first published by Joseph Hollis and Richard Wantz in 1971.

counselor-centered counseling A term used to describe E. G. Williamson's *theory* of *counseling*. See also *directive counseling*.

Counselors for Social Justice (CSJ) A division of the *American Counseling Association* that provides mutual support, information, and ideas for social action to promote community well-being (http://counselorsforsocialjustice.com).

counterconditioning The *process* of unlearning paired associations, with new ones taking their place; a key component of *systematic desensitization*.

counterscript A term in *transactional analysis* for temporarily taking on a *role* that is the opposite of one's *life script*. The individual takes on the role because of a *conflict* between two of his or her *ego states*.

countertransference A term in *psychoanalysis* for the positive or negative wishes, fantasies, and *feeling*s that a *counselor* unconsciously directs or transfers to a *client,* stemming from his or her own unresolved conflicts.

couple group counseling A form of *counseling* developed by John Bell in which *counselors* see more than one couple at a time in a *group setting. Treatment* is conducted in the *group* by having couples discuss their *problem*s in front of other couples. The advantages of this approach are that group members see that some problems are universal; they can identify appropriate and inappropriate *behavior*s and expectations of others; they can develop *insight* and skills through observing other couples; they can receive group *feedback* and support for the ventilation of *feeling*s and *changed* behavior; and they can share the cost.

couples counseling The *counseling* of either *heterosexual* or *homosexual* dyadic pairs about dynamics within their *relationship.* When couples counseling is conducted exclusively with individuals who are married, it is known as *marriage counseling* or *marriage therapy.*

courage An *Adlerian counseling* term for the ability to take a risk without knowing the *outcome.*

court order A *subpoena* to appear in court at a certain time with regard to a specific case.

court-ordered witness A person ordered to appear before a court to testify in behalf of or against someone else.

covered services Professional services of health care providers that have been authorized by a health care plan or *HMO.*

covert A thought, idea, or picture that remains hidden in a person's mind.

covert rehearsal A *cognitive behavioral technique* in which individuals learn new information or *behavior*s through practicing them repeatedly by themselves. It is the opposite of *overt rehearsal.*

covert sensitization A behavioral *technique* in which undesired *behavior* is eliminated by associating it with unpleasantness. For example, when a person does the undesired act, he or she may be "popped" with a rubber band. Covert sensitization is used in treating *client*s who have *problem*s in such areas as smoking, obesity, *substance abuse,* and sexual deviation.

CPI See *California Psychological Inventory.*

crack A highly addictive form of *cocaine.*

crank The injection of methamphetamines into oneself to experience euphoria.

CRC See *Certified Rehabilitation Counselor.*

creative arts Art forms, such as music, literature, dance, storytelling, imagery, play, games, and painting, that express *emotion* in a concrete way.

creative arts therapies Clinical use of the *creative arts* (e.g., music, literature, painting) as a primary or adjunct way of bringing about *change.* See also *National Coalition of Creative Arts Therapies Associations (NCCATA).*

creative imagery A *warm-up technique* that consists of inviting *psychodrama* participants to imagine neutral or pleasant objects and scenes that are not present. The idea is to help participants become more spontaneous.

credentialing Legal regulations of a profession such as *counseling* that take the form of *licensure, certification*, or *registration.* Licensure is the most powerful form of credentialing.

credibility *Counselor* expertness and trustworthiness. See *social influence model.*

criminal law Acts that are considered crimes against society and are prosecuted by the government, not by individuals. Such acts are punishable by fines, imprisonment, or the death penalty.

criminal liability Responsibility for a criminal act. For example, a *counselor* can be held legally liable (or accountable) for working with a *client* in a way that the *law* does not permit.

crisis **1.** An emotionally stressful event or urgent *situation* that involves major changes in a person life or in the life of a community (e.g., an *ecosystemic crisis*). A crisis of this type is usually unsettling and traumatic and outside an individual's control (e.g., an earthquake or tornado). **2.** A crucial or decisive turning point in a person's life that may be developmental and expected, or situational and unexpected. See *developmental crises, situational crises, existential crises.*

crisis counseling A special type of *counseling* that is often *directive* in nature and that focuses on *helping* a *client* find ways to respond productively and constructively in the midst of a chaotically urgent or acute emotionally disturbing *situation,* such as a hurricane or earthquake. See *psychological first aid.*

crisis intervention AKA *crisis management*, a time-limited, action-oriented treatment approach to a specific event that has thrown a person off course and disrupted the individual's life. The objective of the intervention is to help the person cope and return to a precrisis level of functioning.

crisis management See *crisis intervention.*

criterion A standard, norm, or judgment used as a basis for quantitative and qualitative comparison.

criterion-referenced A type of referencing related directly to the dimension (e.g., skill or ability) being measured (e.g., a standard). Criterion-referenced tests focus on specific knowledge or competences. Criterion-referenced is the opposite of *norm-referenced.*

criterion-related validity The predictability of *test scores* with other criteria, such as a person's actual *performance* of a certain skill—such as keyboarding—across time and *situations.*

critical incident in life An event, such as marriage or an automobile accident, that has the *power* to positively or negatively shape or influence a person.

critical parent A term in *transactional analysis* that describes the negative aspect of the *parent ego state* in which the negative *behavior*s (e.g., scolding) of parents are displayed.

critical period A developmental term that describes a time period within children's lives in which they are optimally ready to learn certain *behavior*s, such as reading or speaking a foreign language.

cross-cultural communication The verbal and nonverbal ways in which people from different cultures communicate with one another, from language to facial expressions.

cross-cultural counseling *Counseling* between individuals from different cultural backgrounds. If conducted properly, such counseling transcends or bridges the differences of specific *culture*s and leads to therapeutic results. See also *multicultural counseling.*

cross-dresser Men and women who enjoy wearing the clothing of, or appearing as, the other gender. *The term cross-dresser is now preferred to the term transvestite.*

crossed transaction A communication pattern described in *transactional analysis* in which an inappropriate *ego state* is activated producing an unexpected *response.*

Person 1: Can you help me carry these bags? They must weigh a ton.

Person 2: Those bags weigh approximately 20 pounds, and you are capable of carrying them.

cross-generational alliance (coalition) An inappropriate family alliance that contains members of two different generations within it, for example, a *parent* and *child.*

crossed transaction

cross-sectional research A *research* approach in which large numbers of representative *variables* are studied at a given period in time. A cross-sectional study is frequently the basis for the establishment of normative *data*. It is the opposite of a *longitudinal research*.

cross validation   Readministering a *test* that has been found to be valid with one group to a second group to determine whether it is valid with that group.

crystallization   A *transactional analysis technique* that consists of an adult-to-adult transaction in which the *client* comes to an awareness that individual game playing may be given up if so desired. Thus, the client is free to do as he or she chooses, and the therapeutic *process* is virtually complete.

crystallized intelligence   Mental skills and abilities accumulated through experience and education that continue to increase with age, for example, a knowledge of world events. It is the opposite of *fluid intelligence*.

CS   See *conditioned stimulus*.

CSI   See *Chi Sigma Iota*.

CSJ   See *Counselors for Social Justice*.

cue   A *stimulus,* for example, a word or a gesture, that is intended to communicate information, for example, a yawn.

cuento therapy   A form of narrative modeling in which folktales are modified for use with *children* and *adolescents* to convey cultural *values* and present models of adaptive *behavior.*

cultural bias   The tendency to measure or evaluate characteristics and *behavior*s based solely on one particular *majority culture.*

cultural counseling   See *multicultural counseling.*

cultural diversity   The existence within a society of a number of varied groups with distinct *values* and *lifestyle*s. Cultural diversity allows individual ethnic groups to maintain their own cultural uniqueness while sharing common elements with the *majority culture.* Cultural diversity is also known as *cultural pluralism* and *pluralism.*

cultural-fair assessment   A measurement or assessment that is constructed to minimize or eliminate cultural bias and irrelevant societal influences.

cultural-free assessment   See *cultural-fair assessment.*

cultural identity   The degree to which a person identifies or aligns with a cultural group.

cultural mosaic   A term that suggests various cultures in a society, such as the United States or Canada, coexist, with each maintaining its unique differences.

cultural pluralism   See *cultural diversity.*

cultural relativism   The view that behaviors, attitudes, values, and achievements should be viewed in light of the *culture* that produces them and not judged according to the standards of another culture. Thus, what is acceptable or used in one culture may be inappropriate to another.

culturally encapsulated counselors   A term coined by Gilbert Wrenn for *counselors* who treat everyone the same and in so doing, ignore important cultural differences.

culture   The shared *values,* beliefs, expectations, *worldviews, symbol*s, and appropriate learned *behavior*s of a *group* that provide its members with *norms,* plans, traditions, and *rules* for social living. Culture is transmitted from one generation to the next.

culture shock   The experience of being temporarily confused, *anxious,* disoriented, and *depressed* when entering another *culture* in which one is uncertain of the *rules* and customs.

culture-fair test   A *test* that has been normed on various cultural groups and attempts to be fair to all cultural groups by not penalizing any group because of a lack of relevant experience.

culture-specific treatment   Approaches in *counseling* designed especially for the *need*s or concerns of specific cultural groups, such as *Asian Americans* or *Hispanics.*

curative factors   Eleven *factor*s first researched and described by Irvin Yalom that contribute to the betterment of individuals in a *group*. These 11 factors are instillation of *hope,* universality, imparting of information, *altruism,* corrective recapitulation of the primary *family* group, development of *socialization techniques,* imitative *behavior, interpersonal learning, group cohesiveness, catharsis,* and existential factors.

custody The assignment of children to one or both parents after a *divorce,* along with stipulations concerning living arrangements and visitation rights.

customers Steve deShazer's classification for the type of *client* who wants to do something about his or her *situation.* Such clients are given behavioral tasks. See also *complainants; visitors.*

cut off To physically or psychologically distance oneself from others.

cutoff score A *score* chosen by a *test* administer below which individuals fail.

d

dance/movement therapy The use of dance and movement as a primary or adjunct way of bringing about therapeutic outcomes. Dance/movement therapy is defined by the *American Dance Therapy Association (ADTA)* as "the psychotherapeutic use of movement as a *process* which furthers the emotional, cognitive and physical *integration* of the individual." See also *American Dance Therapy Association (ADTA).*

Darvon See *propoxyphene.*

DAT See *Differential Aptitude Test.*

data Bits of information gathered on some characteristic of an object or group under study; facts or *statistics.*

DCT See *developmental counseling and therapy.*

death instinct A term in *psychoanalysis* for the *unconscious* drive toward destructiveness and death. The death instinct is usually manifested in human *behavior* through unnecessarily risky or dangerous behavior. The death instinct is the opposite of the *life instinct.*

cutting off **1.** Making sure that new material is not introduced too late in a *counseling* session to be adequately dealt with. **2.** Preventing *clients* from rambling when speaking. **3.** Removing oneself either physically or psychologically from others or an *environment.*

cybercounseling See *Internet counseling.*

cybernetics The study of *methods* of *feedback* control within a *system,* especially with regard to the flow of information.

cyclotherapy process The idea that a *group* continues to evolve and can be conceptualized as forever forming, with certain issues returning from time to time to be explored in greater depth.

cyclothymic disorder A mild case of *bipolar disorder.*

debriefing **1.** The process of explaining a research project to participants after they have completed the study. **2.** The process of dealing with the toxic effects of *disaster counseling* by interviewing *counselors* at the end of their shifts and providing services for them as needed.

decile Ranking *percentiles* according to tenths (e.g., 10th percentile, 20th percentile).

decision A cognitive *process* of choosing to take an action and close out other possibilities. Making a decision is an important part of *counseling.* For example, *substance abusers* must make a decision to stop their destructive *behavior* and dry out before they can be rehabilitated.

decision-redecision methods A *transactional analysis technique* emphasized by Robert and Mary Goulding. In this technique, *clients* reexamine *decision* moments in their *childhoods* based on parental *injunctions* (negative messages that begin with don't, e.g., "Don't be that way") that limit personal interactions. They then choose to redecide whether to continue acting in accordance with these messages or to *change*.

decompensation   Refers to a *client* whose condition is deteriorating (e.g., becoming more anxious).

deconstruction   A philosophical *theory* that questions traditional assumptions about certainty, truth, and identity and how words can only refer to other words. For example, in helping a *client* define a general term, the *counselor* might hear the client say that s/he is "depressed" but when this word is explored, it is clear that the client is saying s/he is angry.

deductive reasoning   A form of logical analysis that moves from general observations to a specific hypothesis. For instance, if a *counselor* has found it difficult to work with *substance abusers* before, he or she will assume that it will be hard to work with a new *client* who is a substance abuser. See *inductive reasoning*.

defamation   Injury to a person's character or reputation either through *verbal* means (*slander*) or written means (*libel*).

defense mechanism   A psychological *response* that helps protect a person from *anxiety* and other negative *emotion*s accompanying *stress*. Defense mechanisms originate in the *unconscious* and include *repression, displacement, projection, reaction formation, regression, rationalization, denial, undoing,* and *identification*.

deficit model   A model based on the belief that environmental factors rather than biological factors influence *behavior* and that deficits prevent individuals from performing well. Some federal educational programs, such as Head Start and No Child Left Behind, are based on this model.

deinstitutionalization   The removal of people with chronic or severe *mental health disorders* from state institutions and public hospitals to provide them with quality care in their communities.

delayed-entry women   See *late-entry women*.

delinquency   Antisocial or *illegal* activity. When such *behavior* is connected with a teenager, the action is called *juvenile delinquency*.

delirium, dementia, and amnesic and other cognitive disorders   A diagnostic category in the *DSM* that deals with types of permanent or transient damage to the brain.

delirium   A *cognitive disorder* characterized by a clouding of *consciousness*, reduced environmental awareness, distractibility, disorientation, disorder thinking, and agitation.

delirium tremens   Severe *withdrawal symptoms,* such as *hallucinations,* that sometimes follow heavy and prolonged *alcohol abuse*.

delusion   A false but strongly held belief despite a lack of support for it. The two most common forms of delusions are those of grandeur and persecution.

demand characteristics   A *participant*'s reaction to an *experimenter* or a setting that may influence his or her *behavior*, for example, a two-way mirror may increase *anxiety*.

dementia   The deterioration of intellectual functions such as memory loss or impairment. The onset of dementia is often due to medical conditions such as a stroke, head trauma, or Parkinson's disease. Alzheimer's is an example of a dementia that progresses slowly.

dementia praecox   A historically antiquated name for *schizophrenia*.

Demerol   See *meperidine*.

democratic leader   A leader in a *group* who *trust*s members to develop their own potential and that of others. Such a leader serves as the *facilitator* and not as a director, thereby cooperating, collaborating, and sharing responsibilities.

denial   **1.** A *defense mechanism* in which a person ignores or disavows unacceptable *thought*s or acts as if an experience does not exist or never did. **2.** The first stage in *Elizabeth Kübler-Ross*'s five stages of *grief*.

density of time   Lee Combrinck-Graham's model of *family relationship*s. The model outlines the natural tendencies of three-generational families to be close or distant from each other over time. The fullness of time in regard to events and relationships is greatest during certain periods of the *family life cycle*, such as the birth of a baby.

dependent personality/dependency **1.** A *client* who presents himself/herself as helpless and incapable but refuses to accept constructive *feedback* or to try new ways of behaving. Such clients are help-rejecting complainers and encourage the *behavior* of *advice giving*. **2.** A descriptor of a *relationship* in which one person cannot or will not function without the aid or input of another. **3.** The relatedness of two *scores* in *research*.

dependent variable **1.** In *experimental research*, the *behavior* or *outcome* that is measured as a result of manipulating the *independent variable*. **2.** In *correlational research*, the measure being predicted; also called the *criterion variable*.

depersonalization disorder A condition in which a person experiences the *feeling* that his or her body is unreal.

depressants *Drugs* with an effect similar to that of *alcohol*. Small doses can produce calmness and relaxed muscles; large doses can cause respiratory *depression*, coma, and death. Types of depressants are *barbiturates* and *tranquilizers*. Slang names for depressants include *downers*, *barbs*, *yellow jackets*, *red birds*, and *ludes*.

depression **1.** A common feeling as well as major *disorder* characterized by sadness, dejection, lack of energy, hopelessness, and loneliness. Depression may be chronic or acute, mild or severe. **2.** The fourth of five stages in *Elizabeth Kübler-Ross*'s stages of *grief*.

deprivation To withhold or not provide something that is necessary such as food or love.

derived score A *test score*, such as a *percentile*, *stanine*, or *standard score*, that has been converted from a *raw score* through some type of mathematical operation.

descriptive research A research method that focuses on trends, preferences, opinions, and relationships between variables. Examples of descriptive research include *surveys*, *correlational research*, *historical research*, *case studies*, *field studies*, and *exploratory research*.

descriptive statistics Numbers that summarize, organize, and/or *graph* characteristics of a group of *scores* or a pool of *research data*. *Measures of the central tendency* (i.e., *mean*, *mode*, *median*) as well as variability measures (e.g., *standard deviation*) are descriptive statistics. Descriptive statistics are the opposite of *inferential statistics*.

desensitization See *systematic desensitization*.

desensitized To become less sensitive to a *stimulus* because of repeated exposure to it. One way of *helping* individuals with *phobias* is to desensitize them through exposing them over and over again to the feared stimulus.

designer drugs *Illegal drugs* that have had their molecular structure modified to produce analogs that may be several times stronger than the drugs they were designed to imitate.

despair **1.** An inability in old age to find *meaning* in one's life. Despair is the opposite of Erik Erikson's virtue of *integrity*. **2.** A complete loss of *hope*.

detachment Physical or psychological separateness from others.

determinism The view that *factor*s beyond people's control, such as biology, determine their future. Determinism underlies much of the *theory* of *psychoanalysis* and can be summed up in the phrase "biology is destiny."

detouring coalition A *coalition* in which the pair holds a third member responsible for their difficulties or *conflict*s with one another. See also *coalition*.

detoxification The first phase of dependency treatment; the *process* of removing a harmful *drug* from a person's body through the withholding of the toxic *substance* and providing that person with rest, a proper diet, exercise, *health care*, and so on. Detoxification is typically completed in an *inpatient* setting under medical care.

detriangulate   The *process* of being in contact with others and emotionally separate from them. It is the opposite of *triangulate*.

Developing Understanding of Self and Others (DUSO)   A commercial classroom *guidance* program based on *Adlerian counseling theory*.

development   Predictable physical, mental, and social *changes* over the *life span* that occur in *relationship* to the *environment*. *Counseling* is geared to the development of the *population*s being served, for example, children, adolescents, or adults.

developmental counseling   A *counseling* approach that emphasizes that human *personality* develops based on the interaction between the person and the *environment*. In this approach there is an emphasis on growth, age-appropriate *intervention*, and *prevention*.

developmental counseling and therapy (DCT)   A comprehensive clinical *mental health* approach originated by Allen Ivey for the *treatment* of individuals from a nonpathological, positivistic perspective. DCT suggests that the way *client*s understand and operate in the world is based on two main interacting *systems*: their levels of *cognitive development* and the implications of larger social units in which clients are involved (e.g., *family,* community, and *culture*).

developmental crises   Times of *change* in the *life span* that are expected but that are often accompanied by turmoil and new opportunity, such as marriage, birth, and aging.

developmental disability   A *disability* that is the result of a disease, genetic disorder, or impaired growth pattern that occurs before *adulthood*. Developmental disabilities continue indefinitely and may require specific and lifelong care. Examples of developmental disabilities are *mental retardation,* cerebral palsy, and Down syndrome.

developmental factors   *Variables* such as the age, gender, and maturity level of *client*s.

developmental group counseling   *Counseling* that takes place in a *psychoeducational group*. It is often used for teaching basic *life skills*.

developmental milestones   Marker events or tasks that indicate movement in a person's growth. Developmental milestones are usually in physical, psychosocial, and cognitive *domains*.

developmental psychopathology   The study of psychopathology in the context of maturational and developmental processes that occur in children and adolescents.

developmental stages   Growth and behavioral organization categories in an individual, *group,* or *family*. Each new *stage,* compared to a preceding one, is qualitatively different, novel, and more comprehensive. Developmental stages occur in a fixed sequence of *maturation* and are often age and maturity related.

developmental tasks   Important skills and *achievement*s, such as walking, talking, and reading, that children must master at certain ages if they are to function in a healthy way.

deviation IQ   A *score* on an IQ *test* that compares a person with his/her age or grade group. The fixed *mean* is usually 100 with a *standard deviation* of 15.

diagnosis   An *interpretation*, derived from the use of *assessment* information, about a person's condition (e.g., his or her level of functioning). The *DSM* and *ICD* are often used in making a diagnosis because of the criteria they have established in regard to classifying and labeling physical and emotional categories of diseases and *disorders*.

Diagnostic and Statistical Manual (DSM)   A manual published by the *American Psychiatric Association* that codifies psychiatric *disorders*. The *DSM* contains over 400 different categorical classifications of disorders. It is compatible to the *International Classification of Diseases (ICD)* manual, published by the World Health Organization. The *DSM* is updated and modified on a regular basis, with revisions of the manual being published in between editions. See also *Axes of the DSM*.

diagnostic test   A *test* that is used to help in the *diagnosis* of a *client*. Almost any test can be used as a diagnostic instrument, depending on what the evaluator is seeking to assess.

dialogue **1.** Honest and genuine communication between oneself and others or between different aspects of oneself. **2.** A primary therapeutic tool in *counseling*. **3.** An essential ingredient in an existential *I-Thou relationship*.

dichotomous thinking *Thinking* that categorizes experiences and people in extremes, with no middle ground, for example, all women are alike. Dichotomous thinking, also known as "black-and-white thinking," is common among people with *borderline personalities*.

Dictionary of Occupational Titles (DOT) A U.S. government publication, first published in 1939. Often used in *career counseling*, it provides information and descriptions of current *occupations* within the United States. The DOT has been replaced by *O**Net. See *O**Net.

Differential Aptitude Test (DAT) A multi-aptitude *battery* composed of eight *subtests* used for vocational and educational purposes in grades 7 through 12 and with adults.

differential diagnosis The *process* of choosing which *diagnosis* to make when coexisting diagnoses, such as *addiction* and another *mental disorder*, occur simultaneously.

differentiation A level of maturity that enables persons to separate their rational and emotional selves. Individual are thus able to separate from their *family*. Differentiation is the opposite of *fusion*.

diffuse boundaries Physical and/or psychological arrangements that do not allow enough separation between *family* members, resulting in some members becoming fused and dependent on other members.

diffusion A developmental state where a person is not in *crisis* and is not actively exploring ideas concerning *identity, career,* or *sexuality*.

DINKS An acronym for *double-income-no-kids families*.

directive **1.** An order or instruction given by a *counselor,* for example, when a *client* is upset

and is unable to talk, a counselor might say, "Breathe deeply." **2.** An instruction from a family counselor for a *family* to behave differently. A directive is to *strategic family therapy* what *interpretation* is to *psychoanalysis* (i.e., it is the basic tool of the approach).

directive counseling A counseling *theory* developed by E. G. Williamson in which the counselor functions as a teacher and/or advisor. The theory is sometimes referred to as *counselor-centered counseling, trait-and-factor counseling,* and the *Minnesota Point of View*.

director The individual who guides the *protagonist* in the use of a *psychodrama method* to help that person explore his or her *problem*. The director is roughly equivalent to the *group leader* in other theoretical approaches but serves also as a producer, a *facilitator,* an observer, and an analyzer.

Directory of Counselor Educators The first study of counselor preparation conducted in the United States. This directory was initially published in 1962 by the U.S. Department of Health, Education, and Welfare. Several other editions of the directory were published until Joseph Hollis and Richard Wantz began their more thorough publication, *Counselor Preparation,* in 1971. See *Counselor Preparation*.

dirty game A term used in *Milan family therapy* to describe a *power* struggle between generations sustained by symptomatic *behaviors,* for example, *schizophrenia*.

disability A physical, behavioral, or a mental condition that limits a person's activities or functioning. A disability may be either temporary or permanent.

disassociation A *defense mechanism* in which part of an individual's *personality* appears to split off from the rest and take on an existence of its own. Disassociation is the basis for *multiple personality disorder*.

disaster counseling The *counseling* of *victims* and their families during or immediately after a traumatic event. *Counselors* who participate in this type of counseling receive disaster mental health training. Services they offer include defusing, debriefing, and referrals to help traumatized people cope and readjust both on an immediate and long-term basis.

disaster mental health training   The field application of *crisis* intervention.

disclosure   Providing clients with the information they need to make informed decisions about entering into *counseling*, remaining in counseling, and sharing personal information.

discontinuous change   A dramatic leap to a new level of functioning with *change* occurring in a startling and sudden way. Periods of *stress* and disruption are often preludes to this type of transformation. In families, discontinuous change is more likely to occur around *stages* in the *family life cycle*. In individuals, discontinuous change is manifest in such acts as falling in love.

discontinuous development   *Change* that is unstable, inconsistent, and unpredictable. It involves a major reorganization in *behavior, cognition,* or *emotional* states, for example, restructuring self-talk. Discontinuous development is also known as *qualitative growth*.

discount   A term in *transactional analysis* for either a lack of attention or negative attention that is hurtful. Discounts carry an ulterior put-down.

DISCOVER   A program widely used in the United States for career planning. DISCOVER consists of four components: (1) self-assessment (Self-Information), (2) identification of occupational alternatives (Strategies for Identifying Occupations), (3) reviewing occupational information (Occupational Information), and (4) identification of educational alternatives (Searches for Educational Institutions).

discrimination   **1.** Prejudicial *behavior* against a person or a *group*. **2.** The ability to distinguish between two slightly different stimuli.

discussion team   The dividing of a large *group* into four or five *team*s to get group members involved with one another and a topic under consideration.

disease model of alcoholism   A model held by many *substance abuse counselors* and *mental health* professionals that *alcoholism* is a disease that can best be treated by emphasizing total abstinence.

disengaged   Psychologically isolated from others.

disengagement theory of aging   The idea that detachment and disconnections are inevitable processes as a person ages, and some relationships between an aging individual and others become severed while those remaining are altered in quality. Opposite of *activity theory of aging*.

disidentification   The *process* in which a *counselor* becomes emotionally removed from the *client*.

disorder   A disease or condition that is *dysfunctional* or *abnormal*. See also *mental disorder*.

disorders usually first diagnosed in infancy, childhood, or adolescence   A diagnostic category of the *DSM* that includes *mental retardation, learning* disorders, motor skills disorder, communication disorder, pervasive development disorder (such as *autism*), attention deficit and disruptive disorders, feeding and eating disorders, tic disorders, elimination disorders (*encopresis* and *enuresis*), and others (e.g., *separation anxiety disorder*).

displaced homemakers   Women who have lost their source of economic support and are forced back into the workforce after spending a number of years at home caring for their families.

displacement   A *defense mechanism* in which, on an *unconscious* level, energy is channeled away from a threatening object to an alternative safe target. For instance, a person who has had a hard day at the office may come home and kick the dog instead of yelling at his/her boss.

disputing irrational thoughts   A *technique* of *rational emotive behavior therapy* (REBT) in which a *client*'s *irrational belief*s about an event are challenged by a *counselor*.

dissociative amnesia   See *amnesia*.

dissociative disorders   *Disorders* that involve an alteration in *consciousness,* such as memory *loss* or alternate *personality* states, that is not organic or psychotic in nature. The *DSM* classifies *dissociative identity disorder* (formerly known as *multiple personality disorder*), *dissociative fugue, dissociative amnesia,* and *depersonalization disorder* in this category.

dissociative fugue   See *fugue.*

dissociative identity disorder   See *multiple personality disorder.*

dissonance   The lack of blending or fusing of two aspects of an experience, resulting in discrepancies and discomfort. Dissonance may occur in a number of *situation*s, such as when an inner and outer experience do not fit together well.

distancing   Isolated separateness of *family* members from each other, either physically or psychologically.

distortion   A *defense mechanism* in which *client*s would rather not see the world as it is, therefore changing their take on the *situation* to serve their own agenda. For example, instead of admitting that he is rude, a client may say that others are jealous of him and dislike him.

distractor   **1.** Virginia Satir's term for a person who relates by saying and doing irrelevant things. **2.** Any of the incorrect alternatives on a multiple choice *item.*

distress   A Hans Selye term for being overcome or overwhelmed by *stress* to the point of not being able to function adequately (i.e., being *impaired*). For example, a woman may have so many tasks to do that she does not do any of them well or simply stops doing any of them and becomes despondent.

distribution   The frequency with which a given *variable* occurs. The distribution of variables, which are usually expressed in numbers, are frequently expressed visually on a *graph.*

diversity   Differences, unlikeness, variety. Diversity includes *factor*s such as age, ability/ *disability, culture, sexual orientation, gender,* creed, *ethnicity,* economics, *work* experience,

education, and *personality.* To be competent, counselors must learn to deal effectively with diversity in a number of areas.

Division of Rehabilitation Counseling (DRC)   Established in 1958, a forerunner of the *American Rehabilitation Counseling Association (ARCA).*

Division 17 of the American Psychological Association   Now known as the *Society of Counseling Psychology,* Division 17 of the *American Psychological Association* was founded in 1946. This division of the APA came into existence when the association's Counseling and Guidance Division dropped the term *guidance.* Part of the impetus for the division's formation came from the Veterans Administration. The focus of members of the division is in working with a more "normal" *population* than the one seen by *clinical psychologist*s. Division 17's Internet address is http://www.div17.org/. See *Counseling Psychology.*

divorce   A *legal* term for the dissolving of a marriage prior to the death of either spouse. Most divorces occur in *stage*s, both legally and emotionally.

divorce mediation   A nonadversarial form of arbitration in which two parties, such as a divorcing couple, meet with a *counselor* trained in *mediation* to negotiate a mutually satisfactory settlement on important matters such as *child* custody before entering into *legal* arrangements to end their marriage.

DO A CLIENT MAP   A mnemonic device created by Linda Seligman to address one of the areas to be considered during *diagnosis* and treatment planning using the *DSM* multiaxial system and providing a comprehensive guide to working with a *client.* The letters are as follows:

Diagnosis according to the *DSM* multiaxial system

Objectives of treatment (written as treatment goals)

Assessment procedures (formal and informal procedures)

Clinical (considerations related to clinical background, gender, ethnicity, and other issues)

Location of treatment (inpatient or outpatient)

Interventions (theoretical approach and specific intervention)

Emphasis of treatment (e.g., supportive, probing)

Numbers (individual, group, or family counseling)

Timing (duration and scheduling of sessions)

Medication (determine whether a referral for medication is needed)

Adjunct services (additional activities to supplement the counseling process, such as tutoring)

Prognosis (based on diagnosis, the *GAF* score, and levels of support.

documentation The recorded information about the content of a *counseling* session that is used to guide professional practice and in some cases determine reimbursement for services. Documentation may take the form of *case notes,* clinical entries, and progress notes.

door in the face technique A *counseling technique* in which the *counselor* asks the *client* to do a seemingly impossible task followed by a request that the client perform a more reasonable task.

domains Major aspects of human functioning that include thinking, feeling, relating, conceptualizing, judging, and understanding. Growth is not generalizable across all domains. Therefore an individual can develop in one domain and not another.

domestic violence Physical, emotional, or sexual *abuse* of those within a domestic relationship including partners, children, and the elderly. Domestic violence that occurs between two people in a close relationship is known as *intimate partner violence (IPV).*

dope A slang term for *marijuana.*

DOT See *Dictionary of Occupational Titles.*

double standard of mental health A standard of *mental health* that basically depicts adult female *behavior* as less socially desirable and healthy. Such a perspective lowers expectations for women's behavior and sets up barriers against their advancement in nontraditional *roles.*

double-bind theory The Gregory Bateson *research* group's *hypothesis* regarding the origin of *schizophrenia.* The *theory* states that two seemingly contradictory messages may exist at the same time on different levels and lead to confusion, if not schizophrenic *behavior,* on the part of an individual who cannot comment on or escape from the *relationship* in which this is occurring. For example, a mother may tell her *child* that she loves him or her while discouraging or rejecting any show of affection from the child.

double-blind A *research* procedure where both the participants and the experimenter are unaware of which *group* is being treated until after the *experiment* is completed. See *single blind.*

doubt See *shame.*

downers The street or slang name for any *depressant drugs* such as *barbiturates* or *tranquilizers* that induce extreme relaxation or a sleeplike state.

drama therapy The systematic use of drama and theater *techniques* as a primary or adjunct means to bring about therapeutic *change.* In order to conduct drama therapy, *counselors* must take specialized training in this area. See also *National Association for Drama Therapy (NADT).*

drama triangle See *Karpman Triangle.*

Draw-a-Person Test A *projective test* of *intelligence* and *personality* in which children (ages 3 to 16) are asked to draw a human figure of their choosing.

drawing out The opposite of *cutting off* or *blocking;* the *process* whereby *group leader*s purposefully ask more silent members to speak to anyone in the *group,* or to the group as a whole, about anything on their minds.

dream analysis A *psychoanalytic technique* in which dreams are explored according to *manifest content* (obvious content) and/or *latent content* (hidden content).

dream work   A *technique* based in psychoanalytic and Gestalt theory that dreams are the royal road to the *unconscious* and to the *integration* of people. In this procedure, *clients* recall and talk about their dreams (*psychoanalysis*) or recreate and relive their dreams in the present (Gestalt). In the Gestalt technique, individuals become all parts of their dreams and work alone or in a *group*. When working in a group, members act out different parts of the dream (i.e., dream work as theater).

drug abuse   See *substance abuse*.

drugs   Chemical *substances* that have a marked physiological and often psychological impact on persons.

DSM   See *Diagnostic and Statistical Manual*. This manual of psychiatric *disorders* is periodically updated and published in new editions.

dual-career family   A *family* in which both marital partners are engaged in *work* that is developmental in sequence and to which they have a high commitment.

dual diagnosis   The identification of more than one aspect of *personality* that is open to *diagnosis,* giving the *client* two diagnoses (e.g., a *substance abuser* may also suffer from *depression*).

dual nature of human beings   The idea that individuals have both rational beliefs and *irrational beliefs*, a key concept proposed by Albert Ellis as a part of *rational emotive behavior therapy*.

dual personality   The simplest form of a *multiple personality disorder,* sometimes referred to as a Jekyll and Hyde *personality*.

dual relationship   A *relationship* that is not built on mutuality and may be unethical because the *counselor* assumes a second *role* with a *client* (e.g., that of friend, business associate, or sex partner) in addition to that of *therapist*. Whenever possible, dual relationships should be avoided. The reason is that even if a dual relationship seems harmless, a

conflict of interest frequently exists, and a professional counselor's judgment may be negatively affected because of a *loss* of objectivity. Also, clients may be placed in *situations* in which they cannot be assertive and take care of themselves.

dual therapy   A term devised by Carl Whitaker for conjoint couple *therapy*.

DUD   An informal and cruel *counseling* acronym for people perceived as dumb, unintelligent, and disadvantaged.

DUSO   See *Developing Understanding of Self and Others*.

duty to care   A *legal* obligation on the part of health *providers* to not act negligently. This legal precedent was set in a 1994 California court, when Gary Ramona sued his daughter's *therapist* for implanting in her mind false memories of sexual *abuse*. Ramona won, and the *therapist* was found negligent.

duty to warn   The *legal* responsibility a counselor has to warn others if a *client* is potentially dangerous to *self* or others. This legal precedent was set as a result of the *Tarasoff v. Board of Regents of the University of California* decision.

dyad   A one-to-one *relationship* between two people.

dyadic effect   Reciprocal *self-disclosure* between *counselor* and *client*. See also *self-disclosure*.

dynamics   The interactions of two or more people, usually in a *group*.

dyscalculia   A *learning disability*, specifically a difficulty in or inability to do math.

dysfunctional   *Impaired*; abnormal; unable to function adequately.

dysfunctional thoughts   *Thoughts* that are nonproductive and unrealistic; a key concept in the therapeutic approach of Aaron Beck.

dysgraphia   A *learning disability,* specifically a difficulty in writing or inability to write.

dyslexia   A *learning disability* marked by an impairment in recognizing and comprehending written words. Dyslexia often results in revering letters and difficulty in reading.

e

EAP See *Employee Assistance Program*.

early childhood The period in the human *life cycle* from birth to age 6.

early recollections Memories from *childhood* used in *Adlerian counseling* to assess a person's initial outlook on life and how these memories influence present interactions with others.

eating disorders *Maladaptive* eating patterns in which *clients* starve themselves through eating too little or purging food they have consumed because of obsessive and distorted ideas they have in regard to thinness and body image. The two most prevalent eating disorders are *anorexia nervosa* and *bulimia*.

eclectic counseling Employing concepts from various theoretical systems in the *treatment* of a *client* rather than restricting oneself to a single theoretical approach.

eclecticism A term used to describe a *counselor* who works from a variety of theoretical *systems*. Eclecticism occurs on several levels—*syncretism, traditional eclecticism, theoretical integrationism,* and *technical eclecticism.*

eco-map A graphic representation of the social systems that make up a person's life, such as friends, family, work, worship, and other community and societal links where the individual is involved. Like a *sociogram* or a *genogram*, an eco-map depicts visually where and with whom a person is connected and can provide a more holistic view of a client.

ecological counseling A person–environment interaction approach to *counseling* that states that what people do and how they make meaning in their lives are the result of their interactions with their social and physical environments at any given point in time.

ecological validity The extent to which research conditions mimic real life.

ecosystemic crisis A natural or human-caused disaster that overtakes a person or *group* through no fault of their own but that adversely affects them, for example, a hurricane, wildfire, or war.

ecosystemic thinking A focus on the interconnectedness of the individual, *family,* and *culture*.

ecstasy A synthetic *designer drug*. Ecstasy's structure is similar to that of the *hallucinogen mescaline,* and the *stimulant amphetamine*. It is usually swallowed as a pill but may be inhaled or injected. Ecstasy increases energy and sensuality; it also raises heart rate and blood pressure, causes confusion and severe *depression,* impairs memory, and masks fatigue.

Education of All Handicapped Children Act See *Public Law 94-142.*

Education Resource Information Center/ Counseling and Student Services Clearinghouse (ERIC/CASS) A national information *system* that was established by Garry R. Walz in 1966 and discontinued by the government in 2003. ERIC/CASS provided ready access to an extensive body of education-related literature. Its scope included *school counseling,* school *social work, school psychology, mental health counseling, family counseling, career counseling,* and student development, as well as parent, student, and teacher education in the human resources area.

Edwards Personal Preference Schedule (EPPS) A pencil-and-paper, forced-choice *personality test* developed by Henry Murray and designed to measure 15 important *needs,* such as *autonomy* and *achievement.*

efficacy studies A comparison of methodologies and the usefulness of a specific *helping* methodology for a particular kind of *problem* (e.g., cognitive *therapy* with *client*s suffering from *panic disorders*).

ego **1.** A term that is synonymous with the *self*. People who have an ego can distinguish one person from another and can differentiate themselves from the outside world. **2.** A concept in classical Freudian *psychoanalysis*. The ego describes the *conscious* part of the *personality* responsible for decision making. The ego is sometimes called the "executive of the mind"; it mediates disputes between the *id* and the *superego*. The ego works according to the *reality principle*. A strong ego is necessary for a healthy *personality* to develop. Otherwise, *neurotic* tendencies set in because of the unabated *conflict* between the id and the superego.

ego analysis An analysis of how the *ego* functions, especially how it deals with and resolves *conflict*.

ego ideal A part of the *superego* that *rewards* those who follow parental and societal dictates and do what they have been taught. For example, children who have been taught by their parents that neatness is a virtue feel good when they keep a neat room.

ego identity A term describing any of the eight stages *Erik Erikson* outlined in his *psychosocial* theory of development.

ego states in transactional analysis (TA) A *system* of *feelings* accompanied by a related set of *behavior* patterns. There are three basic *ego* states in *transactional analysis:* parent, adult, and child. See also *adult ego state; child ego state; parent ego state*.

ego strength The ability of persons to maintain a strong *ego* so that they are in contact with reality and free of mental disturbances.

egocentric 1. Preoccupation with oneself and one's importance. **2.** In Piaget's *theory*, the normal state of a *child* under age 6, who believes everyone sees the world from his or her perspective.

egogram A term in *transactional analysis* for a *bar graph* showing how people structure their time in six major ways: *withdrawal, ritual, pastimes, work, games,* and *intimacy*.

egoistic Concerned with one's own *needs* and interests while being indifferent and unresponsive to others.

elasticity A term in *Gestalt therapy* for the ability to move from one set of *needs* to another and back.

Elavil A popular antidepression medicine.

elder hostel A place where older individuals live and study together for a select period of time.

elderly Persons who are 65 years of age and older. The term "older adult" is preferred to the term "elderly."

Electra complex The female version of the *Oedipus complex*. According to Freud's *theory,* during the *phallic stage* (ages 3 to 5) of *psychosexual development,* girls have sexual *feelings* for their fathers and accompanying hostility toward their mothers. This complex is eventually resolved when girls identify with their mothers.

electroshock therapy (*EST*) A medical *treatment* involving the production of electrically induced grand mal seizures. It is used for select *patients* with severe *depression* who have not responded to a pharmacological form of *therapy*.

elegant REBT An emphasis in *rational emotive behavior therapy (REBT)* on the beliefs of *clients* and a focus on their taking responsibility for their own *feelings* and not blaming others. Clients realize in the *process* that success in everything is not essential and that catastrophe is not the result of every unfulfilled want.

elementary school counseling A relatively recent specialty in the field of *school counseling* in which *counselors* in schools work in preventative, developmental, and remedial ways with children in kindergarten through fifth grade. Elementary school counselors are a vanguard in the *mental health* movement. No other *profession* has ever been organized to work with individuals from a purely preventive and developmental perspective. Overall, the elementary school counselor is charged with facilitating optimal *development* of the whole *child*.

ELIZA   An early reflective software *counseling* program with a large vocabulary and the ability to formulate a virtually unlimited number of *response*s. ELIZA's Internet address is http://www-ai.ijs.si/eliza/eliza.html.

EMDR   Eye movement desensitization and reprocessing.

e-mail counseling   See *Internet counseling*.

emic approach to multicultural counseling   A perspective that assumes that *counseling* approaches must be designed to be culturally specific. This approach is sometimes criticized for placing too much emphasis on specific *technique*s as the vehicle for personal *change*. It is the opposite of the *etic approach to multicultural counseling*.

emotion   A strong *feeling* or *affect* of any kind (e.g., joy, anger). The so-called *Big Four feeling words counselors* search for are anger, sadness, fear, and joy.

emotional ambivalence   *Feelings* of *loss,* sadness, and separation mixed with those of *hope,* joy, and accomplishment.

emotional anatomy   The recognition and understanding by *client*s of the way in which *feelings* and *thoughts* are attached (i.e., feelings influence *behavior*s and vice versa).

emotional cutoff   A Murray Bowen concept that describes the avoidance by *family* members of each other, either physically or psychologically, because of an unresolved emotional attachment.

emotional deadness   A condition in which *affect* is seemingly absent or at a minimum in *client*s because they have either suppressed their *feelings* or are unaware of them (e.g., clients who always give *cognitive* answers).

emotional distance   A concept inherent in nuclear family emotional processes, especially in *triangulations*. It is exhibited either by a family member distancing himself/herself from other family members to reduce the intensity of the relationship or by a family member becoming overly connected to the family unit and absorbing too much of the family's anxiety.

emotional impact of separation   The *process*es involved in a separation event that include dealing with *loss,* putting the separation in perspective, becoming aware of the limited value of searching for causes of separation, becoming more cognizant of *system*s interactions (*family, work,* social network), using the past as a guide to the future, and moving from a dyadic to a monadic *identity*.

emotional intelligence   The ability to process emotional information accurately and use it intelligently in social and cognitive situations to promote growth and well-being.

emotional overinvolvement   The *fusion* of *family* members with each other. In this *process*, individuals experience undifferentiated emotional togetherness and lose a sense of who they and others are.

emotional response of separation   The continuing *relationship*s a person has with an ex-spouse, including the influence of the separation on *family,* friends, and children, working and dating, and sexual adjustment.

emotional stimulation   The sharing of *affect* between people (e.g., *catharsis, self-disclosure*).

empathize   To put oneself in another's place in regard to subjective *perception* and *emotion* and yet to keep one's objectivity. Empathizing demands a suspension of judgment and a *response* to another person that conveys sensitivity and understanding. It communicates understanding, fosters *trust,* and encourages deeper levels of *client self-exploration*.

empathy   The *counselor's* ability to see, be aware of, conceptualize, understand, and effectively communicate back to a *client* the client's *feelings, thoughts,* and *frame* of reference in regard to a *situation* or point of view. Empathy operates on at least two levels: *primary empathy* and *advanced empathy*. Empathy is one of the *necessary and sufficient conditions for change,* along with *unconditional positive regard* and *congruence,* according to Carl Rogers.

Employee Assistance Program (EAP)   A program set up by an employer for employees.

EAPs offer *mental health* services or *referrals* to employees to assist them in meeting personal or *family needs*.

empowerment A way of promoting self-efficacy by encouraging and *supporting clients* to think and take action in a positive way. Counselors always try to empower their clients.

empowerment approach A specific perspective when dealing with *clients* in *career counseling* who have disabilities. The approach focuses less on what can be done to or for a client and more on a *process* in which clients must become active, informed participants who learn and control a planning process that they use for short- and long-term *career development*.

empty chair technique A *Gestalt therapy technique* designed to help *group* members deal with different aspects of their personalities. For example, a person may be given an opportunity to *role-play* and speak to a missing person with whom he/she has *unfinished business*.

the empty chair

empty nest A term that describes a *stage* in the *family life cycle* in which couples have launched their children and are without *child*-rearing responsibilities.

enabler **1.** An individual who makes things possible. **2.** In *counseling*, someone who helps another person continue *dysfunctional behaviors*, such as *alcohol abuse*.

enactment **1.** A *client's* actively exhibiting to a *counselor* problematic behavioral sequences instead of just talking about them (e.g., having an argument instead of talking about one). **2.** Jerome Brunner's belief that children represent their world by the activities they perform.

encopresis A lack of bowel control that results in inappropriate defecation. There are emotional and organic causes.

encounter An *existentialist* concept that involves total physical and psychological contact between persons on an intense, concrete, and complete basis in the here and now.

encounter group See *basic encounter group*.

encouragement **1.** The *verbal supporting* of a *client* as he or she struggles in making *changes*. **2.** An *Adlerian counseling technique* of having *clients* take a risk without knowing what its final *outcome* will be.

enculturation The process whereby through socialization individuals learn, accept, and practice particular cultural values, ideas, behaviors, and beliefs prevalent in their society.

end-of-life decisions Decisions related to the imminent approach of death including hospice care, funeral arrangements, the distribution of assets, reconciliation, and issues related to an individual's request to hasten death, usually through the help of a physician. These decisions are filled with a plethora of moral, ethical, and legal concerns.

endorphins Any of a group of peptide hormones that bind to *opiate* receptors mainly in the brain. Endorphins reduce the sensation of pain and positively affect *emotions*.

enneagram A nine factor *personality* system that is measured through a *test*. The nine factors are orderliness, helpfulness, image focus, hypersensitivity, detachment, caution, adventurousness, strength, and calmness.

enmeshment The *loss* of *autonomy* within a *family* due to overconcern and overinvolvement of family members with each other either physically or psychologically. Enmeshment makes individual *autonomy* impossible.

enterprising people   Individuals, according to Holland's *career* typology, who enjoy working in environments where they are able to lead and persuade people (e.g., business, politics, sales). See *RIASEC*.

entropy   The tendency of a *system* to become disorganized.

enuresis   A lack of bladder control that results in the involuntary release of urine, such as in bed-wetting. The cause can be either emotional or organic.

environment   The significant aspects of an individual's surroundings either in the present or the past, including significant events and experiences that influenced a person's *development*.

environment-aimed interventions   In *rehabilitation counseling* interventions targeted toward barriers in the external environment that may need modification to meet the client's goals, for example, use of assistive aids such as prostheses, the removal of architectural barriers, and placing the client in a group home.

environmental conditions and events   Planned and unplanned situations and happenings.

environmental fit   A state in which an *environment* is conducive to *helping* people grow and resolve crises. When the environment does not "fit," people regress or deteriorate.

epistemology   The study of knowledge (i.e., how we know what we know).

EPPS   See *Edwards Personal Preference Schedule*.

equifinality   The idea that similar *outcomes* may result from different origins.

equitability   The proposition that everyone is entitled to have his or her welfare interests considered in a way that is fair from a multilateral perspective. Equitability is the basis for *relationship ethics*.

equivalence   The extent to which two versions of a *test* or *measurement* instrument yield the same or similar results. See also *reliability*.

ERIC/CASS   See *Educational Resources Information Center/Counseling and Student Services Clearinghouse*.

erogenous zones   Sigmund Freud's term for those areas of the body that are most receptive to sexual stimulation.

eros   Freud's term for the life force of the *id*, sometimes equated with the *libido*. Eros is the opposite of *thanatos*. See also *thanatos*.

erotic   Having to do with sexual passion, pleasure, or love.

Esalen Institute   A facility devoted to the human potential movement. The address is Highway 1, Big Sur, CA 93920-9616 (831-667-3000; http://www.esalen.org/).

EST   An abbreviation for *electroshock therapy*.

esteem   The value one attributes to oneself or another. See also *self-esteem*.

estimation   A form of *inferential statistics* in which *sample data* is used to estimate the qualities of the *population* as a whole.

e-therapy   See *Internet counseling*.

ethic of care   A description of what drives morality for women based on a contextual, interconnectedness with others and characterized by nurturance and an emphasis on responsibility to others. This approach is often associated with the *moral development* theory of Carol Gilligan.

ethic of justice   A description of the male approach to morality based on abstract, universal principles, such as fairness and equality, characterized by rationality, with an emphasis on individual rights and autonomy. This approach is often associated with the *moral development* theory of Lawrence Kohlberg.

ethical principles   Principles related to a counselor's *choices* and activities as they pertain to *beneficence, nonmaleficence, autonomy, justice, fidelity,* and the like.

ethics   **1.** The principles from which individuals and social *groups* determine *rules* for right conduct. **2.** Suggested standards of conduct based on a set of professional *values*. **3.** The study and *evaluation* of moral beliefs and actions of *counselors* within certain professional domains.

ethnicity   A group classification in which members believe that they share a common origin and a unique social and cultural heritage such as language, *values,* or religious belief.

ethnocentricism **1.** The development of standards and beliefs based on a person's cultural background. **2.** A belief that your personal *culture* is "right" or "best" when compared to others. **3.** A lack of *flexibility* and openness about other *worldviews* or mindsets.

etic approach to multicultural counseling The perspective that there are universal qualities in *counseling* that generalize across *cultures.* The etic approach can be criticized for not taking important cultural differences into account. It is the opposite of the *emic approach.*

etiology The study of causes such as those associated with *disorders, disabilities,* and conditions.

European American Americans who are descendants from European ancestors. As a group, European Americans have blended together more than other cultural groups. Reasons include a history of intergroup marriages and *relationships* that have simultaneously influenced the group as a whole and made it more *homogeneous.*

euthanasia The act of assisting someone to die who has an incurable disease or injury.

eustress A minimal reaction or even a positive reaction to certain *stressors.*

evaluation The *process* of collecting, analyzing, and judging *data* to make a decision. In *counseling,* such a decision usually involves a *treatment plan.*

evaluative listening A universal tendency to listen to what others say and judge it in such terms as good–bad, right–wrong, acceptable–unacceptable, likable–unlikable, relevant–irrelevant, etc.

evidence-based counseling The selection of counseling interventions based on *outcome research.*

ex post facto research This type of research examines the relationship between variables "after the fact" or after data have been collected.

exchange theory See *social exchange theory.*

executive coaching A one-to-one mentorship program by business-experienced *counselors* that helps *clients* develop specific *job*-related skills or helps them prepare for advanced employment opportunities.

executive function Management by a leader of a *group* as a social *system* that allows the members to achieve specific *goals.*

exercises *Structured activities* that *clients* do for a specific purpose such as to gain awareness (e.g., *role playing*) or to introduce themselves to others (i.e., *icebreakers*).

exhibitionist/exhibitionism **1.** The tendency of someone to show off his or her *traits* or talents to gain the attention of others. **2.** The displaying of one's genitals to others in unacceptable and antisocial ways.

existential counseling An approach to *counseling* that emphasizes a philosophy about the importance of *anxiety, values,* freedom, and responsibility in human life and finding meaning in one's existence. Irvin Yalom, Rollo May, Clemmont Vontress, and Victor Frankl are prominent clinicians who have embraced *existentialism.*

existential crisis Intense, pervasive inner conflict and anxiety associated with issues such as purpose, meaning, freedom, responsibility, and commitment, for example in relationships or work.

existential factors As defined by Irvin Yalom, such human existence *factors* as accepting responsibility for one's life in basic isolation from others and recognizing one's own mortality as well as the capriciousness of existence.

existential guilt *Guilt* associated with the acts of *omission* (not taking action), that is, failure to live up to one's potential or a self-restricted life due to fear of the unknown.

existential isolation Inevitable separation from others and the world. Existential isolation can be reduced but not completely eliminated.

existential vacuum A *feeling* one has of having no value.

existentialism   A philosophical approach that deals with existence. Existential philosophers believe that existence is the only knowable reality because individuals cannot know about their origin or eventual end. Existentialism stresses the importance of authenticity and responsibility, the primacy of the here and now, and the use of experience in the search for knowledge.

exit interview   1. A final *interview* that takes place when a person is terminating *counseling*. The purpose is to assess the *outcome* of *treatment*. **2.** A final *interview* that takes place when a person leaves a *counseling situation* prematurely. The purpose is to find out the reasons for leaving and to assist the person with future life transitions. See also *premature termination*.

experience near research   *Research* that closely approximates what is done in the *counseling* office.

experiential symbolic family therapy   An approach to working with families developed by Carl Whitaker. Its major premise is that individuals in families are not aware of their *emotions*. *Therapists* therefore emphasize expressing *feelings* in the here and now. They also use their own personalities, spontaneity, and creativity during *treatment* to promote *change*.

experiment   A scientific procedure of investigation that involves the manipulation of some aspect of an *environment* to determine what effect the manipulation had.

experimental design   A global term for the procedures used to conduct an *experiment* (e.g., pairing up subjects between comparison groups so that persons are matched along some relevant *variable*).

experimental group   A group that undergoes experimental manipulation (i.e., some aspect of their *environment* is *changed* to observe its effect) as opposed to the *control group*.

experimental research   *Methods* and procedures used to describe, compare, and analyze *data* under controlled conditions. Experimental

research methods used in *counseling* research have their origin in the natural sciences. The purpose of using these methods is to determine the effect of one *variable* on another by controlling other *factors* that might explain the effect. In other words, *researchers* who use this method are seeking to determine causation.

experimenter bias   When a researcher manipulates experimental processes or the interpretation of data to confirm his or her preconceived beliefs about the results.

experimenter drift   When a researcher deviates from the original research protocol.

experiments   Experiences that occur spontaneously in a *Gestalt therapy* session.

expert witness   A person who is asked to testify in a court of *law* about a particular subject because he or she possesses superior knowledge on a matter due to education or experience. The purpose of the expert witness is to assist a jury or judge in understanding complicated and technical subjects that are relevant to a *legal* case or issue.

exploration   The *process* of discovering or uncovering new materials and *insights* related to a *client's* concern(s) so that ideas may be clarified and *goals* generated.

exploratory research   The use of both quantitative and qualitative *methods* to explore phenomenon when there is not an existing measure or *theory* that is applicable.

expressive arts therapies   See *creative arts therapies*.

extended family   1. A *family* composed of three generations or more. **2.** A *family* that includes both immediate and distant relatives. See *multigenerational family*.

external validity   The extent to which *research* results have *generalization* and can be applied to situations outside the confines of a particular study. See *validity*.

externalizing problems   A *narrative family therapy method* of treating a *problem* in which the problem becomes a separate entity outside a *client*. Such a *process* when applied to families helps them reduce their arguments about who owns the problem. Furthermore, externalizing problems helps families form *teams* and enter into *dialogue* about solving their problems.

extinction The *process* of lowering the rate at which a *behavior* occurs through withdrawing the *reinforcers* that have been maintaining it so that the targeted behavior will stop altogether and be eliminated.

extrovert A Jungian concept that describes an individual's basic orientation to the external world and things outside himself or herself. An extrovert tends to be an outgoing and gregarious person. Such a person is the opposite of an *introvert*.

eye contact Looking at someone in the eye when interviewing them. The "e" in *SOLER*.

eye movement desensitization and reprocessing (EMDR) A *process* designed first for *posttraumatic stress,* which requires that *clients* visualize an upsetting memory and accompanying physical sensations. Clients then repeat negative self-statements that they associate with the scene while following the *counselor's* finger as it moves rapidly back and forth. After completing the eye movements, clients stop *thinking* about the scene. The procedure is repeated often until a client's *anxiety* is reduced.

f

F ratio A statistical *technique* in which the larger *sample variance* is divided by the smaller one. When the researcher is conducting an *ANOVA* (one of several statistical procedures that yields an *F ratio*), the between groups mean square is divided by the within-groups mean square. The resulting statistic, known as F, is interpreted for *statistical significance* using an F distribution table. Larger F *values* are more likely to be significant than smaller F values.

face validity The degree to which a *test* appears to measure what it is supposed to measure.

facilitate To help *clients* open up and talk about their concerns.

facilitator A *helping professional* who serves as a catalyst, especially in a *group situation,* by aiding members in choosing and accomplishing *goals*.

FACT See *Fair Access Coalition on Testing.*

factitious disorders Feigned illnesses or disabilities. People with factitious disorders usually are resistant to *treatment* and may leave *counseling* prematurely.

factor A dimension, *trait,* or characteristic that is discovered through the *process* of *factor analysis.*

factor analysis A statistical *method* of analyzing the intercorrelation among a set of *variables,* such as *test scores,* to determine the minimum number of *factors* or dimensions that explain the intercorrelation. Factor analysis is used to discover the essential variables that underlie and summarize information in a larger set of *data.*

fading The gradual removal or withdrawal of *reinforcement,* such as a stimulus, in regard to a *client's behavior* so that the *behavior* eventually disappears.

failure identity A concept from *reality therapy* that describes a person characterized by a lack of confidence and a tendency to give up easily.

Fair Access Coalition on Testing (FACT) A not-for-profit organization that advocates for equitable access to testing services for all appropriately trained professionals (http://www.fairaccess.org/home).

fallible human being   A term used by Albert Ellis in *rational emotive behavior therapy (REBT)* to describe all persons, because no one is perfect. By using the term, *client*s avoid the temptation to judge or label themselves in overly critical or negative ways.

false memory syndrome   AKA *confabulation*. The creation of a memory of an event that did not happen to fill in memory lapses.

false negative error   Failure to identify a phenomenon that is present.

false positive error   Inaccurately identifying the presence of a phenomenon that is missing.

false self   A Rogerian term for a person who is incongruent, not genuine, or not real.

family   A group of two or more persons related by birth, marriage, or adoption and residing together in a household (per the Census Bureau).

family constellation   An *Adlerian counseling* term for the *birth order* of children in a *family* (e.g., firstborns, secondborns, middle children, youngest children, and the only *child*). Adlerians believe that individuals who share a birth order in a family may have more in common with each other than they do with their siblings.

family council   A form of *family group* meeting designed to open up communication between family members. Alfred Adler introduced the idea.

family counseling   See *family therapy*.

Family Educational Rights and Privacy Act (FERPA)   An act, also known as the *Buckley Amendment,* passed by Congress in 1974. The statute gives students access to certain *records* that educational institutions have kept on them.

family group therapy   A *treatment* approach formulated by John Bell that conceptualizes *family* members as strangers in a *group*. Members become known to each other in *stage*s similar to those found in groups.

family homeostasis   The tendency of the *family* to remain in its same pattern of functioning and resist *change* unless challenged or forced to do otherwise. See also *homeostasis*.

family life cycle   A sociological term used to describe the various developmental *stage*s within a *family* over time (e.g., newly married, family with young children).

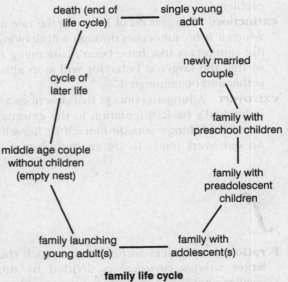

family life cycle
(based on a middle-class family with children)

family life fact chronology   Virginia Satir's *family reconstruction technique* in which the "*star*" creates a listing of all significant events in his or her life and that of the *extended family* that have had an impact on the people in the *family*.

family map   Virginia Satir's *family reconstruction technique* of producing a visual representation of the structure of three generations of the "*star*'s" *family*, with adjectives to describe each family member's *personality*.

family mapping   A symbolic representation of a *family*'s *structure* used by structural family *therapist*s to plan their *interventions*.

family mediation   The *process* of *helping* couples and families settle disputes or dissolve their marriages in a nonadversarial way. See also *mediation*.

family of origin   The *family* into which a person was born or adopted.

family of procreation   The *family* a couple creates through marriage.

family reconstruction   A therapeutic innovation developed by Virginia Satir to help *family* members discover *dysfunctional* patterns in their lives stemming from their *family of origin*.

family rules   The overt and covert *rules* a *family* uses to govern itself (e.g., that you must only speak when spoken to).

family sculpting   See *sculpting*.

family secrets   Overt events and covert fantasies or *thoughts* that are not talked about by a *family* or family members. Family secrets consume the family's energy because members must always be on guard to not disclose information.

family systems theory   See *systems theory*.

family therapy   The *treatment* of a *family* as the *client* through a number of theoretical approaches, including psychoanalytic, Bowen, structural, experiential, strategic, systemic (i.e., Milan), solution-focused, and narrative. In most family treatment, the family is seen together.

fantasy   A form of daydreaming in which a person uses his or her imagination to create mental pictures of desired objects, people, or places.

fantasy exercises   A *group work method* used in *Gestalt therapy* to help group members to (1) be more concrete in assessing their *feelings*, (2) deal with catastrophic experiences, (3) explore and express feelings of *guilt* and *shame,* and (4) become more involved in the *group*. It is not necessary that group members live out their fantasies.

farewell-party syndrome   A syndrome in which group members at *termination* emphasize only the positive aspects of what has occurred in the *group,* instead of what they have learned. This type of focus tends to avoid the pain of *closure*.

faulty logic   Irrational ideas that *clients* think and believe and that are the basis of their *problems* in living and relating to themselves and others (e.g., "Susie spoke to Jim but not to me; therefore, Susie does not like me and I am no good").

fees   The costs associated with *counseling* services.

feedback   **1.** The reinsertion of results of past performances back into a *system*. **2.** The sharing of either a positive or negative *perception* of a *behavior* and relevant information that goes with that perception so that a person can make decisions as to whether he or she would like to *change* or modify what he or she is doing. Feedback information should be given verbally and nonverbally in a clear, concrete, succinct, and appropriate manner. See also *negative feedback; positive feedback*.

feedback loops   Circular mechanisms for the continuous reintroduction of information about a *system's* output back into the system.

feeling   *Emotion; affect*. Unexpressed or repressed feelings are viewed as the cause of *distress* and some *mental disorders*. The expression of feeling in some *counseling* theories (e.g., *psychoanalysis, Gestalt*) is considered therapeutic.

felony   A serious criminal charge or act such as assault, rape, homicide, and burglary.

feminism   A movement to help women advance in society and end *prejudice* toward them.

feminist counseling   *Counseling* from a feminist perspective is based on the idea that women's *problems* are inseparable from societal problems that socialize women to assume inferior *roles*. Therefore, counseling focuses on issues such as the development of *androgyny* and the sharing of *power* between men and women, accepting one's body as is, and a focus on non-sex-biased *careers*. *Techniques* in feminist counseling vary but include *techniques* that are behavioral and cognitive behavioral such as *modeling, assertiveness* training, and *cognitive restructuring*.

Feminist Identity Development Scale (FIDS)   A *career counseling* assessment instrument that uses five different subscales to examine *clients' perceptions* on the influences of gender-related issues in the *career development process*.

feminist movement   A social movement dedicated to removing the prejudicial treatment of women in society and advancing women's issues in general.

feminist theory   An attitude and body of ideas concerning gender hierarchy, *socialization,* and *power* and their impact on conducting *counseling.* Feminists recognize the overriding importance of *sexism* as a *factor* in the *problem*s women have in society and how important it is to eliminate sexist practices that are detrimental to women in particular and society in general.

FERPA   See *Family Educational Rights and Privacy Act.*

fetish   An erotic attraction to inanimate objects (e.g., shoes, clothing) or parts of the body (e.g., hair, the neck). A fetish can become a sexual *disorder* known as *fetishism* when it becomes an *obsession.*

fetishism   A sexual *disorder* where a person becomes obsessed with an inanimate object or parts of the body of another human being.

fiction   An *Adlerian counseling* concept that describes the subjective *evaluation*s people have of themselves and their *environment*s.

fidelity   An *ethical principle* encompassing faithfulness and honoring commitments.

field study   *Qualitative research* that involves spending considerable time in a setting under study and collecting as much relevant information as possible. Field study is the opposite of *laboratory research.*

field theory   Kurt Lewin's approach to *groups* that emphasizes the interaction between individuals and their *environment*s. It is based on the ideas of *Gestalt therapy,* in which there is an interdependence of part/whole *relationship*s.

figure/ground   A *Gestalt therapy* term used to describe focus. *Figure* in one's personal life is composed of experiences that are most important. *Ground* is composed of experiences that are less pressing.

filial therapy   Bernard and Louise Guerney's approach in which parents function as *counselors* and play *therapist*s for their children.

filtered listening   The variety of filters people use to listen to themselves, others, and the world. Personal, familial, sociological, and cultural filters introduce various forms of *bias* into individual's *listening* and do so without people being aware of it.

Finding Your Way   The title of a book by Jeffrey Kottler and a regular column dedicated to how *counselors* have developed as professionals, which is featured in the *ACA* monthly newspaper, *Counseling Today.*

first-degree games   A *transactional analysis* term for the least harmful *games,* in which minor faults are highlighted. For example, in the game "blemish," a minor flaw like the spot on a person's clothing might be pointed out. See also *games.*

first-order change   The *process* whereby someone unable to adjust to new circumstances often repetitiously tries the same solutions as before or intensifies nonproductive *behavior*s. First-order change does not alter the nature or structure of a *system.* For example, a person may try raising his or her voice if another person does not respond to a request spoken in a normal tone; the request remains the same regardless.

fishbowl procedure   See *group observing group.*

Five Factor Model   See *Big Five.*

Five Factor Wellness Inventory   An instrument created by Jane Myers and Tom Sweeney designed to assist individuals in making healthier lifestyle choices based on a model for *wellness.* The inventory can also help clients examine areas of their life that may be out of balance.

fixation   A term in *psychoanalysis* for the cessation of *psychosexual development* at a certain *stage* due to too much or too little gratification at that stage. In fixation, there is a tendency to cope with the outside world in a manner similar to that employed in the earlier stage in which one is stuck. To overcome fixation requires that people regress to that earlier time and come to terms with themselves and *significant other*s who were involved in the fixation *process.*

flashback A mental picture of a historic scene or earlier experience that comes to a person's mind unexpectedly. Flashbacks can be disturbing or comforting. When they occur frequently, they are often the source of *distress* and may be *symptom*s of other *disorder*s.

flat affect Lack of *emotion*; sometimes a *symptom* of *depression* or *schizophrenia.*

flexibility The ability to adjust to new conditions and circumstances. Emotionally mature people and competent *counselors* are flexible.

floating hot seat A *Gestalt therapy technique* in which interaction is promoted by encouraging group members to work on exploring their own personal issues when someone else in the *group* touches on an issue that has personal relevance for them.

flooding A *behavioral therapy* concept that describes the presentation to a fearful person of an imagined anxiety-producing scene that does not have dire *consequences.*

flow A field of behavioral science, conceptualized by Mihaly Csikszentmihalyi, that examines the connections between satisfaction and daily activities. A flow state ensues when one is engaged in self-controlled, goal-related, meaningful actions. The experience is at once demanding and rewarding.

fluid intelligence A person's inherited ability to think and reason, including the *processes* of perceiving *relationships*, reasoning inductively, and solving *problem*s. It is the opposite of *crystallized intelligence.*

focus group A *group* composed of a representative *sample* of individuals concerned with issues, products, and/or *outcome*s. Focus groups are being utilized increasingly by businesses and politicians.

focus on exceptions A *technique* utilized by brief *therapist*s to help people realize that their *symptom*s are not always present and that they have some *power* over what they are presently doing to make *changes.*

focused approach to multicultural counseling A view that sees *multiculturalism* in the United States as focusing on four visible ethnic minority groups: *Native Americans, African Americans, Asian Americans,* and *Hispanics/ Latinos(as).* It is the opposite of the *universal approach to multicultural counseling.*

focused imagery When a *client* actually practices a *behavior* or imagines doing more of a task than he or she had done previously.

follow-up Reconnecting with *client*s after they have left *counseling* and had enough time to *process* what they experienced and work on their *goals* and *objective*s.

foot in the door technique A *counseling technique* in which the *counselor* asks the *client* to comply with a minor request and then later follows with a larger request. It is the opposite of the *door in the face technique.*

forced-choice item test An *objective test* in which each question has several *choices* and a person is required to select at least one of the *item*s. A forced-choice format prevents the development of a certain *response* set.

foreclosure When a person develops a premature identity without exploration by accepting others ideas, opinions, and suggestions, such as: "You should be a pharmacist."

forensic psychiatry A psychiatric specialty that deals with determining the mental competency of individuals in court cases.

formal operations The last of Jean Piaget's four *stages* of *cognitive development.* The formal operations stage usually begins around age 11 or 12. Formal operations is characterized by the increasing ability to use logical *thought processes* and abstract reasoning, and to develop symbolic *meaning.*

formative evaluation See *process evaluation.*

forming The first *stage* of *group development,* which is characterized by initial caution associated with any new experience. During this time, there is an attempt by group members to avoid being rejected by others, the leader, or even themselves.

fourth force A term used by Paul Pedersen to describe *multicultural counseling.* The first, second, and third forces are *psychoanalysis, behaviorism,* and *humanism.*

frame   A mental *perception* or opinion that organizes one's interactions.

framework   The *structure* surrounding the *process* of *counseling*, such as a specific time and place where it will occur or the concern to be addressed. Having a framework promotes the development of counseling.

free association   A *psychoanalysis technique*, especially useful in uncovering repressed *thoughts* and *feelings*. In this procedure a *client* reports everything that comes to mind as soon as it occurs. Through such a *process*, *conflicts* and disturbances from the *unconscious* surface and can be therapeutically dealt with.

free child   See *natural child*.

free consent   The process where clients choose to engage in an activity without undue pressure or coercion.

free-floating anxiety   Feelings of *anxiety* that are not attached to a particular situation or event.

freebasing   The smoking of a *drug* such as *cocaine*.

frequency distribution   A tabulation of *data* that indicates the number of times something occurred in a study.

frequency distribution of math scores

test score	frequency
78	2
85	5
89	4
94	7
99	2

frustration   A negative emotional reaction to being blocked or thwarted in achieving one's *goals*.

fugue   A relatively long period of *amnesia* during which a person takes flight by leaving his or her immediate *environment*. Described in the *DSM* as *dissociative fugue*.

fully functioning person   A term originated by Carl Rogers to describe an individual who is using his or her abilities to the fullest extent possible.

functional autonomy   A concept introduced by Gordon Allport to explain why some human motives have no biological *need* behind them. According to Allport, some acquired motives come to function independently (autonomously), although they may have originally been a means to an end. For instance, a college student who studies a subject in college because it was required may later come to read in the subject for the pleasure of it.

functional family therapy   A type of *behavioral family therapy* that is basically systemic in nature.

functional fixity   Seeing things in only one way or from one perspective or being fixated on the idea that a particular *situation* or attribute is the issue. For instance, seeing all people of a religious persuasion as misguided and to be avoided.

fusion   **1.** In *family therapy*, the merging of intellectual and emotional functions so that an individual does not have a clear sense of *self* and others. It is the opposite of *differentiation*. **2.** In *existential therapy*, an attempt to become part of another person or *group* in an effort to reduce *feelings* of *isolation*.

g

G factor   See *generalized intelligence*.

GA   See *Gamblers Anonymous*.

GAF   See *global assessment of functioning*.

gag clause   A stipulation made by a *managed care* organization that prevents counselors from discussing alternative treatments outside the boundaries of approved services.

Gamblers Anonymous (GA)   A *mutual help group*, similar to *Alcoholics Anonymous*, composed primarily of compulsive gamblers. GA's address is P.O. Box 17173, Los Angeles, CA 90017 (213-386-8789; http://www.gamblersanonymous. org/).

gambling addiction/compulsion The inability to control one's desire to gamble.

game analysis An examination in *transactional analysis* of destructive and repetitive behavioral patterns and their payoffs. Such an analysis involves an *exploration* of the *ego states* and types of *transactions* involved.

games **1.** A competitive contest or interaction where there is usually a winner and a loser even if all the people involved are not sure they are in competition. **2.** A *Milan family therapy* concept that stresses how children and parents stabilize around disturbed *behavior*s in an attempt to benefit from them. **3.** In *transactional analysis,* an ongoing series of complementary *ulterior transactions* progressing to a well-defined, predictable *outcome*. Games are played on three levels (first-, second-, and *third-degree games*), and almost all of them are destructive and result in negative payoffs (i.e., *rackets*). People who play games operate from three distinct *positions*: *victim, persecutor,* and *rescuer*. See also *first-degree games; persecutor; rescuer; second-degree games; third-degree games; victim.*

gang A *group* that arises out of children's *needs* to be independent from their parents and to be with their *peer*s. Members are obligated to participate in the group's activities; outsiders are excluded. Gangs may have secret passwords, explicit or implicit *rules* of conduct, and *rituals* such as initiation rites.

GATB See *General Aptitude Test Battery*.

gatekeepers Individual (usually clinicians) who control access to health care services for members of a specific *group* or individuals (usually academics) who control access to entering a profession such as *counseling*.

gateway behaviors Mildly or moderately distressing activities, frequently self-destructive, which often progress to increasingly deviant *behavior*s, such as smoking cigarettes and then smoking *marijuana*.

gay A term usually used to describe a *homosexual* male.

gender The social expression of a person's sex, especially in regard to one's culture or society.

gender identity The image a person has of himself or herself as possessing feminine or masculine characteristics.

gender identity disorder A *disorder* under *sexual and gender identity disorders* in the *DSM* that is characterized by a strong and persistent cross-gender *identification,* coupled with a discomfort about one's own assigned sex. Such disorders are treatable if client *motivation* is strong.

gender roles The characteristics and *behavior*s assigned by society to individuals because of their sex. Socialization is different for males and females and is often based on assumptions and stereotypes. For example, females may be expected to be nurturing and men competitive. Gender roles often prove untrue for individuals because of their interests, abilities, and *temperament*. See also *sex roles.*

General Aptitude Test Battery (GATB) A *career aptitude test battery* composed of 12 *speed test*s published by the U.S. Department of Labor and administered in state employment services, community colleges, and some high schools. The battery yields nine aptitude *score*s on *cognitive,* perceptual, and psychomotor *factor*s.

general systems theory A *theory* that emphasizes *circular causality* as opposed to *linear causality* and focuses on the interconnectedness of elements within all living organisms.

generalization **1.** The extent to which *conclusions, rules,* principles, and other *behavior*s are applicable in *environment*s outside of where they were originally learned. **2.** The extent to which *research* findings can be applied to people or settings in general.

generalized intelligence (G factor) The *factor* that is measured in most *intelligence tests*.

generativity A goal of *midlife,* according to Erik Erikson, in which people seek to be creative in their lives and work for the benefit of others and the next generation. Generativity is the opposite of *stagnation*.

generation A group of individuals distinguished by sequential birth years that usually share some common peer characteristics and whose time is defined by social movements (e.g., civil rights) or events (e.g., the Great Depression) during their lifetime. An average generation is 22 years.

genetic endowment Innate traits and abilities.

genetic counseling *Counseling* that focuses on inherited *disorders*, such as intellectual disabilities, resulting from a genetic *abnormality*.

genital stage The last of Sigmund Freud's *psychosexual stage*s of development. The geni-

tal stage begins around age 11 or 12 and lasts until about age 18 or 19. If all has gone well previously, each *gender* takes more interest in the other. If there were unresolved difficulties in any of the first three psychosexual stages (collectively known as the *pregenital stages*), the person may have difficulty adjusting to the adult responsibilities that begin at the genital stage.

genius A person with exceptional intellectual or creative ability.

genogram Murray Bowen's visual diagram of a person's family tree over at least three generations depicted in geometric figures, lines, and words. It is used to trace reoccurring patterns within a *family* (see diagram of Gladding genogram).

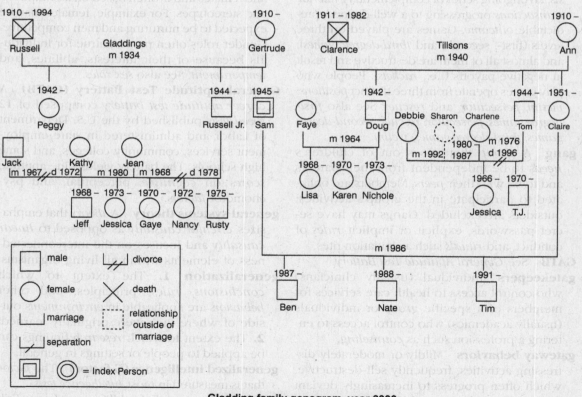

Gladding family genogram, year 2000

genuineness Also known as *congruence,* a quality that is one of the necessary and sufficient conditions for *change,* according to Carl Rogers. Genuineness is characterized by openness, transparency, *self-disclosure, authenticity,* and a lack of pretense.

gerontological counseling A *counseling* specialty that centers around working with the aged.

gerontology The study of *aging,* including biological, mental, psychological, and social components.

gestalt A German word meaning "whole figure"; an integrated whole.

Gestalt therapy A form of *treatment* originated by Fritz Perls and based on the assumption that *clients*' *problem*s arise when they behave according to other people's expectations rather than to their own true *feelings.* The aim of Gestalt therapy is to help the client become more aware of *self* and *emotion* and to act in the *now.* The approach is aimed more at doing rather than talking and uses a number of both *exercises* and *experiences.*

G. I. Bill AKA *Servicemen's Readjustment Act.* Federal legislation enacted in 1944 that paid for a veteran's entire education. The bill encouraged many universities in the United States to expand enrollment and offer *career* and *counseling* services to former service members.

gifted A person, usually a child, with exceptional talents or mental abilities. This term is often used in educational settings to describe students who are above average in one or more areas and who could benefit from special instruction.

glass ceiling phenomenon A term used to describe the barriers to advancement of women or minorities in organizations. The lack of advancement is not due to an organization's official policy but is simply a failure by the organization to promote women and minorities to top-level executive duties, even when they are equal to or better qualified than those who are promoted.

global assessment of functioning (GAF) Axis V in the *DSM* multiaxial diagnosis system, which is based on a scale ranging from 1 to 100. Higher GAF ratings indicate higher levels of functioning.

Gloria,* AKA *Three Approaches to Psychotherapy A film on *counseling* produced by Everett Shostrom in 1964 featuring a *client,* Gloria, in *individual counseling* sessions with Carl Rogers, Fritz Perls, and Albert Ellis.

goals Specific *objective*s that individuals, groups, or families wish to accomplish in *counseling.* Goals are mutually agreed on by *client*s and *counselor*s and may *change* over the lifetime of a counseling *relationship.*

goal-setting A strategy used in *counseling* to help *client*s clarify what they wish from the *process* and define the steps they *need* to take to reach their *objective*s.

going home again A *Bowen family therapy* technique in which the family *counselor* instructs an individual to return home to better get to know the *family* in which he/she grew up. By using this type of information, individuals can *differentiate* themselves more clearly.

good enough mother A mother who lets an infant feel loved and cared for and thereby helps the infant develop *trust* and a true sense of *self.*

go-rounds See *rounds.*

grade equivalent score A *score,* usually on an *achievement test,* that is translated into the grade level, regardless of the age of the individual.

Graduate Record Exam (GRE) An *aptitude test* used to predict success in advanced graduate work. *Test* results are reported along three dimensions: *verbal,* quantitative, and analytical.

graph   A visual representation of a set of *data,* for example, *pie charts, histograms.*

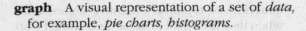

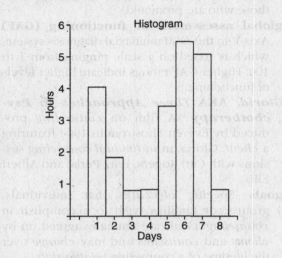

GRE   See *Graduate Record Exam.*

Greek chorus   Observers/*consultant*s of a family or group *treatment* session (i.e., the *team*). The chorus members debate the merits of what a *therapist* is doing to bring about *change.* They send messages about the *process* to the *therapist* and *family or group,* which is helped through this *process* to acknowledge and feel their ambivalence.

grief   AKA *bereavement.* An intense emotional *response* to a *loss* characterized by sorrow and *distress.*

grief stages   A series of five sequential stages, as outlined by *Elizabeth Kübler-Ross,* through which most people pass through when confronting their own death or a major loss: *denial,* anger, bargaining, *depression,* and *acceptance.* Not everyone makes it through all stages.

grief work   A series of *stage*s people in *grief* must go through to resolve their deep *feelings* of sorrow. Among these stages are reminiscing, expressing *emotions,* accepting, adjusting to newness, and forming new *relationships.*

group   A collection of two or more individuals who meet in face-to-face interaction, interdependently, with the awareness that each belongs to the group and for the purpose of achieving individual and/or mutually agreed-on *goals.*

group analysis   A term first applied to the *treatment* of individuals in psychoanalytically oriented *groups* by Trigant Burrow, who emphasized that social forces *affect* individuals' *behavior*s.

group casualties   Members of a *group* who drop out or become worse because of the experience.

group cohesiveness   The degree of togetherness in a *group* expressed in a *feeling* of "we-ness."

group collusion   Cooperating with others on an *unconscious* or a *conscious* level to reinforce prevailing attitudes, *values, behavior*s, or *norms.* The purpose of such behavior is self-protection, and its effect is to maintain the status quo in the *group.*

group counseling   *Groups* that focus on *prevention,* growth, and remedial issues that are both *intrapersonal* and *interpersonal* in nature. Sometimes these groups are known as *interpersonal problem-solving group*s.

group development   The *stage*s that *groups* move through over time, such as *forming, storming, norming, performing,* and *adjourning/mourning.*

group dynamics   A term originally used by Kurt Lewin to describe the interaction among members in a *group.*

group guidance   The *process* of using educational *method*s to help *group* members acquire information and develop needed skills. One type of group guidance is *life skills training.*

group interaction   The way members relate to each other with *nonverbal* and *verbal behavior*s and the attitudes that go with them. *Group* interaction exists on a continuum, from extremely nondirected to highly directed.

group leader   A person who has been specially trained to understand *group dynamics* and *group development* to lead a *group,* especially a *counseling* or *therapy* group.

group leadership style The way a group leader runs a group. Three styles are dominant: authoritarian (*Theory X group leadership*), democratic (*Theory Y group leadership*), and laissez-faire (*Theory Z group leadership*).

group marathon An extended, one-session *group* experience that breaks down defensive barriers that individuals may otherwise use. It usually lasts for a minimum of 24 hours.

group norms The rules, practices, and guidelines which members of a group are expected to follow. Group norms can either be constructive (usually open and facilitative) or destructive (covert and inhibiting).

group observing group The *situation* that occurs when a *group* breaks up into two smaller groups, and the outer group observes the inner group function for a set amount of time. It is sometimes referred to as a *fishbowl procedure*.

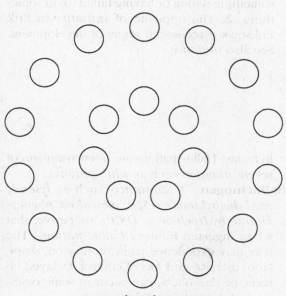

group observing group

group process The interactions of *group* members as the group develops. See also *process*.

group processing A *situation* that occurs when a neutral *third party* (a *group processor*) observes and gives *feedback* to the *group* concerning the interactions between members and in the group itself, in regard to both *content* and *process*.

group processor See *group processing*.

group psychoanalysis A model that emphasizes that the whole *group* is the *client* and that *group dynamics* are an essential feature to analyze.

group psychotherapy A *group treatment* that specializes in *remediation* or *personality* reconstruction. It is meant to help people who have serious psychological *problem*s of a long-term duration. As such, this type of group is found most often in *mental health* facilities such as *clinic*s or hospitals.

group setting The *group*'s physical *environment,* for instance, where the group room is located and how the room is arranged.

group structure Both the way a *group* is set up physically as well as the way group members interact or *structure* themselves in *relationship* to others.

group supervision See *supervision*.

group techniques *Exercise*s, such as *icebreakers,* that are structured in such a way as to get *group* members to interact with one another.

group test A paper-and-pencil *test* given to a number of people at one sitting. A group test has an advantage in its ease of administration and cost, but it does not pick up the subtleties of an *individual test*.

group therapy See *group psychotherapy*.

group work The giving of help or the accomplishment of tasks in a *group setting*. It *involves* the application of group *theory* and *process* by a capable professional practitioner to help an interdependent collection of people reach their mutual *goals*; the goals may be personal, *interpersonal,* or task related. According to the *Association for Specialists in Group Work (ASGW)*, group work is a broad professional practice.

grouping **1.** A statistical procedure for combining individual *scores* into categories or ranking them, such as in *percentiles*. **2.** A way of categorizing people according to common *traits* or characteristics.

groupthink A *group situation* in which there is a deterioration of mental efficiency, reality testing, and moral judgment that results from in-group pressures. The end result is usually a bad decision.

growing times Times at which fresh *learning* occurs on an individual and *interpersonal* level.

guidance A point of view in education that emphasizes the total *development* of individual students and utilizes instructional services to help students develop their abilities and learn to cope. Guidance also deals with *helping* individuals learn to make *choices*.

guidance counselor A term sometimes used to describe a *school counselor* or a *counselor* in an educational setting who provides *clients* with *guidance* activities related to *problem* solving, *career* decision making, and *work* or study habits.

guidance hour Also known as *guidance room*; the term used in the 1930s for time in a homeroom at school that was devoted to *guidance*. The homeroom teacher's responsibilities were to establish friendly *relationships* with students, discover their abilities and *needs*, and develop right attitudes with them toward school, home, and the community.

guidance room See *guidance hour*.

guidance/psychoeducational group A type of *group* that was originally developed for use in an educational setting, specifically a school. The primary function of the group is the *prevention* of personal or societal disorders through the conveying of information and/or the examining of *values*. A guidance/psychoeducational group stresses growth through knowledge. *Content* includes but is not limited to personal, social, vocational, and educational information.

guilt **1.** An emotional *response* to having done something wrong or having failed to do something. **2.** The opposite of *initiative* in Erik Erikson's *psychosocial stages* of development. See also *initiative*.

h

habilitation The education of *clients* who have had disabilities since early life and who have never been self-sufficient.

habituation AKA *satiation*. A situation in which a greater dosage of a *substance* or different *reinforcer* must be used to secure the same result. For example, in *addiction* more of a drug must be taken to achieve the same high.

halfway house A supervised group home for individuals who are making a transition from any type of *treatment* or *rehabilitation* to society.

hallucinations Imagined *perceptions* of an object, sound, or *phenomenon* that is not present in reality. Hallucinations are often *symptoms* of severe *disorders* such as *schizophrenia*.

hallucinogen A *substance*, such as *lysergic acid diethylamide (LSD), mescaline, phencyclidine hydrochloride (PCP),* or *peyote,* that when ingested induces *hallucinations*. The user may experience panic, confusion, suspicion, *anxiety,* and *loss* of control. Delayed effects, or *flashbacks*, can occur in some cases, even after use has ceased.

halo effect The tendency to evaluate individuals in a positive light, according to initial impressions or past *performance* that may be inaccurate in the present. For instance, sometimes skilled athletes may be rated as good leaders even when that is not the case. The halo effect is the opposite of the *horn effect*.

handicap A mental or physical limitation of a person with a *disability*. Such limitations are exacerbated by the presence of various barriers. The words "disability" and "challenged" are preferred to the word "handicap" in describing a person with limitations.

hangover The negative aftereffect of abusing *drugs* or *alcohol* (e.g., a headache, blurred vision).

Hansen effect Third-generation immigrants who wish to capture their lost cultural heritage by engaging in such activities as taking a foreign language or studying their ancestral history.

happenstance A chance event that is unpredictable. Happenstance sometimes plays a part in the development of people's friendships, careers, *lifestyles*, and so forth.

Hawthorne effect A social *research phenomenon* in which *changes* in human *behavior* occur as a result of observing or manipulating a person's *environment*.

health 1. An interactive *process* involving one's mental, physical, spiritual, and social well-being, and associated with positive *relationships* and *outcomes*. 2. A medical term used by *helping professionals* and insurance companies to describe the state of a person's mental, physical, spiritual, and social well-being.

health care Services, including *prevention* and *treatment*, provided to persons to take care of their mental, physical, spiritual and social well-being.

Health Insurance Portability and Accountability Act (HIPPA) Federal legislation passed in 1996 that was intended to promote *standardization* and efficiency in the *health care* industry and safeguard *health* information.

Providers, including *counselors* and other *mental health* specialists, who must comply with HIPAA requirements are those who transmit any health care information in electronic form in connection with a covered transaction.

health maintenance organization (HMO) A comprehensive *health care* organization that provides *health* services to its members for a specific fee or cost over a period of time. See also *managed care*.

hedonistic/hedonist Oriented toward or seeking pleasure for its own sake.

help line A telephone *crisis* or *referral hot line* usually staffed by trained volunteers to provide assistance to those in *need*. See also *hot line*.

helpee Another name for a client. See *client*.

helping 1. Giving assistance or aid to, contributing to the betterment of. 2. The informal or formal *process* of assisting individuals in their times of *need*.

HELPING An acronym for *health, emotions, learning,* personal interactions, imagery, need to know, and *guidance*. HELPING is Donald Keats's multimodal *framework* for *helping counselors* and *clients* focus on what needs to be addressed in *sessions*.

helping process A sequence of events that consists of building a *relationship* and facilitating a positive and productive interaction between a *counselor* and a *client*.

helping profession Any *profession* in which the primary responsibility is to assist individuals in *need*. Examples of helping professions include *counseling, nursing, social work, psychiatry, marriage and family therapy,* and *psychology*.

here-and-now The tendency of a *client* or *counselor* to work in the present with an emphasis on *ahistorical theories* of *counseling*.

heroin An *opiate* related to *morphine*, heroin produces a *feeling* of profound well-being, followed by drowsiness, nausea, and vomiting. Heroin works on the pain and pleasure centers in the brain. It can be injected, smoked, or snorted. Heroin is physically addictive and can cause convulsions, coma, and death. Heroin is also called *smack, horse, junk,* and *brown sugar.*

heterogeneous group   A *group* composed of dissimilar persons. Such groups can broaden members' horizons and enliven *interpersonal* interactions.

heterosexism   The institutionalized assumption that everyone is *heterosexual* and that heterosexuality is inherently superior to and preferable to *homosexuality* or *bisexuality.*

heterosexist assumptions   Views regarding sexuality based on a *culture* that advocates heterosexuality.

heterosexual   A person who is sexually orientated toward sexual *relationship*s with someone of the opposite sex.

hexagon model   Another name for Holland's theory of personality/vocational types.

hidden agenda   Covert, as opposed to overt, agendas or *goals.* For instance, a person may seek *counseling* with the *hope* that a court of *law* may look more favorably on her or him in an upcoming trial.

hierarchy of needs   Abraham Maslow's *theory* that human *needs* occur in ascending order; physical needs must be fulfilled first, followed by safety needs, belonging needs, self-esteem needs, and, finally, *self-actualization* needs.

Maslow's hierarchy of needs

high   A physical or emotion rush usually attributable to the influence of *drugs* or gambling.

high-risk clients   Individuals who are potentially violent, suicidal, homicidal, abusive, or engaged in criminal behavior.

high-stakes testing   The use of standardized test scores, such as those on the SAT, ACT, or Advanced Placement examinations, to make important educational decisions with serious consequences for students and schools, for example, scholarships, remediation, and program funding. High-stakes decisions should be made based on multiple criteria, not a single *test score.*

HIPAA   See *Health Insurance Portability and Accountability Act.*

HIPAA Electronic Transaction and Code Set Standard Requirements   National standards for the electronic exchange of health information. These standards were created to give the *health care* industry a common language.

HIPAA National Identifier Requirements   A regulation within *HIPAA* that requires all *health care provider*s, health plans, and employers to have unique national numbers that identify them on standard *transactions.*

HIPAA Privacy Requirements   These requirements limit how Protected Health Information (PHI) is used and disclosed.

HIPAA Security Requirements   These requirements outline the minimum administrative, technical, and physical *system*s required to prevent unauthorized access to Protected Health Information.

Hispanic   A generic label for people from backgrounds whose origins are in Spanish-speaking Latin America or Spain. This group is the fastest-growing *minority population* in the United States. See also *Latino(a).*

histogram   A *bar graph* that provides a description of the *distribution* of the frequency of *score*s. The horizontal axis of a histogram is marked off in limits of score intervals; the vertical axis is marked off in frequencies.

historical research   The observation and interpretation of past events through qualitative and quantitative means to understand a past person, event, institution, or profession better.

historical time The era in which people live. It consists of forces that affect and shape humanity at a particular point in time, such as in economic depression or war.

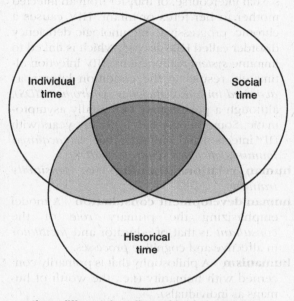

three different time dimensions in human life

histrionic personality disorder A *personality disorder* characterized by all or some of the following: an overreaction to minor events, tantrums, overly dramatic *behavior,* a craving for excitement and attention, manipulation of others, lack of depth or genuineness, and suicidal threats. Individuals with this disorder are sometimes referred to as *hysterics*.

HIV See *human immune deficiency virus*.

HMO See *health maintenance organization*.

holding the focus Concentrating on a specific topic for a set length of time.

holistic The view of humans as complete entities rather than individuals made of separate parts. A holistic perspective is the underlying basis of such *helping* approaches as *existentialism, Gestalt therapy,* and *person-centered counseling*.

Holland Personality Types A typology of six vocational personalities and six work environments used to classify individuals and vocations: *realistic, investigative, artistic, social, enterprising,* and *conventional*. The closer the match between persons and work, the better the fit.

home-based therapy A *method* of *treatment* in which *counselors* spend time with families before attempting to help them. This type of approach is appropriate in working with select families (e.g., some Native American families) unfamiliar with the *helping process*.

homeostasis The tendency of a *system* or organism to remain static and to strive to restore balance if disturbed. This tendency results in resisting *change* and keeping circumstances in a state of equilibrium. Homeostasis is one *factor* affecting *clients* in the *process* of making changes in their lives.

homework Assignments given *clients* to work on outside or between *counseling* sessions to help them practice or refine skills learned in counseling or to try new *behaviors*.

homogeneous group A *group* composed of persons with similar backgrounds.

homonegativity Negative thoughts and feelings about sexual minorities.

homophobic Excessive fear of associating with *homosexuals* or being *homosexual*.

homosexual A person who is sexually oriented toward sexual *relationships* with members of his or her own sex. See also *gay* and *lesbian*.

hope An experience that is important to *client* progress in *counseling,* both cognitively and emotionally. Cognitively, hope is the belief that what is desired is also possible and that events will turn out for the best. Emotionally, hope is the *feeling* that what one believes will occur. The importance of hope is that it energizes and directs clients.

horizontal stressors Stressful events in a person's life related to the present, some of which are developmental, such as *life cycle* transitions (e.g., aging), and others of which are *happenstance* (e.g., accidents).

horn effect The tendency to evaluate individuals in a negative light, according to initial impressions or past performances that may not be accurate in the present. It is the opposite of the *halo effect*.

hospice A philosophy and a program of *caring* for the terminally ill in a nonhospital, homelike atmosphere (usually the home) in which *family,* relatives, and friends can be with the person who is dying.

hospice care The care needed by an individual during their final months or weeks of life.

hot buttons An informal term for the sensitivities that people have about issues. When a hot button is pushed, individuals tend to react emotionally.

hot cognition A powerful and highly meaningful idea that produces a strong emotional reaction.

hotline A *crisis* phone line managed by *helping professionals* and specially trained volunteers. See also *help line.*

hot seat The place in *Gestalt therapy* groups where the person who wants to work sits in a chair facing the *counselor* or leader, whereas the rest of the *group* serve as a kind of *Greek chorus* in the background. The chorus members resonate and *empathize* with the person who is working and gain *insight*s into themselves and others through the *process* of *identification* while giving feedback.

HOUND A cruel but sometimes used *counseling* acronym to describe a *client* perceived as homely, old, unintelligent, *nonverbal,* and disadvantaged.

House-Tree-Person (HTP) test A projective *personality test* in which a person is asked to draw a house, a tree, and a person, in that order. Both *conscious* and *subconscious* dimensions of *personality* are assessed.

how The *process* in *Gestalt therapy* of actually promoting *change* in a *client* through *structure* and *behavior.* How is one of the two legs on which *Gestalt therapy* is based, the other being *now.*

HTP See *House-Tree-Person test.*

human immunodeficiency virus (HIV) A virus that is transmitted by direct exposure to blood and blood derivatives, certain acts of sexual intercourse, or transfer from an infected mother to her fetus or infant. HIV causes a chronic, progressive, immunologic deficiency disorder called HIV disease, which is linked to immune *system* malfunctions. HIV infection ultimately results in the condition known as *acquired immunodeficiency syndrome (AIDS),* although a person may be initially asymptomatic. Some people live for many years with HIV infection and with AIDS. See also *acquired immunodeficiency syndrome (AIDS).*

human relations training See *sensitivity training.*

human-development consultation A model emphasizing the primary *role* of the *consultant* as that of educator and *facilitator* in affective and cognitive *process*es.

humanism A philosophy that is primarily concerned with humanity (i.e., the worth of humans as individuals).

humanistic The philosophical and collective *treatment* approaches in *counseling* and *psychotherapy* that are primarily concerned with the *values,* interests, and welfare of human beings, especially as distinguished from other animals. Theorists associated with the humanistic approach to *therapy* include Abraham Maslow, Carl Rogers, and Gordon Allport. Humanistic psychotherapy is sometimes called the *third force* (*psychoanalysis* is the first force and *behaviorism* the second force).

humor The ability to laugh at oneself and one's circumstances in a healthy, therapeutic, and nondefensive way.

hyperactivity Excessive motor activity and restlessness. See *hyperkinesis.*

hyperkinesis A term synonymous with *hyperactivity* (excessive motor activity and restlessness) and used by some professionals in place of *attention deficit hyperactivity disorder (ADHD).*

hypersomnia A sleep disorder characterized by excessive sleeping or fatigue.

hypnosis An induced state of altered *consciousness* in which a person's suggestibility is heightened. Hypnosis is sometimes used as a complementary treatment to *counseling* to recover repressed memories or to help *clients* become more relaxed.

hypnotherapy The *treatment* or *prevention* of *disorders* through *hypnosis*.

hypochondriasis A *somatoform disorder* characterized by a preoccupation with the idea of having a serious illness.

hypomania A *disorder* with similar *symptoms* to *mania*, but most likely associated with "cheerful or pleasurable" *feelings*. Persons with hypomania may not be able to make rational decisions because of their heightened state. Hypomania can mask *bipolar disorder*, so it should be diagnosed as early as possible to avoid *depression* and/or risk of *suicide*.

hypothesis A hunch or an educated guess or explanation for the occurrence of a *phenomenon*. A hypothesis can be tested to see if it is true.

hypothesis interpretation When a *counselor* conveys to a *client* more than one explanation of a behavior to check out a hunch. Such interpretation begins with phrases like "Could it be?" or "Is it possible that?" This type of interpretation breaks down *resistance*, gives a client an opportunity to think, and lets the counselor know if he or she is on the right track.

hypothesizing A *technique* central to the *Milan family therapy* approach. Hypothesizing involves a meeting of the *treatment team* before the arrival of a *family* to formulate and discuss aspects of the family's *situation* that may be generating a *symptom*. Through hypothesizing, team members prepare themselves for treating the family.

hysteria A historical term for a *conversion reaction*.

hysteric A term used by Sigmund Freud to describe *patients* he worked with who displayed many of the *symptoms* of what is today known as a *histrionic personality disorder*.

i

"I" statements The expression of *feelings* and *thoughts*, using the first person singular "I" in a way that encourages others to express their personal opinions and beliefs.

I.A.A.M. A drug similar to methadone in its effects, with a significantly longer duration of effect than *methadone*, and therefore used in some maintenance programs.

IAAOC See *International Association of Addictions and Offender Counseling*.

IAC See *International Association of Counseling*.

IAMFC See *International Association of Marriage and Family Counselors*.

ICD See *International Classification of Diseases* manual.

ice The street name for methamphetamine.

icebreaker An activity or *exercise* designed to promote initial communication between two or more people, especially in a *group*; for example, having people talk about their favorite color or movie.

id A term in *psychoanalysis* for the part of the *personality* present at birth and expressed as biological urges that strives continually for gratification. The id is where human *instincts* reside. It is amoral and functions according to the *pleasure principle*. The id contains the *psychic energy* (*libido*) of the person.

IDEA See *Individuals with Disabilities Education Act*.

ideal self   A *person-centered counseling* term originated by Carl Rogers to describe what the person is striving to become as opposed to the *real self* (what the person is). The further the ideal self is from the real self, the more alienated and maladjusted a person is or becomes.

ideation   A thought or belief, often used to describe thoughts of *suicide*.

identification   **1.** A "normal" developmental *process* in which individuals see themselves as similar to or different from others. **2.** A *defense mechanism* in which a person takes on the *role* and attitudes of someone more powerful.

identified patient (IP)   A *family* member who is identified as the *presenting problem* or for whom *treatment* is sought and who carries a *family*'s *symptom*s.

identity   **1.** The sense of oneself as a unique person. **2.** A virtue that is part of the fifth *stage* of *psychosocial development* conceptualized by Erik Erikson. Identity occurs between ages 12 and 18 and is the period at which adolescents establish a clear idea of who they are in regard to *values* and *roles* in life. Identity is the opposite of *role confusion* (which often leads to an *identity crisis*).

identity crisis   Confusion and doubt over one's *role* in life. An identity crisis is most likely to happen during *adolescence*.

ideographic   Geared toward or focused on an individual person. Much of *counseling* has traditionally been ideographic.

idiot   An antiquated term to describe persons with an *IQ* of 20 or below or an *adult* with the mentality of a *child* 2 years old or younger.

idiot savant   A mentally disabled person who seems to be a genius in a few areas such as in mathematics or memorization.

IEATA   See *International Expressive Arts Therapy Association*.

IEP   See *individualized educational program*.

illegal   An action or *behavior* that is in violation of the *law*.

illicit drug   An unlawful *drug*, such as *cocaine*, an *opiate*, and *marijuana*.

illusion   A misperception due to physical or psychological reasons.

image/imagery   **1.** A mental picture created in one's mind. **2.** An impression one has of a person, place, or thing.

imagery techniques   *Technique*s that help people imagine other people, scenes, smells, *feeling*s, *thought*s, and *behavior*s as vividly as possible. Arnold Lazarus is one of the more noted authorities in devising imagery techniques.

imaginal disputation   A *rational emotive behavioral therapy (REBT) technique* that has participants see themselves in stressful *situation*s and examine their *self-talk*.

Imago (Image) Relationship Therapy   An *eclectic* approach to couple work that includes elements of *psychoanalysis*, *transactional analysis*, *Gestalt therapy*, *cognitive therapy*, and *systems theory*.

imbecile   An antiquated term once used to describe a person with a *mental age* of a 3- to 7-year-old.

imitation   *Learning* new knowledge and *behavior* by observing other people and events without engaging in the behavior itself and without any direct *consequences* to oneself. Imitation is also known as *observational learning*, *social modeling*, and *vicarious learning*.

immanent justice   The idea, especially in young children, that *punishment* for a wrongdoing is absolute and inevitable.

immediacy   **1.** The ability of the *counselor* to discuss with the *client* the quality of their *relationship* and current interactions. **2.** A *response* by a *counselor* to something that just took place in a *counseling* session.

impaired   Unable to function adequately or at the level of one's potential or ability.

impasse layer   A term in *Gestalt therapy* for a *client* who is adrift in a sea of helplessness and dread without any sense of direction.

implosive therapy   A form of *behavioral counseling* in which the *client* is taught to image vividly the things that he or she most fears through a *process* called *flooding*. As a result, the client becomes desensitized to and less anxious about previously feared stimuli.

impotence The inability of a male to achieve an erection.

impulse control disorders *Disorders* that are characterized by clients' difficulty in resisting impulses, drives, or temptations. For many of these disorders a built-up tension is released when the act is committed followed by feelings of remorse or guilt. Examples of these disorders include *kleptomania, pyromania, pathological gambling, trichotillomania, and intermittent explosive disorder.*

in loco parentis A Latin phrase that means "acting in the place of the parent." In loco parentis is a theoretical model in which parents entrust others to act in their place. This model is sometimes used in educational institutions.

in vivo A Latin phrase that means "in life." In vivo refers to therapeutic procedures that take place in the *client*'s natural *environment.*

inappropriate affect *Emotions* that are not appropriate to the *situation* at hand, such as laughing at the death of a loved one. Inappropriate affect is a *symptom* of a *mental disorder.*

incapacitated Unable to take care of oneself because of diminished physical or mental functioning.

incest Sexual *relationships*, specifically intercourse, between close relatives, such as a father and daughter or between two siblings.

incompetent A *legal* term for the inability of a person to make legal decisions or to stand trial.

incoherent A person who cannot communicate in a clear, logical, and effective way.

incongruence Disparity between two things that are supposed to be in harmony, such as words and actions. *Counselors* and *client*s do not make progress when things are incongruent in the *counseling process.*

incorrigible An antiquated term used to describe a juvenile delinquent who was impossible to control.

incremental Small steps or increases. *Clients* often modify their behavior incrementally.

independent variable A term used in a *research experiment* for the *factor*, experience, or *treatment* that is under the control or manipulation of the experimenter and that is expected to have an effect on the subjects as assessed by *changes* in the *dependent variable.*

indigenous healing Helping approaches that originated in a *culture* before modern medicine.

individual counseling One-on-one *counseling* between a *counselor* and a *client.* See also *ideographic.*

individual differences The differences among people regarding *trait*s and quantifiable *factor*s, such as height or weight, that make them unique and distinguishable from others.

individual psychology **1.** The name given to Alfred Adler's approach to *counseling* and *psychotherapy.* See also *Adlerian counseling.* **2.** The branch of *psychology* that investigates differences between individuals.

individual test A *test* administered to only one person at a time. Often these tests are measures of *intelligence* (such as a *Wechsler Adult Intelligence Scale*) or *personality* (such as a *Rorschach Ink Blot Test*). It is the opposite of *group test.*

individual time The span of life between one's birth and death. Notable individual *achievement*s are often highlighted in this perspective, for example, being recognized as "teacher of the year."

Individuals with Disabilities Education Act (IDEA) A *law* that provides for a free and appropriate education in the least restrictive environment to almost 7 million children with special needs.

individualized educational program (IEP) An educational program tailored to the specialized *need*s of a certain child. *Counselors,* especially in schools, engage in either direct *intervention*s or support services with students for whom IEPs are drawn up.

individuation   The *process* by which an individual comes to understand himself or herself as an indivisible and integrated whole person who is different from others.

inductive reasoning   A form of logical analysis that moves from specific observations to a *generalization*. Therefore, a *profession* may be judged by who someone knows in it. See *deductive reasoning*.

industry   A virtue that is a part of the fourth *stage* of *psychosocial* development conceptualized by Erik Erikson. Industry occurs between ages 6 and 12 and is conceptualized as the setting and attaining of personal *goals*. It is the opposite of *inferiority*.

infancy   The period in human life that begins after birth and lasts for approximately 2 years.

inferential statistics   A set of procedures for making *generalization*s about a *population* by studying a *subset,* or *sample,* of the population. Sample *survey*s use inferential statistics (e.g., the Gallup Poll).

inferiority   **1.** The opposite of Erik Erikson's concept of *industry*. Inferiority occurs between ages 6 and 12. If children come to feel that they are inferior to others, they fail to set and attain *goals* because they think they cannot. **2.** An *Adlerian counseling* concept for *feeling*s of inadequacy that stem from being born with a physical or mental defect, being pampered by parents, or being *neglected*. The feelings must be corrected and inappropriate forms of *behavior* stopped. To do so, the *counselor* assumes the *role* of teacher and interpreter of events.

inferiority complex   An *Adlerian counseling* concept denoting the unresolved *feeling* of inadequacy and insecurity a person has in regard to others. An inferiority complex may lead to *overcompensation*.

infliction of mental distress   Outrageous and inappropriate *behavior* toward a *client* by a *therapist* that causes undue mental anguish and suffering.

influencing skills   Counseling proficiencies such as the use of *interpretation, feedback, self-disclosure,* and the giving of information that help a *client* move toward growth and *change*.

information giving   Providing a *client* with information needed to help make a decision. For example, in *career counseling* specific information may help a client decide on a *vocation*.

informed consent   A document *client*s sign acknowledging that they have been informed of the activity or experience they are about to participate in and are entering it voluntarily.

Informed Consent Statement
(counseling)

I, _____, acknowledge that counseling is an activity that involves my being open, honest, and willing to participate with my counselor as I strive, to reach personal goals. I may experience negative, as well as positive, feelings in this process. I am entering this relationship voluntarily and pledge to work hard in this process.

_____
date

_____
client signature

_____
counselor signature

inhalant A toxic vapor found in such products as glue, gasoline, nail polish remover, aerosols, anesthetics, cooking sprays, and organic nitrites that when inhaled gives their users a quick high with a minimal *hangover.* Inhalants damage the nerves that control breathing, and sniffing them can lead to a coma or death. Yet inhalants are readily available, inexpensive, and *legal.*

inherent inferiority An *Adlerian counseling* concept that refers to the belief that everyone is born with a built-in *feeling* of *inferiority* because of their helplessness and *dependency* as an infant. This inferiority is a motivator for people to achieve.

inherited cultures *Identification* based on *grouping*s such as *ethnicity* or *religion.*

initiative A virtue that is a part of the third *stage* of *psychosocial* development conceptualized by Erik Erikson. Initiative occurs between ages 3 and 5 and emphasizes the child achieving a sense of competence and motivation through encouragement to discover, experiment, and learn. The opposite of initiative is *guilt* (i.e., a sense of badness that results in passivity because of rejection, *punishment,* and restriction).

injunction **1.** A *transactional analysis* concept for negative messages in an individual's *life script,* such as parent commands (e.g., "Do as you are told") recorded by the child that call for the child to adopt certain *role*s. Injunctions often begin with the word "don't" (e.g., "Don't be that way") and limit personal interactions. **2.** A *legal* term for a court *process* that forbids taking a particular action.

innate A trait or quality an individual is born with that may or may not manifest itself until later in life.

innovation When *client*s turn possibilities into a practical program for *change.*

innovative creativity group a group where members examine an issue from alternative viewpoints.

inpatient A person who is treated in a residential setting such as a hospital. Inpatient is the opposite of *outpatient.*

insane A *legal* term for a person with a severe *mental disorder* that keeps them from functioning normally.

insight Self-understanding and increased awareness about one's *problem*s and the *factor*s that are influencing one's *behavior*s. Insight often occurs during or after the experience of *catharsis.* It is sometimes sudden but more often gradual. Insight comes about as a result of reorganizing ideas and *perception*s. See also *aha reaction.*

insomnia The inability to sleep, especially when such an inability is chronic.

inspection A *process* whereby a state agency periodically examines the activities of a *profession*'s practitioners. In doing so, the agency ascertains that the practitioners are performing in a fashion consistent with the public safety, health, and welfare. Many state agencies that employ *counselors,* such as *mental health* centers, are subject to having their personnel and programs regularly inspected.

instinct Inborn tendencies to act in a certain way; a natural tendency or ability. Instinct is the opposite of *learning.*

Institute for Family Counseling An early *intervention* program at the Philadelphia Child Guidance Center for community *paraprofessionals.* It proved to be highly effective in providing *mental health* services to the poor.

Institute for Rational-Emotive Behavior Therapy See *Albert Ellis Institute.*

Institute for Reality Therapy Now known as the *William Glasser Institute,* this is the center that William Glasser established in California to train *counselors* and other *helping professionals* in the *theory* and *technique*s of reality therapy/ choice theory. The institute's address is 22024 Lassen Street, Suite 118, Chatsworth, CA 91311 (800-899-0688; http://www.wglasser.com/).

institutional barrier Institutionalized inconveniences *minority population*s must endure to receive *mental health* services, such as an inconvenient *clinic* location, the use of a language not spoken by one's *family,* and the lack of diversified practitioners.

institutional review board (IRB)   A board set up by any institution that applies for federal funding involving human subjects. The board reviews research proposals to protect the rights and ensure the safety of participants in such studies.

institutionalization   The placement of a person in a long-term care facility such as an *inpatient* hospital.

intake interview   The initial *interview* a *client* undergoes to screen or *diagnose* his or her *situation* and determine whether he or she is a good candidate for *counseling*. Usually intake interviews involve taking a history of the person and his or her *presenting problem*.

integration   **1.** The ability of a person or *group* to bring together ideas and experiences into a unified whole. **2.** The bringing together of different ethnic, culture, or social groups into harmonious *relationships*. **3.** The last phase of *psychodrama*, which involves discussion and *closure*.

integrity   **1.** A state of being complete, undivided, whole. **2.** A virtue in Erik Erikson's eighth and last *stage* of *psychosocial* development that occurs from about age 65 on. Integrity describes the total *integration* of life experiences into a meaningful whole. It is the opposite of *despair* (i.e., the *feeling* that one's life has been *meaningless*).

intellectualization   A *defense mechanism* that is characterized by an emphasis on abstraction with a minimal amount of *affect*; it is as if a person used *thoughts* and a sophisticated vocabulary to avoid dealing with personal *feelings*.

intelligence   Higher-level *thought process*es, including the ability to learn from experiences, *problem* solve, remember, and successfully manipulate the *environment*. There are multiple forms of intelligence and a number of individual and group *intelligence tests*.

intelligence quotient (IQ)   The *score* on an *intelligence test* that defines a person's relative standing in a *group*. An intelligence quotient may be derived by a ratio or deviation *method*. In the *ratio IQ* method, IQ equals a person's *mental age* divided by one's *chronological age* times 100 ($IQ = MA/CA \times 100$). In the *deviation IQ* method, one's IQ is computed according to how far one's score deviates from the *mean* score obtained by individuals of the same chronological age. The deviation method assumes a normal *distribution* of scores for each age group.

intelligence test   A standardized way of assessing a person's current mental ability, intelligence tests are given either on a group or an individual level.

intensity   A *structural family therapy method* of changing *maladaptive transactions* by having the *counselor* use strong *affect*, repeated *intervention*, or prolonged pressure with a *family*.

intentionality   The capability of a *counselor* to choose *response*s to *client*s from a wide *range* of possibilities based on the counselor's *assessment* of *situation*s.

intentional civil liability   Intentional violations of a person's civic rights through *battery*, *defamation*, *invasion of privacy*, and infliction of mental distress.

interest inventory   A *test* or *questionnaire* that records an individual's preference for, interest in, or *motivation* for various activities. Interest inventories are often used as part of *career counseling*; some have been normed on individuals who *work* in select *occupation*s.

interlocking pathology   A term created by Nathan Ackerman to explain how families and certain of their members stay *dysfunctional*. In an interlocking pathology, there is an *unconscious process* that takes place between family members that keeps them together in an unhealthy relationship.

interlocking triangles   Murray Bowen's idea that the most stable and basic unit within a *family relationship* consist of three-person sets of interactions (e.g., father/mother/child).

intermittent explosive disorder A disorder characterized by engagement in aggressive or destructive behavior.

intermittent reinforcement A *schedule of reinforcement* that varies over time and that is used once a *behavior* has been established through *continuous reinforcement*.

internal consistency analysis A form of *reliability* in which the *scores* of two randomly selected halves of a *test* are compared.

internalization **1.** The *process* of taking in *thoughts* and *behaviors* from others and making them one's own. **2.** The process of incorporating the *norms* from one's *culture* and making them one's own.

internalized homophobia The way *gay, lesbian,* and *bisexual* persons are affected by societal beliefs and messages regarding intimate *relationships* between members of the same sex.

International Association for Analytical Psychology A training institute in Zurich for individuals interested in Carl Jung's theory (http://www.iaap.org/).

International Association of Addictions and Offender Counseling (IAAOC) A division within the *American Counseling Association*. Founded in 1972, IAAOC was formerly the *Public Offender Counselor Association*. The association is composed of *counselors* who have an interest in or *work* in settings that counsel with addicts and those convicted of crimes (http://www.iaaoc.org/).

International Association of Counselling (IAC) An international organization of *counselors* from throughout the world who meet for a conference annually (http://www.iac-irtac.org/).

International Association of Marriage and Family Counselors (IAMFC) A division of the *American Counseling Association*, founded in 1989. IAMFC is composed of *counselors* who work with families and couples. IAMFC's Internet address is www.iamfc.com.

***International Classification of Diseases (ICD)* manual** A manual that codifies

psychiatric *disorders* and is published by the World Health Organization. It periodically is updated in new editions. The ICD is the parallel publication to the DSM. See also *DSM*.

International Expressive Arts Therapy Association An association that supports "artists, educators, consultants and therapists using multimodal expressive arts processes for personal and community transformation" and promotes the uses of the expressive arts "as a powerful tool for psychological, physical and spiritual wellness" (http://www.ieata.org/). See *creative arts, creative arts therapies,* and *Association for Creativity in Counseling*.

International Transactional Analysis Association (ITAA) An association that was founded by Eric Berne, the creator of *transactional analysis*. It helps advance the *theory, methods,* and principles of transactional analysis and offers *certification* and training in various categories. ITAA's address is 436 14th Street, Suite 1301, Oakland, CA 94612-2710 (510-625-7720; http://www.itaa-net.org).

intercultural communication A symbolic transaction, *verbal* or *nonverbal,* between people of different *cultures*. Such a transaction is open to a multitude of *interpretations,* expectations, and *meanings*.

Internet counseling A sometimes controversial but prevalent form of individual, group, and family *counseling* in which *clients* use computers to interact with *counselors* via e-mail, chat rooms, and video on the Internet. Sessions are for fixed periods of time for a fee. *Nonverbal cues* and messages are difficult, if not impossible, to *process*. Empirical evidence of effectiveness is scarce. However, clients may benefit from being able to express their *thoughts* and *feelings* at any time, not just at appointed times. Persons with limited mobility or who live in isolated regions may benefit too. Counselors may also benefit from Internet counseling by getting to consult with colleagues prior to responding. Internet counseling is known by a variety of names such as *cybercounseling, Web counseling, e-mail counseling, e-therapy,* and *therap-e-mail.*

internship A clinical training experience in a *counselor education* program following a *practicum,* in which the counselor-in-training essentially works full time in a clinical setting under the *supervision* of a more experienced *counselor,* both on-site and at the institution from which the counselor-in-training is receiving his or her degree.

interpersonal Between two or more people.

interpersonal attractiveness *Counselor behavior* that conveys to *clients* that they are liked and that they share meaningful similarities. See *social influence model.*

interpersonal problem-solving groups See *group counseling.*

Interpersonal Process Recall An approach to *supervision* originated by Norman Kagan. It utilizes *feedback* to the *counselor* through the use of videotaped playbacks.

interpretation 1. An explanation or clarification of concepts or data whose *meaning* is not obvious. See *test interpretation.* 2. A *verbal technique* that focuses on *helping clients* gain *insights* into their past or present *behavior.* Interpretation offers possible explanations for certain *behaviors, feelings,* or *thoughts,* usually from a theoretical perspective, such as *psychoanalysis.* When used successfully, interpretation helps a client explain or understand a *situation* better, develop *insight,* and become more open to *change.* There are three levels of interpretation: constructional, situational, and thematical. See also *constructional interpretation; situational interpretation; thematical interpretation.*

intersex A person with an intersex condition is born with sex chromosomes, external genitalia, or an internal reproductive *system* that is not considered "standard" for either male or female. (Replaces the outdated term hermaphrodite.)

interval scale A *measurement* scale that can be used to classify and order measurements. An interval scale does not have a true zero point but does have *score* points that are of equal distance from each other. An *IQ test* is an example of an instrument based on an interval scale.

intervention *Treatment* initiated by a *counselor* that is aimed at disrupting and/or alleviating *client problems,* for example, giving a *directive* to a client to do the opposite of what he or she has been doing.

interview A *method* of seeking clinical information or *research data.* An interview almost always involves two-way *verbal* communication between the interviewer and the interviewee.

intimacy 1. A close association and familiarity. 2. A virtue in Erik Erikson's sixth *stage* of *psychosocial* development that occurs between ages 18 and 35. The emphasis in intimacy is on achieving intimate *interpersonal relationships.* Intimacy is the opposite of *isolation* (i.e., facing life alone).

intimate partner violence (IPV) A form of domestic violence that occurs between two people in a close relationship.

intoxication The physical/psychological state induced by consuming *alcohol* or other *drugs.*

intracultural communication Communication between members of the same *culture.*

intrapersonal A synonym for *intrapsychic*; literally, "within the person."

intrapsychic Within the mind of the person.

intrinsically neutral An approach that views individuals as neither positive nor negative (i.e., without a predetermined set of *responses*).

introjection A *defense mechanism* in which a person internalizes messages from another person, such as a parent, and applies them to his or her life.

introspection The *process* of examining one's *thoughts.*

introvert A Jungian concept for a person who tends to direct his or her life energy inward rather than toward the *environment.* Introverts are more concerned with their own *thoughts* and *feelings* than with others. Introvert is the opposite of *extrovert.*

intuition An awareness of the rightness or wrongness of a solution to a *problem* or a possibility often based on information and logic that may not be obviously apparent to outside observers.

invariant prescription A specific kind of *ritual* in *Milan family therapy* given to parents with children who are *psychotic* or anorexic in an attempt to break up the *family*'s dirty game. An invariant prescription requires parents to unite so that children cannot manipulate them as "winners" or "losers" and thereby side with them.

invasion of privacy A violation of the right to be left alone.

inventive creativity group A group where members offer unique solutions to a problem.

inventory A list of questions, statements, or words to which an individual responds (e.g., agrees or disagrees). Inventories are designed to measure a dimension of *personality,* interest, aptitude, or other behavioral characteristic.

inverse correlation A statistical term for a negative *correlation* in which one *variable* goes up while another goes down.

investigative people Individuals, according to Holland's *career* typology, who enjoy working in precise, scientific, and intellectual environments studying and solving scientific and mathematical problems (e.g., scientists, mathematicians). See *RIASEC.*

investment syndrome A *situation* that occurs when *counselors* are reluctant to work with *older adult*s because they feel their time and energy are better spent working with younger people who may eventually contribute to society. Professionals who display this attitude are banking on future payoffs from the young and may well be misinformed about the possibilities for *change* in older adults.

invisible disability A *disability* that is not readily observable like a psychiatric disorder.

invisible loyalty An *unconscious* commitment that a grown child makes to help his or her *family of origin,* especially his or her parents (e.g., phoning to see how the parents are doing or sending money).

invitational skills *Nonverbal skills* and *opening skills* that are used in building a helping relationship.

in vivo In real time; the attempting of *behaviors* in the present as in *systematic desensitization.*

involuntary client A *client* who is ordered to receive *counseling* but does so unwillingly. Such clients are usually *reluctant* (referred by a *third party* and unmotivated to seek help) or *resistant* (unwilling or opposed to *change*).

Iowa Law Review Note A 1971 ruling that legally recognized *counselors* as professionals who provided personal as well as vocational and educational counseling. This *legal* ruling was among the first to view *counseling* as a *profession* separate from other *helping* specialties.

Iowa Test of Basic Skills A *battery* of *achievement test*s covering kindergarten through grade 8. The tests are designed to measure basic educational skills and include reading, math, language, and study skills.

IPV See *intimate partner violence.*

IQ See *intelligence quotient.*

irrational belief (IB) The generation of an upsetting and disturbing *thought.* Adlerian and cognitive theories of *counseling* emphasize the part that irrational beliefs play in people becoming upset or distraught. Albert Ellis classifies irrational beliefs under three main headings dealing with *self,* others, and the *environment.* All contain the word "must" and when believed lead to various kinds of emotional disturbance.

irrational thinking A concept associated with Albert Ellis's *rational emotive behavior therapy (REBT)* that describes how illogical *thinking* of *client*s is based on wants and desires (e.g., "I must have all of my wishes filled"). See also *awfulizing; musturbation.*

isms The suffix of many words that have an impact on counselors and *clients*. Negative isms include *sexism* and *racism*. Positive isms include *optimism* and *altruism*.

isolation **1.** A style of living in which a person is disconnected socially and emotionally from others. **2.** The opposite of *intimacy* in Erik Erikson's sixth *stage* of *psychosocial development*. If a person does not achieve intimate *relationship*s, he or she becomes socially isolated. **3.** A *defense mechanism* that people employ to separate an idea from its emotional content. **4.** A term sometimes used synonymously with "*time-out*." **5.** A basic concept in *existentialism* where persons realize they live and die apart from others.

j

Jaffee vs. Redmond The 1996 U.S. Supreme Court decision that held that communications between licensed *psychotherapists* and their *patients* are *privileged* and do not have to be disclosed in cases held in federal court.

JCD See *Journal of Counseling and Development*.

job A definite piece of *work* undertaken for a fixed price.

job analysis A procedure used to determine the *factor*s or tasks that make up a *job*.

job satisfaction The degree to which individuals like or dislike a *job*.

Johari Awareness Model (Johari Window) A representative square with four quadrants that, when the *process* works well, is often used in *counseling* to show what happens with an individual or in *group* interactions. If the group works well, the first three quadrants (the *public self,* the *blind self,* and the *private self*) grow, and the last one (the *unknown self*) shrinks.

ITAA See *International Transactional Analysis Association*.

item The individual questions, that compose a *test*.

item analysis The examination of *test* questions to determine the effectiveness of each in measuring the concepts the test is purported to measure.

I-Thou relationships An existential term originated by Martin Buber to describe *relationship*s that focus on interactions and dialogue with persons in a deep and intimate way rather than relationships with things, which are considered I-It relations.

I statement Taking responsibility for one's *actions, emotions,* or *thoughts* by using the word "I" at the beginning of any statement.

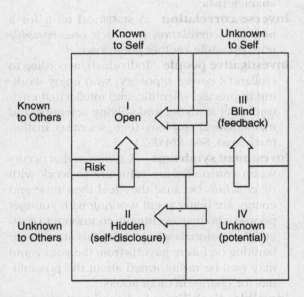

Johari Window.

Source: From *Group Processes: An Introduction to Group Dynamics,* Third Edition, by Joseph Luft. Copyright © 1963 by Joseph Luft. Reprinted by permission of Mayfield Publishing Company.

joining The *process* of "coupling" that occurs between the *counselor* and the *client,* leading to the development of a therapeutic *relationship* and *change.*

joint A term for *marijuana* that is wrapped in cigarette paper and smoked.

joint custody A *legal* term for the right of both parents, after a divorce, to share in making major decisions for their children.

Jonah complex A term coined by Abraham Maslow for a defense that involves a person trying to run away from his or her responsibilities, potential, and talents, just as the biblical character Jonah tried to escape his fate.

journal/journaling **1.** Also known as a *log;* the writings of one's reactions to a *counseling* session or daily events. This *process* enables *client*s and *counselor*s to spot patterns, *thought*s, and themes more quickly than otherwise. See also *scriptotherapy.* **2.** A term often used in the official title of a *professional association*'s regularly published periodical.

Journal of Counseling and Development (JCD) The flagship *journal* of the *American Counseling Association* (ACA).

k

K-ABC See *Kaufman Assessment Battery for Children.*

KAIT See *Kaufman Adolescent and Adult Intelligence Test.*

Karpman triangle Also known as the *drama triangle,* a way of conceptualizing game interactions in *transactional analysis* for the three *position*s (*victim, persecutor, or rescuer*) people assume during transactional analysis *games.* To keep games going there is often a switch-off, in which people assume new *roles.* For example, in the game "Why Don't You/Yes, But," one person plays the rescuer, responding to a complaint by the victimized other person by saying, "Why don't you . . .?" The *victim* answers, "Yes, but . . . [I've tried]."

Journal of Counseling Psychology The flagship *journal* of the *Society of Counseling Psychology* (Division 17) of the *American Psychological Association* (APA).

Journal of Marital and Family Therapy The flagship *journal* of the *American Association for Marriage and Family Therapy (AAMFT).*

justice An ethical principle encompassing fairness and referring to the equal *treatment* of all people. This virtue advocates that everyone's welfare should be promoted and that visible differences in people, such as *gender* or *race,* should not interfere with the way individuals and groups are treated.

juvenile **1.** A general term for a young person who is under age 18 and not considered an adult. **2.** A *legal* term for a young person who has not reached the age at which he or she would be tried as an adult in a court of *law.*

juvenile delinquency See *delinquency.*

juvenile offender An individual, usually under the age of 18, who has been charged and tried in a court of law.

After this game becomes tiresome, the rescuer may switch to a more punishing, persecuting role. When the *victim* complains, the *persecutor* may respond sarcastically, "Ain't it awful," until the game ends. See also *games.*

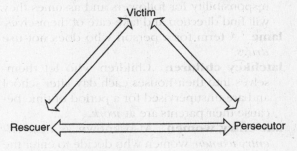

Drama (Karpman) triangle.

Kaufman Adolescent and Adult Intelligence Test (KAIT)   An individually administered *intelligence test* for use with adolescents and adults. The KAIT provides three broad measures of *intelligence*: a crystallized scale, a fluid scale, and a total *score*. See also *crystallized intelligence; fluid intelligence*.

Kaufman Assessment Battery for Children (K-ABC)   An individually administered measure of *intelligence* and *achievement* containing 16 *subtests* of mental and processing skills for children 2 years 6 months to 12 years 6 months.

kinesics   Communication through facial and body movement.

kleptomania   A *neurotic* compulsion to steal objects that are not needed. Kleptomania is considered an *impulse control disorder*.

KOIS   See *Kuder Occupational Interest Survey*.

Kuder Occupational Interest Survey (KOIS)   An activity-preference, *item*-type, untimed, forced-choice, triad-*response* interest *test*, in which a person is asked to respond to each triad by picking his or her least and most preferred activity. There are six forms of the KOIS, which was first published in 1939 and has continued to evolve. *Scores* on the KOIS correlate highly with commonly expressed interests of select *career* groups and college majors. The test's 10 broad career areas are social services, persuasive, clerical, computational, musical, artistic, literary, mechanical, outdoor, and scientific.

Kuder Preference Record—Vocational   An instrument that measures interest in 10 career areas: outdoor, mechanical, computational, scientific, persuasive, artistic, literary, musical, social service, and clerical.

l

labeling   The use of a label, such as a *diagnosis,* to characterize or name a *client's behavior* (e.g., schizophrenic).

labile   A tendency for abrupt *changes* in a person's *mood* or *emotion*.

laboratory research   Investigation within a controlled *environment,* such as a *counseling* laboratory, in which the researcher has control over experimental and environmental conditions.

laissez-faire leader   A leader who does not take responsibility for followers and assumes they will find direction and take care of themselves.

lame   A term for a person who does not use *drugs*.

latchkey children   Children who let themselves into their houses each day after school and are unsupervised for a period of time because their parents are at *work*.

late-entry women   Also known as *delayed-entry women*; women who decide to enter the *job* market after considerable time at home, often raising children.

latency   A period between ages 6 and 12 in which there is little manifest interest in sexuality, according to Sigmund Freud. Instead, energy is focused on *peer* activities and personal mastery of cognitive *learning* and physical skills.

latent content   The symbolic features of the dream that escape first analysis (e.g., water as a *symbol* for life). Sigmund Freud believed that in dreams, the presumed true *meaning* is hidden behind the *manifest content*. See also *dream analysis*.

Latino(a)   A person from Spanish-speaking Latin America who stresses his or her Latin American heritage. See also *Hispanic*.

law   A body of *rules* recognized by a nation, state, or community as binding on its members.

law of effect   Edward Thorndike's proposition about learning in which he stated that reward is more powerful than punishment in acquiring new behaviors.

law of triviality An axiom that states that the time spent discussing an issue is in inverse proportion to the *consequences* of the issue. The law of triviality is important in attending to the *content* of a *group*.

lay analyst A trained psychoanalyst who does not have a medical degree.

layers of neurosis A *Gestalt therapy* term for aspects of people's lives that keep them from being healthy (e.g., the *phony layer,* the *phobic layer,* and the *impasse layer*). See also *impasse layer; phobic layer; phony layer.*

leader-centered group An autocratic *group* in which the leader instructs the followers. The leader-centered group is based on obedience from followers.

leaderless group A *group* that rotates the leadership *role* among its members (e.g., a *self-help group*).

lead/leading A term coined by Francis Robinson to describe certain deliberate *behaviors* counselors engage in for the benefit of their *clients.* Leads vary in length, and some are more appropriate at one *stage* of *counseling* than at another. Robinson used the analogy of a football quarterback and receiver to describe a lead: A good quarterback anticipates where the receiver will be on the field and throws the ball to that spot. The same type of dynamic is true of counselors and clients. Counselors anticipate where their clients are and where they are likely to go and then respond accordingly. If there is misjudgment and the lead is either too far ahead (i.e., too persuasive or direct) or not far enough (i.e., too uninvolved and nondirect), the counseling *relationship* suffers.

learned helplessness Martin Seligman's idea that when people have been in *situations* in which they were not able to control their *environment* (e.g., in dire poverty), they will fail to take initiatives to influence their surroundings when they are in circumstances in which that is possible because they have learned to be *helpless* (i.e., they do not think they can make a difference in improving their lot in life).

learned optimism Martin Seligman's idea that when people practice cautious *optimism* in their thinking, they are less likely to become *depressed,* ill, or a victim of *learned helplessness.*

learning A general term referring to *processes* that lead to relatively permanent *changes* in *behavior* resulting from past experiences. Learning can occur on a number of levels (e.g., overt or covert, *conscious* or *unconscious*). Although there are multiple theories on how learning takes place, there is general agreement on what learning entails.

learning curve A graphic presentation of the *changes* in *learning* over time. Although learning curves differ, a classic learning curve is steeper when beginning new tasks and then, after a time, plateaus.

learning disability A term for a child of average or above average *intelligence* who has difficulty *learning.* Specific difficulties are *dyslexia* (reading difficulty), *dysgraphia* (writing difficulty), and *dyscalculia* (math difficulty).

learning experiences Instructional and associated learning (i.e., gathering of knowledge).

learning theory The idea that all human *behavior* is learned; the foundation for *behavior therapy.* It is the opposite of *instinct.*

learning theory of career counseling (LTCC) Specific applications of *social learning theory* to the practice of *career counseling* as developed by John Krumboltz. According to LTCC four interactive factors influence a person's career decision making: *genetic endowment, environmental conditions and events, learning experiences,* and *task-approach skills.* The goal of LTCC is to help clients develop skills, interests beliefs, values, work habits, and personal qualities that will enable them to have satisfying lives in a dynamic work environment.

least restrictive environment   A mandate from *Public Law 94-142* that states that persons with *disabilities* must be placed in the most normal *situation* possible in schools.

leaving a legacy   Leaving something behind to prove the worth of one's existence.

legal   The *law* or the state of being lawful.

leisure   Activities that are a part of a person's self-expression and that one does for enjoyment and relaxation when not engaged in *work*. Leisure is a part of *career* life planning.

lesbian   A term used to describe a female *homosexual*.

level of care   The treatment alternatives on a continuum of care (e.g., outpatient, inpatient).

leveling   A term used by Virginia Satir to describe a congruent communication, in which the straight, genuine, and real expression of one's *feelings* and wishes are made in an appropriate context.

liability   A *legal* term that involves issues concerning whether *counselors* have caused harm to *clients*. Liability may be *civil* (e.g., for failing to perform one's duties as required by *law*) or *criminal* (e.g., for failing to report suspected child *abuse* or sexual misconduct). Liability issues are intertwined with *malpractice*. See also *malpractice*.

liability insurance   Insurance designed to protect a person from the financial risks of a lawsuit (see *professional liability insurance*).

libel   Injury to a person's character through written means.

libido   A *personality* component, according to *psychoanalysis*, that includes the basic sexual *instincts*, desires, and impulses with which all people are born.

licensed professional counselor (LPC)   The title often given (in states that license counselors) to a *counselor* who successfully passes all criteria for *licensure*.

licensing board   An official agency that is given jurisdiction over the regulation of licenses for a particular *profession* (e.g., *counseling*).

licensure   *Permission* granted by a government, usually on the state level, allowing practice of an *occupation*, such as *counseling*, by an individual meeting professional criteria. Once licensure requirements are established, individuals cannot practice a *profession* legally without obtaining a license.

Life Career Assessment (LCA)   A qualitative *assessment* procedure that uses a structured *interview* to focus on *clients*' levels of functioning in their life *career development* and the internal and external dynamics that may be involved.

life events   Experiences that occur in the daily lives of individuals, such as births, weddings, illness, moves, basically short-lived transitions as opposed to enduring conditions (e.g., poverty).

life expectancy   The expected duration of human life.

life instinct   A *psychoanalysis* term for an *unconscious* drive toward preserving and enhancing life. The life instinct is the balancing force to the *death instinct*.

life review   The review of one's life in old age to find themes, *meaning*, understanding, and acceptance of what one has done.

life script   A concept created by Eric Berne; a plan based on the interpretation of one's life experiences, which helps determine how a person interacts.

life script analyses   A component of *transactional analysis* that examines people's basic plans involving *transactions* and *games*.

life skills   Learned *behaviors* (e.g., *problem* solving, communication, planning), on both the *interpersonal* and *intrapersonal* level, necessary for effective living.

life skills training   A type of *guidance* or *psychoeducational* activity (often carried out in *groups*) especially designed to help those who have a deficit of *behaviors*. Emphasis is on a "how-to" approach to *learning* new *behaviors* and may include the use of films, plays, demonstrations, *role plays,* and guest speakers.

life span   **1.** The average number of years men and women normally live. **2.** The particular number of years a specific person lived.

life span development The way a person matures from conception to death on a number of dimensions (e.g., physical, mental, behavioral, emotional, and moral).

life tasks According to Adlerian *theory,* the basic challenges and obligations people face in life.

lifestyle 1. A way of life or a style of living that reflects a person's *values* and attitudes or the values and attitudes of the group to which he or she belongs. **2.** An *Adlerian counseling* concept for a person's unique, directional pattern of *behavior* based on a judging of both oneself and the outside world.

Likert scale A *technique* developed by Rensis Likert that measures (on a multipoint scale) a person's degree of agreement or disagreement with a statement.

Most days I wake up happy.

5	4	3	2	1
strongly agree	mildly agree	don't know	mildly disagree	strongly disagree

Likert scale

limbic system A complex set of structures that lies on both sides and underneath the thalamus in the brain and includes the hypothalamus, the hippocampus, and the amygdala. The limbic system is primarily responsible for a person's emotional life (e.g., fear, aggression). Memory and sexuality are also linked to the limbic system. Clients dealing with chronic pain, stress, or struggling with cognitive functioning may be especially affected by limbic system responses.

limited license A term that is used in connection with the protection of a title only. For instance, persons cannot call themselves *National Certified Counselors (NCCs)* unless they have successfully completed the requirements for and been granted this title by the *National Board for Certified Counselors (NBCC).*

linear causality Also known as *linear thinking;* the concept of *cause and effect* (i.e., forces are seen as moving in one direction, with each causing the other). It is the opposite of *circular causality.*

linear thinking See *linear causality.*

linking The *process* of connecting a person with *themes* in his or her life or connecting persons with one another by pointing out what they share in common. Linking strengthens the bonds within and between individuals.

listening A skill that is one of the primary means of conducting *counseling.* Listening involves hearing not only the *content* of a *client*'s words but also the tone and inflection of what is being said (i.e., the *nonverbal*). Furthermore, listening in counseling involves hearing what is not being said as well as deciphering patterns.

living will A legal document that specifies what to do if a person becomes very sick and is unable to communicate his or her wishes. Usually a living will contains a "Do Not Resuscitate" order that withholds life support measures to keep a person alive.

locus of control The idea espoused by Julian Rotter that individuals live their lives according to their view of controlling forces as either internal or external. When the locus of control is internal, people view themselves as being in charge of their own destinies. When the locus of control is external, people believe they are controlled by outside forces.

log See *journal.*

logical consequences An *Adlerian counseling* concept that stresses the negative social consequence for a *client* when actions are ill timed (e.g., not knowing about a class function because of not paying attention in a class).

logico scientific reasoning Reasoning that is characterized by empiricism and logic.

logotherapy An existential *psychotherapy,* developed by Victor Frankl, that helps the *client* restore *meaning* to life by placing his or her *problem*s in a larger spiritual and philosophical context. Logotherapy is uniquely existential in that it attempts to offer solutions to human concerns as they exist in the moment, rather than attempting to locate their roots in the past.

long brief therapy *Therapy* so named because of the length of spacing between sessions (usually a month) and the duration of *treatment* (up to a year). Long brief therapy is also known as *systemic family therapy.*

longitudinal research An investigation that collects information on the same individuals repeatedly over time in an effort to determine how phenomena *change* as people develop. Longitudinal research is considered more valid in most cases than *cross-sectional research,* but it also takes considerably longer.

long-term therapy *Treatment* for *disorders* or *problems* that is extensive and extends over a number of sessions and at least a 6-month period.

loss The *process* of ending, *terminating,* or losing a *relationship,* person, experience, or function. Loss is often, but not always, associated with *grief.* When such is the case, people must work through their *feelings* and come to resolution if they are to avoid *depression* and live a full life.

lost child A *child* within a family with *alcohol* abuse who separates himself or herself from the *family system.*

low facilitative responses *Responses* that are minimally helpful. Three such responses are (1) *advice/evaluation* (telling people how to behave or judging them), (2) *analyzing/ interpreting* (explaining the reasons behind *behavior* without giving the *client* an opportunity for self-discovery), and (3) *reassuring/ supportive* (trying to encourage someone, yet dismissing the person's real *feelings*).

LPC See *licensed professional counselor.*

LSD See *lysergic acid diethylamide.*

LTCC See *learning theory of career counseling.*

lucid A term that refers to an individual who is in touch with reality and can accurately convey what he or she is experiencing.

ludes See *depressants.*

lysergic acid diethylamide A *hallucinogen,* sometimes called *acid.*

m

MAC See *master addiction counselor.*

macrosystem The outermost layer of a child's environment (e.g., cultural values, customs, laws).

magic shop A *warm-up technique* in *psychodrama* that is especially useful for *protagonists* who are undecided or ambivalent about their *values* and *goals.* It involves a storekeeper (the director or an *auxiliary ego*) who runs a magic shop filled with special qualities. The qualities are not for sale but may be bartered for.

magical thinking The belief that *thinking* influences the *environment* and is equivalent to *behavior.* Magical thinking is dysfunctional and is found mainly in *psychotics* and young *children.*

magnification An exaggeration of something significant.

main effects The individual effects of the *independent variable* on the *dependent variable.*

mainstreaming **1.** The injection of a *narcotic* directly into the bloodstream through a vein. **2.** The placing of developmentally delayed children into a regular classroom setting.

maintenance A *behavior therapy process* in which a *client* consistently performs desired actions without relying on external help.

maintenance role A *role* that contributes to the social-emotional *bonding* of members and the overall well-being of the *group*. When *interpersonal* communication in the group is strained, there is a need to focus on *relationships*. Persons who take on such roles are socially and emotionally oriented. They express themselves by being encouragers, harmonizers, compromisers, commentators, and followers.

majority culture The primary group of people that sets the standards and tone for life within the *culture* in which it dominates. See also *minority*.

making the rounds A *warm-up exercise* in *Gestalt therapy groups* in which *confrontation* is heightened and group members are asked to say something they usually do not verbalize. A milder form of making the rounds, in which there is less confrontation but yet participation by all group members, is called *rounds* or *go-rounds*.

making wishes into demands Using "should," "ought," and "must" in regard to an action. According to Albert Ellis, individuals who do this make themselves miserable.

maladaptive *Behaviors*, *thoughts*, *feelings*, or characteristics that are ill suited for the demands of life and that do not help a person obtain personal or societal *goals*.

malingering Faking or inducing a physical symptom or a mental *disorder*.

malpractice The failure to fulfill the requisite standard of care expected of a professional either because of *negligence* or ignorance that may occur through *omission* or commission.

malpractice insurance See *liability insurance*.

malpractice suit A claim against a professional made by a "plaintiff" who seeks a monetary award based on a specific amount of physical, financial, and/or emotional damages.

maltreatment Actions that are abusive, neglectful, or otherwise threatening to another person's welfare. Maltreatment is often used as a general term for *abuse* or *neglect*.

managed care A wide *range* of *techniques* and *structures* that are connected with obtaining and paying for medical care, including mental *health care* such as *counseling*. Managed care involves the participation of a *third party* other than a *caregiver* and a *client*. The two most common third-party participants are a *preferred provider organization (PPO)* and a *health maintenance organization (HMO)*.

mandala A *symbol* found in most *cultures* that represents, according to Carl Jung, the striving for the total unity of *self*.

A Mandala

mandatory ethics The level of ethical functioning characterized by required compliance with basic, minimal standards.

mania/manic A *mood disorder* in which there is elation and euphoria as well as a preoccupation with an activity or object.

manic-depressive illness See *bipolar disorder*.

manifest content The obvious *meaning* of dreams in dream analysis.

manipulators Individuals, often in *groups*, who use *feelings* and *behaviors* to get their way or exploit regardless of what others want or *need*. Frequently, they are angry.

MANOVA A statistical procedure often thought of as an extension of *ANOVA* used to measure significance with two or more *dependent variables* or *independent variables*.

mantra A word or phrase a person says repeatedly to induce *meditation*.

manualization The systemized *techniques* of *behavior therapy* where a step-by-step approach to *treatment* can be written down and used by other *therapists, counselors,* and *client*s themselves.

mapping   **1.** In *brief therapy,* the sketching out of a course of successful *intervention.* **2.** In *structural family therapy,* the mental *process* of envisioning how the *family* is organized. See *family mapping.*

marathon group   A type of *encounter group,* originated by George Bach and Fred Stoller in 1964, that seeks to help people become more *authentic* with themselves. Marathon groups usually are held for extended periods of time (e.g., 24 or 48 hours), during which group members are required to stay together. As time goes by, members become tired and experience a breakdown in their defenses and an increase in their truthfulness.

marijuana   Often referred to as *pot* or *dope,* marijuana is a commonly used and controversial *drug* employed for recreational and, sometimes, medical purposes. Recreationally, marijuana produces a euphoric state, but prolonged use of marijuana impairs short-term memory, inhibits alertness, and causes lung infections. As a medical drug, marijuana is used primarily with cancer *patient*s as a hypnotic, an analgesic, an anticonvulsant, and an antinausea drug.

marital schism   Overt marital *conflict* that is pathological.

marital skewness   A *dysfunctional* marriage in which one partner dominates the other.

marker events   The tern Daniel Levinson gave to experiences in a man's life that require some type of adaptation, such as being fired or getting a divorce. Although Levinson wrote about the lives of men, marker events are pertinent for women too.

marriage counseling   Working with a married couple in remedial and preventive ways. Marriage counseling is usually conjoint, but sometimes it is concurrent. Marriage counseling is also known as *marriage therapy.* See also *couples counseling.*

marriage enrichment   The concept and practice that couples and families stay healthy or get healthier by actively participating in activities that include other couples.

marriage therapy   See *marriage counseling.*

masculine mystique   The belief that men are superior to women and therefore have the right to devalue and restrict women's *values, role*s, and *lifestyle*s.

masochism   **1.** A tendency for a person to seek out ways of being physically or psychologically hurt. **2.** A sexual *disorder* in which a person gets sexually excited by being threatened or harmed.

MAST   See *Michigan Alcoholism Screening Test.*

Master Addiction Counselor (*MAC*)   A specialized *certification* in *substance abuse counseling* that is obtained after a professional becomes a *National Certified Counselor (NCC).*

masturbation   The stimulation of one's own genitalia.

MAT   See *Miller Analogies Test.*

mattering   To feel significant to others; to be wanted or needed by others.

maturation   Growth and development common to members of a species.

MBTI   See *Myers-Briggs Type Indicator.*

MCMI   See *Millon Clinical Multiaxial Inventory.*

mean   A statistical *measure of the central tendency* that is the arithmetic *average* of the *score*s in a set of *data.* See also *average.*

meaning   Having significance and purposefulness.

meaning attribution   **1.** Assigning worth and importance to an event or experience (e.g., *client*s' beliefs that their times of *depression* have been valuable in *helping* them understand what happiness is). **2.** A *group leader*'s ability to explain to members in a cognitive way what is occurring in their *group.*

meaningless   Without significance or purposefulness.

mental disorder   "A clinically significant behavior or psychological syndrome or pattern that occurs in an individual and that is associated with present *distress* (e.g., a painful symptom) or *disability* (i.e., an impairment in one or more important areas of functioning) or with a significantly increased risk of suffering death, pain, disability, or an important loss of freedom" (*DSM-IV-TR*, 2000, p. xxxi).

measure of the central tendency A statistical term for describing the typical, middle, or central *score* in a *distribution* of scores. The *median*, the *mean*, and the *mode* are all used as *measures of the central tendency*. All these measures encompass different *meaning*s of the term *average*.

measurement A procedure used to assign numbers to objects (e.g., *test* answers) in such a way that the numbers have quantitative *meaning*.

median A *measure of the central tendency* that is the halfway point or the midpoint of a *distribution*. In a set of *data*, the median is the point at which an equal number of *score*s are above and below it. The median corresponds to the 50th *percentile*.

mediation The practice of having a *third party* hear arguments about a *situation* and then render a decision.

Medicaid A government-sponsored *health care* program available to anyone unable to afford private health insurance and unable to meet the qualifications for *Medicare* benefits. Medicaid is unique in that it is funded by federal, state, and local funds; is run by state guidelines; and is designed to assist low-income persons by paying for most medical expenses.

Medicare The largest government health insurance plan, Medicare covers most Americans 65 years of age and older and certain disabled persons of any age who have received Social Security benefits for at least 2 years.

medical model An approach to *helping* that is patterned after the orientation used by physicians in which the *client* is seen as having a disease or *disorder*.

meditation A purposeful self-regulatory *process* that produces relaxation. Meditation can lower heart rate and blood pressure. In order to meditate, a person *needs* a quiet *environment*, an object to dwell on, a positive attitude, and a comfortable *position*.

melancholia Intense *depression* or sadness accompanied by a lack of activity.

melting pot A way of describing how homogeneous societies develop and ways that different cultures blend so that they lose their distinct identity. Critics of this theory in America state it is unrealistic and racist because it focuses on Europeans and excludes non-European immigrants.

mental age A *score* on an *intelligence test* that is representative of one's mental ability regardless of one's *chronological age*. Mental age was first used by Alfred Binet as a term for the age at which a given number of *test item*s were passed by the average child.

mental disorder/mental illness A clinically significant behavioral or psychological syndrome or pattern that occurs in an individual, according to the *American Psychiatric Association*. At least one of three features must be present for a mental disorder to be diagnosed: *distress*, impairment, and/or significant risk. See also *disorder*.

mental health A state of *positive wellness* and emotional well-being free from excessive *stress*.

mental health counseling An interdisciplinary *counseling* specialty that is community based and comprehensive. Mental health counseling includes an emphasis on *development, environment, prevention*, and *treatment* issues. This specialty is recognized by the *Council for Accreditation of Counseling and Related Educational Programs (CACREP)* and the *National Board for Certified Counselors (NBCC)*.

mental health counselor An individual who provides professional *counseling* services to individuals, couples, families, and groups for the purpose of treating *psychopathology* and promoting optimal *mental health*. Mental health counselors work in a variety of settings, such as community agencies and hospitals, as well as in *private practice*. Some states, such as Florida, license counseling professionals as mental health counselors.

mental health professionals   Individuals who have received advanced, specific degrees and are duly licensed in professions that work to promote *mental health* and treat *mental disorders* (e.g., *counselors, psychologists, psychiatrists, social workers, marriage and family therapists*).

Mental Measurement Yearbook   One of the most comprehensive and definitive reference books published. It describes and reviews commercially published *tests*. Information on the Mental Measurement Yearbook can be found on the Internet at http://www.unl.edu/buros/. See also *Buros Institute of Mental Measurements*.

Mental Research Institute (MRI)   Since 1959, a leading source of ideas in the area of *systems* studies, *psychotherapy,* and *family therapy.* MRI is located in Palo Alto, California; its Internet address is www.mri.org/

mental retardation   See *retardation.*

mental status exam (MSE)   An exam that provides information about a client's level of functioning and self-presentation. Data gathered during a mental status exam is frequently used for initial *diagnosis.*

meperidine   The leading painkiller drug (after *morphine*) with a rapid onset. Meperidine is *addictive* and is marketed under the name *Demerol.*

Mescaline   A *hallucinogen*, also known as *peyote.*

Mesmerism   Named for F. A. Mesmer, the original term for *hypnosis.*

meta-analysis   The analysis of a number of *research* studies on the same subject to decipher patterns and determine across-study findings or results.

metacommunication   The implied message within a message typically conveyed in a *nonverbal* manner. For example, a *client* who is not happy may cross his or her arms and frown.

metaphor   A *verbal* or *nonverbal* experience that occurs when two dissimilar objects are compared to one another for the sake of understanding one of the objects better. For example, on a verbal level, a *client* may describe himself or herself as "a dot who stays in one spot"; on a nonverbal level, a father who runs around in the morning waking up his *family* may be deemed "the family alarm clock." *Counselors* use metaphors to help *clients* gain *insight* into themselves and formulate their *goals*. For example, a counselor may say to a client who is trying to hold his or her family together, "You want to be the Velcro in your family."

methadone   A potent synthetic *narcotic* that is less addictive than *morphine* or *heroin* and is used as a substitute for these drugs in some *addiction* recovery programs.

method   **1.** The means by which *counselors* accomplish their purposes or *goals* in *treatment.* **2.** A procedural tool used in *research* that can be applied in various disciplines.

Metropolitan Achievement Tests   A *test* used in school districts for standardized testing programs. The tests are used in kindergarten through grade 12 and focus on eight basic skills: vocabulary, reading, mathematics, spelling, language, science, social studies, and writing.

Michigan Alcoholism Screening Test (MAST)   A widely used and researched diagnostic instrument, composed of 25 *items*, that is self-administered. The MAST has been shown to correctly identify up to 95 percent of people who have alcohol abuse *problems*.

microcounseling   An approach to teaching basic *counseling skills* (i.e., *microskills*), initiated by Robert Carkhuff and Alan Ivey. The approach is based on the assumption that interviewing skills are complex and can be taught best if broken down into discrete behavioral units.

microcounseling supervision model (MSM)   A *supervision* model that strives to help supervisees learn to identify and classify essential *interviewing counseling skills.*

microskills   Human relations skills common to all theories of *counseling,* such as *active listening* and *empathy.*

microsystems   All of the individuals in direct, close relationship with a child over a period of time (e.g., parents, teachers, peers).

middle adulthood/middle age   Ages 40 to 65; the period in which individuals realize that life is half over and death is a reality. These years are often full of *family* and *work* responsibilities.

middle childhood   Ages 6 up to puberty.

middle old   Ages 65 to 74.

middle school counseling   *Counseling* in school grades 6 through 8 or sometimes grades 7 through 9 by *counselors* educated to deal with the developmental and situational aspects of children and their parents at this time of life. Middle school counseling is both preventative, including the use of *psychoeducational processes*, and *treatment* oriented.

middlescence   A term used to describe the pluses and minuses of *middle adulthood*.

midlife   Ages 40 to 65. See also *middle adulthood*.

midlife transition   A time in *midlife* when individuals evaluate and make necessary adjustments to their lives to compensate for physical or psychological *factors*. This period—a time when people must give up their dreams and come to terms with reality and their own mortality—can be difficult for some individuals.

Milan family therapy   An Italian approach to working with families formulated by the clinical *research team* of Mara Selvini-Palazzoli, Luigi Boscolo, Gianfranco Cecchin, and Guiliana Prata, who in the 1970s became the most prominent leaders in *systemic family therapy*, their own approach to *strategic family therapy*.

milieu therapy   A form of *therapy* that focuses on changing the environment rather than the person.

Miller Analogies Test (MAT)   A *power test* consisting of 100 complex analogy *items* drawn from a number of academic disciplines. The MAT is a screening devise for predicting success in advanced graduate work.

Millon Clinical Multiaxial Inventory (MCMI)   A widely used instrument, periodically updated and employed to assess *DSM* categories of *personality disorders* and clinical syndromes. The MCMI yields 20 clinical scales divided into three categories: basic *personality* patterns (e.g., antisocial, narcissistic), pathological personality disorders (e.g., borderline, paranoid), and clinical *symptom* syndromes (e.g., *anxiety, alcohol abuse*).

mimesis   A way of *joining* with a *family* in which the *counselor* becomes like the family in the manner or *content* of their communications, for example, joking with a jovial family.

mindfulness   Paying attention to the here and now in a purposeful, nonjudgmental manner.

minimal encouragers   Brief supportive statements that convey attention and understanding (e.g., "I see," "Right," "Okay," "Hmm," and "I hear you"). Minimal encouragers help *clients* reveal and explore information, especially in the beginning *stages* of *counseling*.

minimization   Making an event less important than it was or is. This strategy is sometimes used in *denial* or when clients wish to decrease how upset they are.

Minnesota Model of Alcohol Treatment   Also known as the Minnesota Model; a *treatment* approach that integrates self-help with professional *counseling* and involves three levels of treatment: *detoxification, rehabilitation,* and *aftercare*. The model is nationally publicized by the Hazelden Foundation (800-257-7810; http://www.hazelden.org/).

Minnesota Multiphasic Personality Inventory-2 (MMPI-2)   A revision of one of the oldest and most widely used *personality tests* in the world. The MMPI-2 is a pencil-and-paper *objective* personality test designed to be administered to *clients* ages 16 and above. *Test* results, which are translated into *T scores*, provide *data* on nine abnormal or potentially abnormal dimensions (e.g., *hypochondriasis, depression, hysteria, paranoia,* and *schizophrenia*).

Minnesota Point of View A student personnel point of view, originated by E. G. Williamson, that was directive in nature. See also *clinical counseling*.

minority A group of persons who, because of cultural or physical distinctions, are fewer in number and less powerful in a *culture* or society than a *majority*. Minorities are distinctive in regard to such dimensions as *ethnicity, religion,* and *race*. Often minorities are discriminated against.

minority model A model, especially in *rehabilitation counseling,* in which people with disabilities are assumed to be a *minority* group.

miracle question A *brief therapy technique* in which the *counselor* asks the *client* a question that is intended to help the client obtain a clearer picture of when he or she will be better. The question is a variation of the following: "If a miracle happened tonight and you woke up tomorrow and the *problem* was solved, how would you know it? What would be different?"

mirror technique A *psychodrama* activity in which the *protagonist* watches from offstage while an *auxiliary ego* mirrors the *protagonist's* posture, gesture, and words. This *technique* is often used in the *action phase* of psychodrama to help the *protagonist* see himself or herself more accurately.

misdemeanor A minor criminal offense.

mistrust One of the *outcomes* in Erik Erikson's *psychosocial theory* of development that occurs when from birth to 1 year of age, a child is given inconsistent *treatment* or experiences. Mistrust is the opposite of *trust*.

mixed thoughts One of four *rational emotive behavior therapy (REBT) types of thoughts*. Mixed thoughts contain elements of each of the other three thought *processes*. See also *rational emotive behavior therapy (REBT) types of thoughts*.

MMPI See *Minnesota Multiphasic Personality Inventory*.

mode The *score* or value that occurs most frequently in a *distribution* of scores; a *measure of the central tendency*.

model minority A *stereotype* description of *Asian Americans/Pacific Islanders* that is the result of the significant educational and economic success of some members of this *minority* group in the United States. In fact, many members of this *population* live in poverty or suffer psychological *distress*. See also *Asian Americans/Pacific Islanders*.

modeler of appropriate behavior A *group leader* who, through passive and active demonstrations, consciously models actions that he or she thinks group members need to learn. The ways of *modeling* can include deliberate use of *self-disclosure, role plays,* speech patterns, and acts of creativity.

modeling *Observational learning;* a social behavioral *method* used to teach complex *behavior*s in a relatively short period of time by copying or imitating. Modeling is a part of Albert Bandura's *social learning theory*. See also *imitation*.

monodrama Also known as *autodrama;* a *psychodrama technique* in which the *protagonist* plays all the parts of an *enactment,* with no *auxiliary ego*s used. The person may switch chairs or talk to different parts of the *self*.

monopolizer A *group* member who, because of his or her own *anxiety,* dominates conversations by not giving other persons a chance to verbally participate.

monopolizing Taking up the group's time by talking and not giving others in the *group* a chance to participate.

mood An emotional state of mind. The pervasive way a person feels most of the time.

mood disorders *Disorder*s that have an emotional base and cause clinically significant distress in people's lives, including impairing their ability to fulfill important life roles. Mood disorders are classified by the *DSM* as those that are primarily of a *bipolar* or *depressive* nature.

Mooney Problem Check List A checklist that is used to identify *client problems* in different *content* areas (e.g., health, economic security, self-improvement, *personality,* courtship, family life, sex, *religion,* and education). Different forms are available from middle school through *adulthood.* No scale *scores* are given; rather, *counselors* are helped to identify and discuss different types of problems that may be affecting clients.

moral development The *processes* in which individuals, starting in *childhood,* learn about and come to adopt principles of right and wrong. Through these processes, they come to enact acceptable social *behavior* and to resist unacceptable conduct. Lawrence Kohlberg's *theory* of moral development, based on Jean Piaget's *cognitive development theory,* serves as an example of the *stages* involved in this process.

moral principle *The principle that guides the superego* so that it operates according to what is ideal (i.e., the moral teachings of a child's parents). Under this principle, there is a striving to be perfect.

moral therapy An approach of the late 1800s to working with mental *patients* that included using the arts and a type of *occupational therapy.*

morality The judgment or *evaluation* of action. Morality is associated with such words as "good," "bad," "right," "wrong," "ought," and "should."

moratorium Being in a *developmental crisis* but not being committed to a specific plan of action or *identity.* In such a state a person is in the process of *becoming* but is still exploring preferences.

morita A Japanese *therapy* for treating *anxiety.* In this approach, a *client's* attention is directed away from the *self.* Absolute rest and avoidance of distractions is emphasized.

morphine A *drug* extract from *opium* that is used to relieve pain and that may become *addictive* with continuous use.

morphogenesis The ability of an organism, such as a *family,* to modify its functioning to meet the changing demands of internal and external *factors.* Morphogenesis usually requires a *second-order change* rather than a *first-order change.* For example, instead of talking, family members may need to try new ways of behaving. See also *first-order change; second-order change.*

morphostasis The tendency of a person or *system* to resist *change* and remain the same way.

motivation *Behaviors* initiated by *needs* and directed toward *goals.* Motivation is biologically based as well as acquired.

motivational interviewing A directive, client-centered counseling interview method effective with a wide variety of problems, but first used by Stephen Rollnick and William R. Miller in addiction settings. The approach incorporates many basic *counseling skills,* such as active listening, reflection of feelings and content, in order to help the client explore and resolve ambivalence and motivate the client to engage in the *change* process.

mourning **1.** The expression of sorrow and *grief* that follows a *loss.* Mourning varies according to the person and the degree of loss. Prolonged mourning may lead to pathological *behavior.* **2.** The final *stage* in a *group's* development in which group members reflect on their past experiences, *process* memories, evaluate what was learned, acknowledge ambivalent *feelings,* and engage in cognitive decision making. Mourning is also known as *adjourning* or *termination.*

MRI See *Mental Research Institute.*

MSM See *microcounseling supervision model.*

MST See *multisystemic therapy.*

multiaxial assessment A way of organizing information about a *client's symptoms* along a continuum of five axes that is used in the *DSM.* See also *Axes of the DSM.*

multicultural A term used to refer to the major cultural groups within a region, territory, or nation.

multicultural counseling According to Paul Pedersen, two or more persons with different ways of perceiving their *environment* (or two different *worldviews*) working together in a *helping relationship*. Differences may be the result of specific *socialization, development,* or environmental *factor*s or a combination of such factors. The debate in multicultural counseling centers on how broadly to define the term *"multicultural."* One side advocates that the term be confined to ethnic groups; another side proposes that the term be more inclusive and refer to, people who are disabled, people who are aged, and people with different sexual orientations.

Multicultural Counseling Competencies and Standards A set of competencies and standards for working with *client*s who are from different cultural backgrounds. Published in 1992 in the *Journal of Counseling and Development* by Derald Wing Sue, Patricia Arredondo, and Roderick J. McDavis, the competencies revolve around acquiring a set of proficiencies in the following areas: attitudes and beliefs, knowledge, and skills. These competencies have been widely discussed and adopted by a number of *counseling* groups and associations.

multigenerational family A household that includes members of more than one generation (e.g., a child, a parent, and a grandparent). See also *extended family.*

multigenerational transmission process Coping strategies and patterns of coping with *stress* passed on from generation to generation in families. In poorly differentiated persons, *problem*s may result, including *schizophrenia.*

multimodal distribution A *distribution* in which two or more *score*s have the same (also the greatest) frequency.

multimodal method The use of *verbal* and *nonverbal* means for conveying information.

multimodal therapy A *cognitive behavioral therapy* introduced by Arnold Lazarus. A basic assumption of this approach is that *client*s are usually troubled by a multitude of specific *problem*s that should be addressed by a multitude of specific treatments. Thus, multimodal therapy utilizes *method*s from various approaches in an effort to help people make positive *change*s in their *BASIC ID.* See also *BASIC ID.*

multiple baseline design A *research* design that permits greater *generalization* of the results. There are three types of multiple baseline research designs: across individuals, across *situation*s, and across behaviors. Each emphasizes a different focus. The common *trait* of all three is that *intervention* is initially employed with a select individual, situation, or *behavior* while the researcher continues to gather *baseline data* on other persons, situations, or behaviors.

multiple intelligence The idea that there are a number of kinds of *intelligence.* They include *verbal*/linguistic, logical/mathematics, visual/spatial, body/kinesthetic, musical/rhythmical, *interpersonal,* and *intrapersonal.*

multiple personality disorder A term that describes the appearance of more than one *personality* within a person. This *disorder* is rare and dramatic and is known as a *dissociative identity disorder* in the *DSM.* It has been popularized in such books and movies as *The Three Faces of Eve* and *Sybil.*

multiple relationships See *dual relationships.*

multiple transferences A *phenomenon* in *psychoanalytic groups* in which group members can experience *transference feeling*s with others in the *group* as well as with the *group leader.*

multiple-family group therapy A procedure for the *treatment* of several families together at the same time. Created by John Bell in the 1960s, multiple-family group therapy requires the use of *coleader*s and has many advantages, including the fact that families can often serve as co-*therapist*s for each other.

multisystemic therapy (MST) An intensive, short-term, home- and family-focused treatment service for youth with behavioral and emotional disturbances. MST intervenes directly in a young person's family, school, neighborhood, and peer group by identifying factors that contribute to the problem behavior.

MUM effect An effect that occurs when a *counselor* avoids confronting a *client*'s *behavior.* As a result, the counselor is less effective than he or she would be otherwise.

Münchhausen syndrome The more severe and chronic form of a *factitious disorder.*

Muse v. Charter Hospital of Winston-Salem A 1995 court ruling that found it was the duty of the mental health facility to provide care to patients based on patients' medical conditions, not the need of insurance companies.

music therapy The systematic and primary or adjunct use of music as a way of bringing about therapeutic *change.* See also *American Music Therapy Association (AMTA).*

musterbation A word coined by Albert Ellis that refers humorously to the irrational *thought process* of demanding. When musterbation occurs, *client*s think they must have everything go their way. This "must" theme

leads to emotional difficulties when life does not go the way *clients* think it must or should.

mutism The inability to speak.

mutual-help group A group in which members mutually assist one another; another term for a *self-help group.*

Myers-Briggs Type Indicator (MBTI) A pencil-and-paper self-administered *personality test* based on the *theory* of Carl Jung. The MBTI is widely used in a variety of settings and yields *score*s on four dimensions of an individual's personality: extroversion-introversion, sensing-*intuition,* thinking-*feeling,* and judgment-*perception.*

mystification **1.** A deliberate *distortion* and misrepresentation of another person's experience by misinterpreting it. **2.** A term used to describe how some families mask what is going on between *family* members by giving conflicting and contradictory explanations of events.

mythopoetic A *treatment* for men developed by Robert Bly. Mythopoetic treatment involves the use of ceremony, drumming, *storytelling*/poetry reading, physical movement, and imagery *exercise*s designed to create a "ritual *process.*"

n

N A *symbol* for the number of people, *scores,* or objects in a group.

N of 1 research The study of a single qualitative entity, such as a person. N of 1 research is usually employed in a historical study or a *case study.*

NA See *Narcotics Anonymous.*

NACCMHC See *National Academy of Certified Clinical Mental Health Counselors.*

NADT See *National Association for Drama Therapy.*

NAPT See *National Association for Poetry Therapy.*

narcissism An excessive preoccupation with, concern for, and love of oneself to the exclusion of others.

narcissistic group A *group* that develops *cohesiveness* by encouraging hatred of an out-group or by creating an enemy. As a result, group members are able to overlook their own deficiencies by focusing on the deficiencies of the out-group.

narcolepsy A sleep disorder characterized by irresistible attacks of sleep.

narcotics A group of *depressant drugs,* such as *heroin, methadone, codeine, morphine, cocaine,* and *opium,* that relieve pain and *anxiety* but are *addictive* and may have major side effects (e.g., drowsiness, nausea, and vomiting). An *overdose* can produce shallow breathing, clammy skin, convulsions, coma, and possible death.

Narcotics Anonymous (NA)   A *mutual-help group* based on the *Alcoholics Anonymous (AA)* philosophy and using a variation of AA's 12-step program. Narcotics Anonymous is inclusive in its definition of *addiction* and includes anyone who has used a *mood-changing, mind-altering substance.* NA's address is P.O. Box 9999, Van Nuys, CA 91409 (818-773-9999; http://www.na.org).

narrative therapy   A postmodern and *social construction* approach to *change* based on narrative reasoning, which is characterized by stories, meaningfulness, and liveliness. *Counselors* are seen as collaborators and masters of asking questions. According to the narrative family viewpoint, people live their lives by stories. The approach emphasizes developing unique and alternative stories in the *hope* that families will come up with novel options and strategies for living. In changing their stories, families are encouraged to externalize *problem*s to solve them; blame is alleviated, and *dialogue* is generated as everyone works to solve a common problem. See also *reauthoring.*

narrowband assessment instruments   *Tests* or instruments that measure a narrow range of *characteristics, behaviors,* and *symptoms* and are used to monitor symptom severity once a *diagnosis* is made (e.g., Beck Depression Inventory). Opposite of *broadband assessment.*

NASP   See *National Association of School Psychologists.*

NASW   See *National Association of Social Workers.*

National Academy of Certified Clinical Mental Health Counselors (NACCMHC)   A *certification* group originally established, in 1978, as an independently incorporated unit of the *American Mental Health Counseling Association (AMHCA).* In 1993, the NACCMHC

merged with the *National Board for Certified Counselors (NBCC).* A professional who wishes to obtain the *Certified Clinical Mental Health Counselor (CCMHC)* credential must first become a *National Certified Counselor (NCC).*

National Association for Drama Therapy (NADT)   A nonprofit association incorporated in 1979 to establish and uphold high standards of professional competence and *ethics* among *drama therapist*s. Its members use drama and theater to bring about *symptom* relief, emotional and physical *integration,* and *personal growth.* NADT mailing address is *44365 Premier Plaza, Suite 220, Ashburn, VA 20147* (1-888-416-7167; http://www.nadt.org/).

National Association for Poetry Therapy (NAPT)   A nonprofit organization incorporated in 1981 and affiliated with the *National Coalition of Creative Arts Therapies Associations (NCCATA).* Members are interested in the *power* of the healing word and represent a wide *range* of professional experience, schools of *therapy,* educational affiliations, artistic disciplines, and other fields of training in both mental and physical health. NAPT mailing address is 777 E. Atlantic Avenue, #243, Delray Beach, FL 33483 (1-866-844-NAPT; http://www.poetrytherapy.org/).

National Association of Alcoholism and Drug Abuse Counselors (NAADAC)   A professional membership organization that serves *counselors* who specialize in *addiction counseling* (www.naadac.org).

National Association of Guidance and Counselor Trainers   One of the four original group to establish the *American Personnel and Guidance Association* in 1952. This association evolved into the *Association for Counselor Education and Supervision.*

National Association of School Psychologists (NASP)   The largest association of *school psychologist*s in the world. Its purpose is to promote *research*-based programs that prevent *problem*s, enhance independence, and promote optimal *learning.* NASP is located at

4340 East-West Highway, Suite 402, Bethesda, MD 20814 (301-657-0270; http://www.nasponline.org).

National Association of Social Workers (NASW) The largest organization of professional *social workers*. NASW promotes, develops, and protects the practice of *social work* and social workers in the United States. NASW's address is 750 First Street NE, Suite 700, Washington, DC 20002-4241 (866-331-NASP; http://www.naswdc.org).

National Board for Certified Counselors (NBCC) An independent not-for-profit credentialing body, founded in 1982, that established and now administers and monitors national *counselor certification*. NBCC identifies those *counselors* who have voluntarily sought and obtained certification and also maintains a register of certified counselors. This process recognizes counselors who have met predetermined NBCC standards in their training, experience, and *performance* on the *National Counselor Examination (NCE)*. NBCC certifies counselors in the counseling specialties of, *school counseling, mental health counseling,* and *addictions counseling.* NBCC's address is 3 Terrace Way, Greensboro, NC 27403 (336-547-0607; http://www.nbcc.org).

National Career Development Association (NCDA) A division of the *American Counseling Association (ACA)*. NCDA's mission is to promote the *career development* of all people across the *life span*. Their Internet address is http://www.ncda.org/.

National Certified Counselor (NCC) A *counselor* who is certified nationally by the *National Board for Certified Counselors (NBCC)*. Complete information on becoming an NCC can be found on the Internet at http://www.nbcc.org.

National Clearinghouse for Alcohol and Drug Information (NCADI) An information service of the *Substance Abuse and Mental Health Services Administration (SAMHSA)*, a component of the U.S. Department of Health and Human Services. NCADI is the world's largest resource for current information and materials concerning *substance abuse.* Their address is P.O. Box 2345, Rockville, MD 20847-2345 (800-487-4889; http://www.health.org/).

National Coalition of Creative Arts Therapies Associations (NCCATA) An alliance of *professional associations*, founded in 1979 and dedicated to the advancement of the arts as therapeutic modalities. NCCATA represents members of six creative arts therapies associations: *art therapy, dance/movement therapy, drama therapy, music therapy, psychodrama,* and *poetry therapy*. The association is located at c/o AMTA, 8455 Colesville Rd., Ste. 1000, Silver Spring MD, 20910 (http://www.nccata.org/).

National Counselor Examination (NCE) The exam a *counselor* must pass to become a *National Certified Counselor (NCC)*. The exam comprises 200 multiple-choice questions (recorded on a separate answer sheet) and is scheduled for a 4-hour period. For more information, visit the *National Board for Certified Counselors (NBCC)* Web site at http://www.nbcc.org.

National Defense Education Act (NDEA) An enactment by Congress in 1958 following the Soviet Union's launching of its first space satellite, Sputnik I. The act's primary purpose was to identify scientifically and academically talented students and promote their development. It provided funds through Title V-A for upgrading *school counseling* programs and through Title V-B to train *counselors* and established *counseling* and guidance institutes. In 1964, NDEA was extended to include *elementary school counseling.*

National Defense Education Institutes Specialized training programs set up by the U.S. government at select colleges and universities from 1959 to 1967 that supported the expansion and improvement of *guidance* and *counseling* services nationally. These programs varied in length from long term (a year) to short term (a few months). They were located outside regular academic programs and did much to increase the number of *counselors* in secondary and elementary schools and the professional image of counseling.

National Employment Counseling Association (NECA)   One of the divisions of the *American Counseling Association (ACA)*. NECA was originally established in 1966. Their internet address is http://www.employment-counseling.org/.

National Fair Access Coalition on Testing (FACT)   See *Fair Access Coalition on Testing*.

National Institutes of Health (NIH)   The principal biomedical and behavioral *research* agency of the U.S. government. NIH is a component of the U.S. Department of Health and Human Services. Their address is 6001 Executive Boulevard, Room 8184, MSC 9663, Bethesda, MD 20892-9663 (301-443-4513; http://www.nih.gov/).

National Institute of Mental Health (NIMH)   An institute that is a part of the *National Institutes of Health (NIH)*. The mission of NIMH is to diminish the burden of mental illness through *research*. NIMH's address is 6001 Executive Boulevard, Room 8184, MSC 9663, Bethesda, MD 20892-9663 (301-443-4279; http://www.nimh.nih.gov/).

National Mental Health Association (NMHA)   Established in 1909, the country's oldest and largest nonprofit organization addressing all aspects of *mental health* and mental illness. NMHA's address is 2001 N. Beauregard Street, 12th Floor, Alexandria, VA 22311, 703/684-7722 (www.nmha.org).

National Occupational Information Coordinating Committee (NOICC)   A federal interagency organization that works with the Department of Defense; the Department of Labor; and the Department of Education to promote excellence in the way occupational information is compiled.

National Organization for Victim Assistance (NOVA)   A private, nonprofit organization of victim and witness assistance programs and practitioners, criminal justice agencies and professionals, mental health professionals, researchers, former victims and survivors, and others committed to the recognition and implementation of victim rights and services (http://www.trynova.org/).

National Association of Peer Program Professionals (NAPPP)   Founded in 1984, this nonprofit organization provides leadership and promotes excellence in the field of *peer helping*. NPHA's address is Box 28564, Gladstone,, MO 64188 (888-691-1088; http://www.peerprogramprofessionals.org/).

National Rehabilitation Counseling Association (NRCA)   The oldest association dedicated to promoting the rights of persons with disabilities. NRCA's mission is to provide *advocacy*, awareness, and career advancement for professionals in the fields of *rehabilitation*. Their address is P. O. Box 4480, Manassas, Virginia 20108 (703-361-2077; http://nrca-net.org/).

National Training Laboratories (NTL)   A group training facility in Bethel, Maine, established by Kurt Lewin and associates in the late 1940s.

National Vocational Guidance Association (NVGA)   The forerunner of the *American Counseling Association (ACA)*. Founded in 1913, it offered *guidance* literature and united those with an interest in vocational *counseling* for the first time.

Native American   An individual who belongs to one of the 478 tribes recognized by the U.S. Bureau of Indian Affairs or another 52 tribes without official status. There is tremendous *diversity* among Native Americans, including 149 languages. However, there are common *identity values* among many Native Americans, including a harmony with nature, cooperation, holism, a concern with the present, and a reliance on one's *extended family*.

natural child   Also known as the *free child*. A *transactional analysis* term for a division of the *child ego state*. It includes the spontaneous, *feeling*-oriented, impulsive, pleasure-loving, creative, intuitive, and expressive part of one's *personality*. The natural child is responsive to *nonverbal* messages and can be self-centered.

natural consequences An *Adlerian counseling* concept that emphasizes living with the results of a particular ill-timed *behavior* that brings a negative result to the *client* (e.g., damaging a piece of art through carelessness).

natural observation The collection of *data* on *clients* by observing them in their natural *environment*.

NBCC See *National Board for Certified Counselors*.

NCADI See *National Clearinghouse for Alcohol and Drug Information*.

NCCATA See *National Coalition of Creative Arts Therapies Associations*.

NCC See *National Certified Counselor*.

NCDA See *National Career Development Association*.

NCE See *National Counselor Examination*.

NDEA See *National Defense Education Act*.

NECA See *National Employment Counselor Association*.

necessary and sufficient conditions for change The conditions *Carl Rogers* outlined in 1957 that must be present for *change* to occur. These core conditions of *counseling* are *empathy, unconditional positive regard (acceptance),* and *congruence (genuineness).*

necrophilia Sexual contact or sexual attraction to dead bodies.

need A necessity (e.g., food) that is required for one's welfare and overall well-being. A need may be psychological as well as physiological (e.g., love). The deficit of something that is a need motivates people to behave in ways to satisfy it.

need theory A *theory* based on Abraham Maslow's *hierarchy of needs* that states that people act to satisfy their basic psychological and physiological needs.

needs assessment A structured *survey* that focuses on the systematic appraisal of the types, depth, and scope of *problem*s or concerns within a specific *population. Counselors* in school and community settings can obtain a great deal of information about the populations they serve through the regular use of *needs assessments*.

negative feedback The input of corrective information to a person or a *system* to help keep a person or a system functioning within prescribed limits. Negative feedback diminishes or stops output, such as "grounding" an adolescent who stays out past curfew.

negative group variables *Factor*s in *group*s that include but are not limited to avoiding *conflict,* abdicating group responsibilities, group members anesthetizing themselves to contradictions within the group, and the group becoming *narcissistic.*

negative reinforcement An aversive *stimulus* whose removal is contingent on *performance* of a desired action. The removal of the aversive stimulus is reinforcing for the person involved. For example, a mother nags her daughter until the daughter washes the dishes. The nagging could be viewed as negative reinforcement, especially if peace and quiet is valued by the daughter.

negative thoughts One of four *rational emotive behavior therapy (REBT) types of thoughts.* Negative thoughts concentrate on painful or disappointing aspects of an event. See also *rational emotive behavior therapy (REBT) types of thoughts.*

neglect *Omission* of responsibilities; not paying attention to or taking care of. Children in neglect *situation*s are often left to take care of themselves in regard to *basic needs,* such as food, shelter, hygiene, medical attention, or management of their everyday lives.

negligence Failure on the part of a *helping professional* (e.g., a *counselor*) to take due care within accepted standards of *treatment*.

neo-Freudian Followers of Sigmund Freud who put more emphasis than Freud did on *adulthood* and *defense mechanism*s and who challenged Freud's concepts of the instinctual drive, the *Oedipus complex*, and the motivational primacy of sex and aggression. Leading neo-Freudians include Anna Freud, Harry Stack Sullivan, Karen Horney, and Eric Fromm.

NEO Personality Inventory   The most comprehensive and widely used instrument to assess the five domains in the *Big Five* or *Five Factor Model* of *personality.*

network therapy   A type of *therapy*, usually carried out in the home of a *client*, in which *family*, friends, neighbors, and others may be involved. It may include several *counselors* and 20 to 80 people.

networking   See *professional networking.*

neurofeedback   A form of brainwave feedback that enables people to alter their own brain waves using information about their brain-wave characteristics made available to them through electroencephalograph recordings, which may be displayed in auditory or visual means.

neurolinguistics programming (NLP)   A *theory* of communications originated by Richard Bandler and John Grinder. Human *behavior* is understood by NLP practitioners as the way people *process* information in their *environment* through using one or more dominant senses. For example, a person with a dominant auditory ability might be one who picks up information best through *listening.*

neurosis   **1.** In *psychoanalysis,* a functional *disorder* of the nervous *system* that is psychological rather than organic in nature; a disruption of *ego* functions. **2.** In present-day *treatment,* an antiquated but still widely used term to describe individuals who have some emotional disorders but who are not *psychotic.* The word *disorder* is now used in place of the word *neurotic* when a *diagnosis* is made using the *DSM.*

neurotic   A person suffering from a *neurosis.*

neurotransmitters   Chemicals, such as dopamine or serotonin, that are released by the terminal buttons at the end of a neuron and received at receptor sites on the dendrite of other neurons.

neutral cognitions   One of four *rational emotive behavior therapy (REBT) types of thoughts.* Neutral *cognitions* are those that are neither positive nor negative. See also *rational emotive behavior therapy (REBT) types of thoughts.*

new epistemology   An idea from the general *systems* approach of Gregory Bateson; also referred to as *cybernetics.* New epistemology emphasizes that the impact of the family counselor's inclusion and participation in a *family system* must be incorporated into *family therapy.* This emphasis is known as *second-order cybernetics.*

nicotine   A *stimulant* found in tobacco products that produces a physical dependence and a euphoria in the brain similar to that of *amphetamines* and *morphine.* Nicotine is dangerous to the health of those addicted to it and is a major cause of cardiovascular disease, cancer, obstructive lung disease, and complications during pregnancy.

night-terror   A dream that is usually more terrifying than a nightmare and wakes a person up screaming or in a panic.

NIMH   See *National Institute of Mental Health.*

NLP   See *neurolinguistic programming.*

No Child Left Behind Act of 2001   An act of Congress signed into *law* in January 2002. This act redefined the federal *role* in K–12 education and strove to help close the *achievement* gap between disadvantaged and *minority* students and their *peers.*

no excuses   The sixth of eight steps in William Glasser's *reality therapy* in which the *counselor* accepts no excuses after a *client* has committed to a plan of action.

no punishment   The seventh of eight steps in William Glasser's *reality therapy* in which the counselor does not punish a *client* for failing to follow a plan of action. Instead, a new plan is devised.

NOICC See *National Occupational Information Coordinating Committee.*

nominal scale The assigning of numbers for categories that represent the way individuals differ (e.g., the number 1 is assigned to *European American*s, 2 to *African Americans,* 3 to *Asian Americans,* 4 to *Native Americans*, and 5 to *Hispanic*s). A nominal scale simply classifies without ordering.

nominal-group technique A six-step *process* involving the generation both verbally and in writing of a number of ideas/solutions connected with a *problem.* The *process* requires less open exposure of members than *brainstorming*; ends with a vote, discussion, and revote on priorities for resolving a *situation*; and takes between 45 minutes and 1.5 hours. Although this *group* procedure does not lend itself to statistical analysis and may not yield a representative *sample* of opinion, it is an enjoyable process and a fairly quick and efficient way for *counselors* to obtain a good idea of major issues.

nondevelopmental factors Events in the lives of *client*s that are unpredictable but important in *counseling* (e.g., the nature of a *problem,* the suddenness of its appearance, the intensity of its severity, and the present coping skills).

nondirective counseling See *nondirective therapy.*

nondirective therapy See *client-centered counseling; person-centered counseling.*

nonevent The nonmaterialization of an expected occurrence in life, such as getting married, having children, or advancing in one's *career.* A nonevent can cause a *crisis* just like an event.

nonexperimental research The detailed observation, description, and documentation of variables as they naturally occur.

nonlinear causality See *circular causality.*

nonlinear thinking See *circular causality.*

nonmaleficence An ethical principle of *helping* that focuses on not inflicting harm on the *helpee.* The phrase "first do no harm" is one that is often used in defining nonmaleficence.

nonparametric statistics Statistical *test*s that are used when there is an assumption of sharp dichotomies but not of a normal curve *distribution.* Nonparametric tests require larger *sample* sizes to yield a level of significance similar to *parametric tests.* Examples of nonparametric tests are the Spearman rank-order correlation, *chi-square test*, and Mann-Whitney U test.

nonstandarized test A *test* that does not have a formalized administrative procedure and that does not allow for a standardized comparison of results, such as fill-in-the-blank or some projective *personality tests.* The opposite of a *standardized test.*

nonsummativity The idea that a *family* is greater than the sum of its parts, making it necessary to examine the patterns within a family rather than the actions of any specific family member.

nontraditional career A *career* in which people of one *gender* are not usually employed and/or are employed in low numbers, such as men employed as secretaries.

nontraditional college student A student older than age 25 or a student whose background or circumstances differ significantly from the majority of students on a college campus.

nontraditional family A term historically used to describe a non*nuclear family.*

nonverbal Responses that are other than *verbal*; messages expressed through nonlinguistic means.

nonverbal cues Body language, such as gestures and smiles, and a person's physical appearance that make up more than 50 percent of the messages communicated in social *relationships. Nonverbal behaviors* are usually perceived as more honest and less subject to manipulation than *verbal* behaviors.

nonverbal skills The use of *nonverbal* behaviors such as eye contact, body position, and physical distance in building a *helping* relationship.

non-zero-sum game A game based on the assumption that there can be two winners and on the principle of *equitability*. At its best, marriage is a non-zero-sum-game in which disagreements and differences occur without one spouse being right (a winner) and the other being wrong (a loser). It is the opposite of a *zero-sum game*.

noogenic neurosis A *disorder* characterized by Victor Frankl as the *feeling* that one has nothing to live for. This disorder is found in self-indulgent people who experience an *existential vacuum* (a sense that life has lost all meaning) and, in the extreme, feel a sense of normlessness and valuelessness.

norm group The group on which a *test* is standardized.

normal curve See *bell-shaped curve*.

normal distribution A smooth *bell-shaped curve* frequency *distribution*; the underlying basis for *inferential statistics*. Large-*group test* results are frequently distributed in this way with the greatest number of cases near the *mean* and the frequency of cases trailing off on either side of the mean.

normalizing When *clients* realize they are not alone in their difficulty (e.g., most people have experienced mild *depression* in the course of their lives).

norming The third *stage* of *group development* (following *forming* and *storming*) in which members form an *identity* as a group and a sense of "we-ness" (i.e., cohesion). Norming, like storming, lasts only for a few sessions; it sets the pattern for *performing* (i.e., working), which is the fourth stage.

norm referenced A *test* or *behavior* in which the *score* or *outcome* is compared to that of other members of a *group. Standardized tests* are norm referenced. The opposite of *criterion referenced*.

norms 1. *Rules* and standards of *behavior* held to by a *group* or society that are both formal and informal; the expected behavior within a society. Two types of norms important in *counseling* are *prescriptive norms* and *proscriptive norms*. 2. The average performance and varying degrees of deviation of a set of *test scores* standardized on a representative *sample* that provide a basis for interpreting the *scores* of other individuals or groups.

NOS A term used in the *Diagnostic and Statistical Manual* meaning "Not Otherwise Specified."

no-shows *Clients* who do not keep their appointments and do not notify the *counselor* beforehand that they will miss their appointments.

NOVA See *National Organization for Victim Assistance*.

now An important concept in *Gestalt therapy* and other *humanistic counseling* approaches. Now can be expressed in the following formula: Now = experience = awareness = reality. The past is no more and the future not yet. Only the now exists.

NRCA See *National Rehabilitation Counseling Association*.

NTL See *National Training Laboratories*.

nuclear family A core *family* unit of husband, wife, and their children.

null hypothesis A *hypothesis* used in *experimental research* that predicts there will be no *significant difference* between *experimental group* and *control group outcomes*.

nurturing parent A *transactional analysis* term that describes the positive aspect of the *parent ego state* in which nurturing *behaviors* toward others are displayed.

NVGA See *National Vocational Guidance Association*.

nymphomania An excessive, insatiable sexual appetite in females.

O

OA See *Overeaters Anonymous*.

obesity An individual who weighs in excess of 20% of what would be considered his or her normal body weight.

object A term in *object relations theory* and in Piaget's *theory* for a *significant other* outside oneself (i.e., another person such as one's mother) with whom a child forms an interactional, emotional bond.

object loss A term used in *object relations theory* for the *loss* of love from someone external from oneself.

object permanence Jean Piaget's idea of an understanding by infants that *objects,* such as people, do not disappear once they are out of sight. This ability is acquired in the *sensorimotor stage* of development.

object relations A *psychoanalytic theory* that explains *relationships* across generations. According to this theory, human beings have a fundamental motivation to seek *objects,* that is, people, in relationships, starting at birth. An individual's relationships in later life are based on parent–child interactions and the *internalization* of images that accompany early object interaction.

objective **1.** A term that refers to *research, theory,* or experimental *methods* dealing with observable, actual events that are not affected by the observer. **2.** A purpose, aim or *goal.* 3.Unbiased, balanced, fair, nonsubjective (as in questions on an *objective test*).

objective test A *test* that yields *scores* that are independent of any opinion or judgment of the scorer. An objective test is usually multiple choice in nature. Examples include the *Minnesota Multiphasic Personality Inventory-2* (MMPI-2), the *Myers-Briggs Type Indicator (MBTI),* and the *Edwards Personal Preference Schedule (EPPS).*

observation method A *research* procedure in which the investigator directly observes a person or *environment* for periods of time and records *data* on what is seen.

observational learning See *imitation*.

obsession A persistent, recurring, and uncontrollable *thought* or idea.

obsessive-compulsive personality disorder A *disorder,* listed under the broader category in the *DSM* of *anxiety disorders,* characterized by perfectionist *behavior,* insistence on having others do things a certain way, preoccupation with trivial matters and *rules,* inability to make decisions or prioritize, and a limited ability to express *warmth* or tenderness.

occupation A group of similar *positions* found in different industries or organizations (e.g., a programmer or a manager).

Occupations: The Vocational Guidance Magazine A forerunner of what is now the *Journal for Counseling and Development; Occupations* was published between 1944 and 1952.

***Occupational Outlook Handbook* (OOH)** A U.S. government reference book that contains information (e.g., career descriptions, *job* outlook, salaries) on select *occupations*.

occupational stress The chronic psychological and physiological strain associated with ongoing *work* (e.g., events, conditions, demands).

occupational therapist A *helping professional* who focuses on assisting people with *disabilities* increase their independent functioning, maximize their *environment,* and enhance their quality of life.

occupational therapy The American Occupational Therapy Association defines occupational therapy as "the therapeutic use of self-care work and play activities to increase independent function, enhance development, and prevent *disability*. It may include adaptation of task or *environment* to achieve maximum independence and to enhance the quality of life."

OCEAN An acronym for the five bipolar dimensions of the *Big Five* or *Five Factor Model* of personality: openness, conscientiousness, extraversion, agreeableness, and neuroticism.

odd-even reliability The correlation between the total *score* on the odd-numbered and even-numbered *item*s on a *test*.

Oedipus complex A *conflict* that occurs during the *phallic stage* (ages 3 to 5) of *psychosexual* development. According to the *theory*, during this stage, boys have a sexual desire for or erotic interest in their mothers together with hostile *feeling*s for and fear of castration by their fathers. The complex is resolved when boys *identify* with their fathers and vicariously possess their mothers through such an identity. The *Oedipus complex* is the opposite of the *Electra complex* in girls.

offender A person who broke the *law*.

offender counseling *Counseling* that is focused on working with persons who violate the *law*s of society and are in correctional or prison facilities or on probation. It is also referred to as *correctional counseling*.

OK positions The four life *position*s in *transactional analysis theory* that influence a person's interactions with others. The positions are **1.** "I'm OK; you're OK" (a "get-on-with" position); **2.** "I'm OK; you're not OK" (a "get-away-from" position); **3.** "I'm not OK; you're OK" (a "get-nowhere-with" position); and **4.** "I'm not OK; you're not OK" (a "get-rid-of" position). Everyone operates from each of these four positions at various times, but well-functioning individuals learn to recognize unhealthy positions and modify *thought*s and *behavior*s accordingly. See also *scripts*.

old People who are ages 75 to 84.

old epistemology Dated ideas that no longer fit a current *situation*.

old old People who are age 85 and older.

old-timer A term that refers to a more experienced member of a *self-help group*.

OLSAT See *Otis-Lennon School Ability Test*.

omission **1.** A term used in connection with *malpractice* or *neglect* for someone not doing something that should have been done. **2.** A term used in *existentialism* in connection with guilt a person has for not taking action. See *existential guilt*.

omnibus test A *test* (e.g., the *Otis-Lennon School Ability Test*) that measures a variety of mental operations.

One-Stop Career Centers Centers that provide a single location where an applicant can gain information needed to choose an *occupation*, find access to training, be placed in a job, and have access to all public services needed to continue in employment.

O*NET A computer-based *career* information system that provides up-to-the-minute sources of information on *occupations* (http://online. onetcenter.org/).

online counseling See *Internet counseling*.

online group counseling A counselor-coordinated computer-assisted group counseling experience where members exchange ideas and help one another with different concerns.

online support groups Computer-assisted *mental health* groups that provide opportunities for global communication among individuals dealing with issues such as *grief, depression,* or chronic illness.

ontology Any matter related to the study or science of being or existence.

OOH See *Occupational Outlook Handbook*.

open marriage A marital arrangement in which marital *rules* and *relationship*s, including sexual *fidelity,* are constantly being worked out as the couple focuses on their independence and *autonomy*.

open panel Where a *Health Maintenance Organization (HMO)* allows members, for an additional fee, to receive services out of the provider's network without a referral authorization.

open system A *system* with relatively permeable *boundaries* that exchanges information with the world outside it.

open-ended group A *group* that admits new members at any time.

open-ended question A question that leads to *self-exploration* into the "what" and "how" of *behavior*. Open-ended questions invite more than a one- or two-word *response*. See also *questioning*.

opening skills The use of such procedures as *open-ended questions, closed-ended questions*, and *minimal encouragers* in building a helping relationship.

operant B. F. Skinner's term for a *response*.

operant conditioning A type of *learning*, originating out of *research* by B. F. Skinner, which emphasizes that *behavior* is a function of its *consequences*. The acquisition or elimination of a *response* is a function of *rewards* and *punishments*. The way people operate in regard to their *environments* is dependent on the *consequences* of their actions.

operation Jean Piaget's term for a type of mental activity or *thought process*. An operation follows logical *rules*, whereas a *preoperation* is intuitive, egocentric, and less logical.

opiate Any of various sedative *narcotics* containing *opium* or one or more of its natural or synthetic derivatives.

opium A *narcotic* extracted from poppies and processed to make other *drugs* (e.g., *morphine, codeine,* and *heroin*).

oppositional defiant disorder (ODD) A disorder in children characterized by an ongoing pattern of uncooperative, defiant, and hostile behavior toward authority figures. This behavior seriously interferes with the child's day-to-day functioning. Symptoms of ODD may include: frequent temper tantrums, excessive arguing with adults, active defiance and refusal to comply with adult requests and rules, deliberate attempts to annoy or upset people, blaming others for his or her mistakes or misbehavior, hateful talk when upset, and seeking revenge.

oppression The systematic subjugation, suppression, and unjust treatment of a *group* of people by another group of people with access to social *power*.

optimism A tendency to expect, *hope,* and work for the best in *situations*. One of the positive *isms* in *counseling*.

oral personality A term from *psychoanalytic theory* that describes a person whose satisfaction in life comes from orally oriented activities such as smoking, drinking, eating, and talking.

oral stage The first *stage* in Sigmund Freud's *psychosexual* stages of development. This stage occurs during the first year of life. The infant derives pleasure from orally oriented activities such as sucking, biting, and swallowing.

ordeal A *strategic family therapy process,* developed by Jay Haley, in which the *counselor* assigns a family or family member(s) the task of performing an activity (i.e., an ordeal) whenever the family or individuals involved display a *symptom* they are trying to eliminate. The ordeal is a constructive or neutral *behavior* (e.g., doing *exercise*) but not an activity that those involved want to engage in.

ordinal position See *birth order*.

ordinal scale A scale that orders or ranks *scores* or individuals according to some characteristic.

organism A form of life composed of mutually dependent parts and *processes* standing in mutual interaction.

organismic A descriptive term for a person as a whole entity with interrelated and interdependent parts.

orientation A term used both to describe a *counselor*'s preferred mode of *treatment* (e.g., *behavioral, existential, client-centered*) and a person's sexual preference (e.g., *gay, heterosexual,* transexual.)

orthopsychiatry An interdisciplinary field that emphasizes the development of *mental health* in human life and the *prevention* of mental illness.

Otis-Lennon School Ability Test (OLSAT) One of the most widely used group-administered general *intelligence tests* with levels for

Analogous stages of counseling practice and the research process

Stages in Counseling	Stages in Outcome Research
1. Identification of problems or difficulties	1. Identification of research question(s)
2. Formulation of goals	2. Formulation of research design
3. Determine interventions	3. Determine methods for ensuring treatment integrity and measures of outcome
4. Implementation of counseling	4. Data collection
5. Appraisal and evaluation of progress	5. Data analysis
6. Termination	6. Interpretation and conclusions

Source: Reprinted from "Accountability through Action Research: Research Methods for Practitioners," by S. C. Whiston, 1996, *Journal of Counseling and Development, 74*, p. 617. © 1996 by ACA. Reprinted with permission. No further reproduction authorized without written permission of the American Counseling Association.

primary through high school grades. The OLSAT is employed primarily for predicting success in cognitive and school-related areas.

outcome The results of *counseling*. Outcome in counseling is usually linked to preplanned *goals* and *objectives* (i.e., a *treatment contract*) by *counselors* and *clients*.

outcome research *Research* that emphasizes results rather than the *factors* producing them. It is typified by *measurement* before and after *treatment* on specified dependent *variables*. An example of outcome research is the effect of *person-centered counseling* on depressed persons.

outpatient A *client* who receives *counseling* services in a nonresidential setting.

outreach Initiating behavior toward people in need for the purpose of making a helpful difference.

overcompensation The continuous striving by a *client* to overcome or offset a perceived or actual weakness. *Motivation* for this striving comes from *feelings* of *inferiority*.

overcorrection A *technique* in which a *client* first restores the *environment* to its natural state and then makes it "better than normal." For example, children who throw food in the lunchroom might be required to clean up their mess and wax the floor.

overculturalization The mistaking of people's reactions to poverty and *discrimination* for their cultural patterns.

overdose An excessive dose, especially of a *narcotic*. Overdoses are a leading cause of death in people who are addicted to *drugs*. Overdoses occur usually because of an attempt to reach a certain level of effectiveness in a drug after *tolerance* has developed or because of ignorance in regard to the impact of a drug.

Overeaters Anonymous (OA) A *mutual-help group* for individuals with compulsive *eating disorders*. The organization is based on the philosophy of *Alcoholics Anonymous (AA)* and a variation of AA's 12-step program. OA's address is 6075 Zenith Court NE, Rio Rancho, NM 87124 (505-891-2664; http://www.oa.org/).

overgeneralization Applying *learning* from a particular incident too broadly so that matters related to that incident are viewed as being the same in all circumstances or matters.

overidentification A form of *countertransference* in which the *counselor* loses the ability to remain emotionally distant from the *client*.

overlearning *Learning* material through repetition and practice to a point well beyond simple mastery.

overt behavior An *observable act*.

ownership of problems An agreement within a *helping relationship* between a *counselor* and a *client* of who owns the *problem*(s) being discussed. Ownership determination assists the counselor and the client in perceiving the problem clearly.

p

PA See *Parents Anonymous*.

Pacific Islander See *Asian American/Pacific Islander*.

palliative care Includes *hospice care* and refers to a compassionate, comprehensive team approach to care that focuses on quality of life for anyone coping with a serious illness, including the patient and family members.

panic attack See *panic disorder*.

panic disorder Also known as a *panic attack*, the sudden onset of intense fear and *anxiety* that is completely unexpected and not linked to any *environmental* event. A panic disorder is accompanied by such *symptoms* as sweating, dizziness, chills, nausea, and fear of losing control. Panic disorders usually last only a few minutes.

panphobia An exaggerated fear of everything.

pansexual A person who exhibits or suggests a sexuality that has many different forms, objects, outlets, and expressions.

paradox **1.** A form of *treatment* in which *counselors* give *clients* *permission* to do what they were going to do anyway, thereby lowering client *resistance* to *treatment* and increasing the likelihood of *change*. **2.** A form of *treatment* in which counselors ask *resistant clients* to do the opposite of what would be an ideal treatment in the *hope* that they will disobey and as a result get better.

parallel relationships *Relationships* in which both complementary and symmetrical exchanges occur as appropriate.

oxycodone A *morphine* derivative mainly used for short-term pain. As a prescriptive narcotic, oxycodone is marketed under the name *Percodan*.

parallel reliability A type of *reliability test* in which two equivalent forms of the same test are administered to see how closely they correlate. See also *equivalence*.

parameter The descriptive measure of a *population* (e.g., *mean, standard deviation*).

parametric statistics Statistical *tests* used when it is thought that the *population* being described has evenly distributed characteristics that could be represented by a *bell-shaped curve*. An example of a parametric statistical test is a *t-test*.

paranoia An unsubstantiated and unfounded suspicion of others and the fear that one is being watched, followed, talked about, and persecuted. In the extreme, paranoia can become a *personality disorder* in which the person becomes extremely distrustful and suspicious of others.

paraphilias *Sexual and gender identity disorders* characterized by sexual urges and *behaviors* that interfere with social adjustment and *relationships* (e.g., *exhibitionism, fetishism, voyeurism, pedophilia,* and sexual *sadism*). Paraphilias are difficult to treat.

paraphrasing A reflective statement by the *counselor* of what a *client* has said but restated in different words and in a nonjudgmental way. Paraphrasing helps a client know that the counselor is aware of the client's perspective.

paraprofessional A category of helpers who do not have terminal degrees in *counseling* or in other *helping* professions but who provide direct services to *client*s to supplement the services of professionals (e.g., a nurse's aide).

parent education group A *group* that is *psychoeducational* in nature and that focuses on the raising of children. Rudolph Driekurs began setting up these groups in the 1950s using Alfred Adler's *theory* and ideas.

Parent Effectiveness Training (PET) Thomas Gordon's parent education program that emphasizes communication skills. In PET, parents are encouraged to recognize their positive and negative *feelings* toward their children and come to terms with their own humanness. A major *hypothesis* of this approach is that *active listening* and *acceptance* will decrease family *conflict*s and promote individual growth.

parent ego state A *transactional analysis* term for the controlling, limit-setting, and rule-making part of the *personality*. The parent ego state is dualistic: It is both nurturing and critical (or controlling). The function of the *critical parent* is to store and dispense the *rules* and protection for living. The function of the *nurturing parent* is to provide affectionate care and attention.

parentified child A child who is forced to give up *childhood* and act like an adult parent even though he or she lacks the knowledge and skills to do so.

Parents Anonymous (PA) A national mutual-help organization with local chapters patterned after *Alcoholics Anonymous (AA)* to help parents who are at risk for abusing their children. PA's address is 675 West Foothill Boulevard, Suite 220, Claremont, CA 91711-3475 (909-621-6184; http://www.parentsanonymous. org/paIndex10.html).

Parents Without Partners (PWP) A national mutual-help organization with local chapters that help single parents and their children deal with the realities of *single-parent family* life in educational and experiential ways. PWP's address is 401 North Michigan Avenue, Chicago, IL 60611-4267 (312-644-6610; http://www. parentswithoutpartners.org/).

parent-skills training An educational model of teaching parent skills in which *counselors* serve as social *learning* educators whose prime responsibility is to *change,* through experiential activities as well as discussions, a parent's *response* to a child. Examples of parent-skills training programs are *Parent Effectiveness Training (PET)* and *Systematic Training for Effective Parenting (STEP)*.

parsimony The idea that explanations of *behavior* should be as simple as possible and consistent with observations.

partial reinforcement Also known as *intermittent reinforcement*, a *schedule of reinforcement* used to maintain a *behavior*, once it is established, through *continuous reinforcement*. In partial reinforcement, a *reward* is given at intervals that vary but are frequent enough to maintain the *client*'s interest.

participant A person who takes place in a research study or experiment.

passive-aggressive behavior *Behavior* that is covertly angry but overtly docile. A person with a passive-aggressive *personality* tends to pout and procrastinate as well as be obstructive, obstinate, and inefficient. Anger is often *unconscious* or hidden just below the surface.

pastimes A *transactional analysis* term for superficial exchanges between people that allow them to spend time together without getting involved at a deeper level. An example of a pastime is talking about the weather.

pastoral counseling A specialized form of *counseling* rendered by clergy who have been trained in counseling and who also deal with spiritual matters. See *American Association of Pastoral Counselors (AAPC)*.

pat on the back A closing *group counseling exercise* in which members draw the outline of their hands on a piece of paper that is then taped on their backs. Other group members then write positive and constructive closing comments about the person on the hand outline.

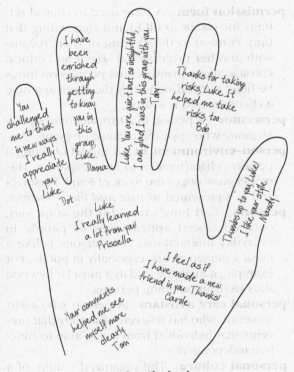

a pat on the back

pathological gambler A person who is unable to resist impulses to gamble.

pathological view of minorities The view that some *minority culture* persons can never be helped sufficiently to fit in with the *majority culture*.

pathology The study of disease, *disorder*s, and dysfunction.

patient The term used in the *medical model* for *client*s or counselees who receive help or *treatment*.

PCP See *phencyclidine hydrochloride*.

Peabody Picture Vocabulary Test (PPVT) An individually administered *test* of vocabulary that is sometimes used as an abbreviated test of general ability. The PPVT, which is revised and updated periodically, consists of 175 plates with four pictures each. The examinee points to the picture that best illustrates a *stimulus* word given by the examiner.

peak experiences Abraham Maslow's term for the both mystic and intense emotional *feeling*s of joy experienced during *self-actualization*. At such times, self-actualizing people feel at one with the world.

pedophilia A *disorder* that can take a number of forms but, in all cases, involves gratification on the part of an adult through sexual contact with a child. Most pedophiles are males; most *victim*s of pedophilia are female children.

peer A person who is of equal status to another such as students in a school or adults in a *group*.

peer group A *group* of equals along some notable dimension such as social status, *intelligence,* or age.

peer counselors/helpers Students in educational settings who are specially trained to help their *peer*s in dealing with developmental or situational concerns both by *listening* and referring them to appropriate sources for help.

peer mediation The use of a third impartial person or party to assist in resolving a dispute between two or more people.

peer supervision *Supervision* between practitioners of equal status on a regular basis concerning issues and treatment of difficult *client*s or *situation*s.

peer-counselor model An aspect of *rehabilitation counseling* in which it is assumed that people with direct experience with a *disability* are the most capable of *helping* individuals with recently acquired *disabilities*.

penis envy Sigmund Freud's idea that during the *phallic stage* girls initially envy boys for their external sex organ and wish one for themselves.

people of color A term used to describe non-white individuals in the United States other than those who are European–North Americans.

percentage score A final score that expresses a raw score on the basis of 0 to 100. For example, if a person gets 4 out of 10 questions correct, the person will have a score of 40%.

p

percentile A value on a scale of 100 that indicates the percentage of cases at or below a given *score*. Percentile scores are often expressed as *decile*s and *quartile*s.

percentile rank A widely used *method* for showing the relative *position* of a person's *score* on a *norm-referenced test*. Percentile rankings *range* from 1 to 99, with a percentile rank of 50 being the *median*. Percentile ranks provide descriptive interpretation clearly and concisely by showing the percentage of persons in a reference group who score lower than a targeted person.

perception The sensing of information through any of the five senses (i.e., sight, sound, touch, taste, and smell).

peripheral nervous system (PNS) – One of two systems within the nervous system, the PNS is comprised of nerves extending from the spinal cord and the rest of the body (e.g., organs and muscles).

Percodan See *oxycodone*.

performance The way in which someone accomplishes a task or the outcome of a person's or persons' work on such a task. For example, his performance on the *intelligence test* indicated that he had above-average ability.

performance assessment/test A *measurement* that requires minimal verbal communication and that a person is required to make motor *response*s other than writing to show a certain skill or competence level. Performance assessments/tests are sometimes known as *work samples*. They reduce cultural bias and assess a broad range of attributes.

performing The fourth *stage* of *group development,* in which members become involved with each other and strive to achieve certain *goals.*

permission **1.** Authorization by a government agency. **2.** *Consent* by a *client* to share information, usually *records,* with another professional. **3.** A *transactional analysis* term for giving group members *directive*s to behave against the *injunction*s of their parents.

permission form A form used in clinical settings for *client*s to fill in and sign stating that they *consent* to the sharing of their *records* with another professional. *Legal* and ethical considerations mandate that permission forms be filled out and signed by the client any time a client's record is shared.

persecutor A person in a *transactional analysis game* who appears to cause *problem*s.

person–environment fit A model of fitting a person's characteristics to an *occupation*. This model grew out of the work of Frank Parsons's and is represented in *trait and factor theories*.

persona Carl Jung's term for the *conscious,* outward, social appearances of people in everyday interactions. The persona is like a mask a person wears, especially in public. For example, it might be said that most Hollywood stars have an outgoing persona.

personal care assistant A person who assist someone who has a severe *disability* that prevents that individual from being able to function independently.

personal culture The organized totality of a person's *identity* comprised of historical moments, unchangeable human *factor*s such as *gender* and age, and a *range* of sociocultural factors such as region, *work* experience, and *family* background. The interaction of these dimensions makes the person dynamic.

personal growth A term that stresses *development* as a result of experiences such as travel or encounter and interaction with others.

personal growth group See *basic encounter group.*

personal growth issues Perceived deficits or *need*s within a person.

Personal Orientation Inventory (POI) A *personality test* created by Everett L. Shostrom. The POI is designed to measure *values* and *behavior* that seem to be of importance in the development of self-actualizing persons.

personal myths Stories people tell themselves about who they are and what they cherish in themselves and their *cultures*, how they got where they are, and how they see their lives developing in the future.

personal power A source of *power* employed more frequently in mature *relationship situations*. It is derived from the individual and his or her ability to persuade others to follow a select course of action. See also *power to resolve conflict*.

personal unconscious See *collective unconscious*.

personality A global concept that includes all the physical, mental, emotional, and social characteristics of someone that make that person unique.

personality disorders Long-standing, deeply ingrained, *maladaptive behaviors* that take many forms (e.g., *antisocial, avoidance, borderline, dependent, paranoid, narcissistic, obsessive-compulsive*). Personality disorders are highly resistant to *treatment*. They are listed on Axis II in the *DSM multiaxial assessment system*.

personality inventory Any of a number of *objective* or *projective methods* that analyze one or more aspects of an individual's *personality* (e.g., attitudes, *temperament, values*). Examples of methods include the *California Psychological Inventory (CPI)* and the *Rorschach Inkblot Test*.

personality test Any of several *methods* (e.g., *checklists, personality inventories,* and *projection*) of analyzing *personality*. A personality test may be either objective *(MMPI)* or projective *(Rorschach Ink Blots)*.

personalization A tendency for individuals to relate external events to themselves, even when there is no basis for making this connection. For example, if a *client* does not show up for a *counseling* session, the *counselor* may become convinced that he or she did something wrong.

person-centered counseling The name for the *theory* of *counseling* originated by Carl Rogers. It was previously known as *nondirective therapy* and *client-centered therapy*.

person-environment interaction A *theory* that refers to the *congruence* between *clients* and their *environments*. Congruence is believed to lead to satisfaction, *stability,* and, perhaps, *development*.

Personnel and Guidance Journal The name of the flagship *journal* of the *American Counseling Association (ACA)* from 1952 to 1984.

persuasion The *process* of trying to positively influence a *client* to take needed action. Two direct persuasion *techniques* employed in *counseling* are the *foot in the door* and the *door in the face*.

pervasive development disorders Neurological conditions that are first *diagnosed* in infancy, *childhood*, and *adolescence* but that are manifested later. These disorders include *autistic disorder*, Asperger's disorder, Rett's disorder, and childhood disintegrative disorder.

pessimism A tendency to stress the negative and worse that could happen. The opposite of *optimism* and a cognitive outlook on life that is potentially detrimental in helping people find resolutions to their *problems*.

PET See *Parent Effectiveness Training*.

peyote A *hallucinogen*; also known as *mescaline*.

PFA See *psychological first aid*.

phallic stage The third *stage* in Freud's stages of *psychosexual development*. In this stage, in which the chief zones of pleasure are the genitalia, children (between ages 3 to 5) attempt to resolve their sexual identities by *working through conflicts* (for boys, the *Oedipus complex*; for girls, the *Electra complex*). If this stage of *psychosexual* development is not resolved, individuals will experience future *intrapersonal* and *interpersonal* difficulties. Freud thought the basic ingredients of the adult *personality* had formed by the end of the phallic stage.

pharmacotherapy The *treatment* of *mental disorders* with prescribed medications.

P

phase of life   A predictable and developmental transition in the *life cycle* such as *adolescence* or retirement.

phases of sexual responsiveness   Periods of sexual responsiveness including excitement, plateau, orgasm, and resolution.

phencyclidine hydrochloride   An *illegal hallucinogenic drug* also known as *PCP* and *angel dust*. A water-soluble white powder *substance,* it can be ingested a number of ways (e.g., orally, smoked, snorted, or intravenously injected). It produces euphoria and numbness when taken in low dosages but may produce delirium, convulsions, and violent *behavior* when taken in higher dosages.

phenomenological perspective   The idea that what is important is the person's *perception* of reality rather than an event itself.

phenomenology   The *theory* that individuals behave according to the way they perceive their worlds.

phenomenon   An occurrence that is perceived by an observer through the senses.

PHI   *Protected Health Information.*

phobia   An irrational, exaggerated, and/or unrealistic fear of a specific object or *situation*.

phobic layer   A term in *Gestalt therapy* for the *client*'s attempt to avoid recognition of the aspects of the *self* that he or she would prefer to deny.

phony layer   A term in *Gestalt therapy* for a *client*'s pretense to be something that he or she is not.

photocounseling   The use of photography as the primary or adjunct means of working therapeutically with a *client*.

physiological characteristics   Characteristics such as skin and eye color, shape of head, and so forth.

pie chart   A type of *graph* used to display the percentage of *data* in a category. A pie chart is circular in form, with a wedge of the circle identified with each category.

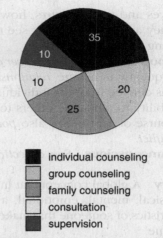

- ■ individual counseling
- □ group counseling
- ▨ family counseling
- □ consultation
- ▩ supervision

piggybacking   *Helping client*s use one idea in a *session* as a takeoff point for another. For example, after talking about what he will say to his *family,* a client may be encouraged to put his words into action.

pilot study   A small *experimental research* study that precedes a larger study to test proposed methodologies.

placater   One of Virginia Satir's four *role*s that a person takes when the person is not *leveling* (i.e., communicating clearly and directly). A placater is characterized as a person who avoids *conflict* at the cost of his or her *integrity*. Therefore, a placater may ingratiate, apologize, or eschew disagreement when just the opposite *behavior* is called for.

placebo effect   A sham *treatment* that has no known therapeutic value and is given in double-blind *research* to test whether the targeted *treatment* has an impact. *Placebos* (i.e., inactive *substance*s or preparations) are often given in medical research in the form of agents, such as sugar pills, that look identical to the *drug* being tested. Research suggests that the placebo effect is greatest in people who are under psychological *stress*.

placement   The locating and placing of people in *job*s. A placement service is often performed by *rehabilitation counselors*.

play Activities that have no goal other than the enjoyment that is derived from them.

play therapy The use of *play* as a means of establishing *rapport*, uncovering what is troubling a person (often a child), and bringing about resolution. There are a number of theoretical approaches to play therapy. Play therapy takes place in a playroom that is specially designed, decorated, and furnished with the toys and equipment children need to use as tools for the dramatic scenes they create and talk about with their *counselors*.

pleasure principle The principle by which the *id* operates in Freud's schema of the *personality*. The id is dominated by the pleasure principle, seeking immediate gratification of its *needs* and avoiding unpleasantness or pain. It is the opposite of the *reality principle*.

pluralism See *cultural diversity; cultural pluralism*.

POCA See *Public Offender Counselor Association*.

poetry therapy The use of the language arts as a primary or adjunct means of working with *client*s in *treatment*. The goals of poetry therapy are to promote an understanding of the *self* in society, to accept and *change feelings* and *behavior*, and to enhance mental and social *wellness*. See also *National Association for Poetry Therapy (NAPT)*.

POI See *Personal Orientation Inventory*.

polarization The division of a *group* into different and opposing *subgroups* or camps. Such a division can lead to a stalemate, a *conflict*, or the forming of a *coalition*.

polarized thinking *Thinking* that involves interpreting events and/or people in all-or-nothing terms, or categorizing experiences in either/or extremes (e.g., good versus bad).

polysubstance abuse The *abuse* of two or more *substance*s simultaneously.

pops A street name for *codeine*.

population **1.** A statistical term for all members of some defined *group*. **2.** All the people inhabiting a certain area or within a specifically defined *group*.

portability The ability to carry, move, or transfer a license between states.

possible self A term used in *counseling* to represent an individual's ideas of what he or she might become, would like to become, and is afraid to become.

postcrisis counseling Counseling that takes place with victims of *trauma* after *crisis management* has ended.

position **1.** The way in which something is placed. **2.** A *group* of tasks performed by one person. **3.** The status or rank of a person or object. **4.** A point of view.

position power A source of *power* most often used when there are immature *relationship*s between individuals. Position power is derived from the status of people's titles, such as "president" or "chair." See also *power to resolve conflict*.

positioning Acceptance and exaggeration by *counselor*s of what *client*s are saying or doing. If conducted properly, positioning helps clients see the absurdity in their words and in their *nonverbal* actions, such as in *sculpting*. Positioning is often used in *family counseling*.

positive addiction William Glasser's idea that some activities, such as *meditation* and jogging, may be therapeutically beneficial.

positive connotation A type of *reframing* in which a *client's behavior* is labeled as *benevolent* and motivated by good intentions.

positive correlation A pattern of points in a *scattergram* that tend to run from lower left to upper right and to occur when high *score*s on one *variable* are associated with high scores on the other variable.

positive feedback Any *stimulus* that when added to a *situation* increases the likelihood that a *response* will occur. For example, instructing a baseball player on how he may hit a curve ball is positive feedback.

positive psychology   A term associated with Martin Seligman that focuses on understanding and building on human strengths such as positive emotions and strength-based character. See *authentic happiness.*

positive regard   Love, *warmth,* acceptance, and respect given to a *client* by the *counselor.* See also *unconditional positive regard.*

positive reinforcer   A material (e.g., food, money, medals) or a social action (e.g., smile, praise) that individuals find significant and rewarding and are willing to work for.

positive risk   A unilateral action not dependent on another for success. See also *caring days.*

positive thoughts   One of four *rational emotive behavior therapy (REBT) types of thoughts.* Positive thoughts focus on helpful aspects of an event. See also *rational emotive behavior therapy (REBT)* thoughts.

positive wellness   Health-related activities that are both preventive and remedial and have a therapeutic value to individuals who practice them consistently. Such activities include eating natural foods, taking vitamins, going to a health spa, *meditating,* participating in regular exercise, and exploring a variety of *humanistic* and *transpersonal* approaches to *helping.*

possibility therapy   See *solution-focused family therapy.*

postconventional morality   The last two *stage*s of Lawrence Kohlberg's six stages of *moral development,* in which *behavior* is governed by a set of consciously held ethical principles. See also *moral development.*

postsecrets   A Web site that describes itself as "an ongoing community art project where people mail in their secrets anonymously on one side of a postcard." The project is a type of *bibliotherapy* and cathartic experience for some (http://postsecret.blogspot.com/).

posttest   The administration of a *questionnaire* to a person after he or she has received *treatment.* Comparison is made between *pretest* and *posttest* results.

posttraumatic stress disorder (PTSD)   A *disorder* following a *trauma* (e.g., an accident, *rape,* combat). PTSD is characterized by a cluster of *symptom*s such as sleep disturbance, nightmares, *flashback*s, and *anxiety.*

postvention   AKA *rehabilitation counseling,* focuses on helping people with permanent or chronic physical, psychiatric, and mental *disorders* or *disabilities* cope successfully and better adjust to life.

pot   A slang term for *marijuana.*

potency   The use of appropriate *counseling technique*s in certain *situation*s to bring about *change.*

power   **1.** The ability to get something done or to control access to resources. In families, power is related to both authority and responsibility. **2.** A term in *research* for the ability of a statistical *test* to find a difference in *data* when there is one.

power difference   An unequal *relationship,* such as between a *counselor* and a *client,* due to more *power* or prestige from one party, making the other party less free or more dependent in regard to initially making independent *choices.*

power test   A *test* in which ample time is provided so that those taking it can complete all the *item*s. The items are usually arranged in order from easiest to most difficult (though most are difficult). Examples include *intelligence, achievement,* and *aptitude test*s.

power to resolve conflict   A strategy that involves the imposition of someone's will on someone else. The source of *power* may either be derived from one's *position* (*position power*) or one's person (*personal power*). By using *power,* a leader is able to quickly resolve a *crisis,* but the use of power creates a win–lose atmosphere.

PPO   See *preferred provider organization.*

PPVT   See *Peabody Picture Vocabulary Test.*

practicum   A supervised short-term experience in which students preparing to be *counselors* learn to do *counseling* through *supervision.* A practicum experience is usually a prerequisite to an *internship* in *counseling.*

preadolescents   Ages 8 to 12 years.

preauthorization   The authorization by an insurance company or *managed care provider* to treat a *client* before the client is given *treatment.* In many cases, preauthorization is necessary for reimbursement.

preconscious   A term in *psychoanalytic theory* for the area of the mind in which materials not immediately available can be recalled to *awareness* if given enough prompting.

preconventional morality   The first two *stages* in Lawrence Kohlberg's six-stage *theory* of *moral development.* See also *moral development.*

predictive validity   A type of *validity* that exists when the *criterion* for what a *test* is measuring is not available until after the test is administered.

predisposition   The tendency to develop in a certain way under the right conditions. For example, the child of parents who have a schizophrenic disorder may be predisposed to develop *schizophrenia,* especially if placed in a stressful and nonsupportive *environment.*

preferred provider organization (PPO)   A *health care* organization in which the PPO contracts with select *mental health* practitioners, physicians, and hospitals in a community for services. *Client*s can go outside the PPO network (unlike in an *HMO*), although they pay more for a nonnetwork *provider*'s services. See also *managed care.*

pregenital stages   The first three *stages* (*oral, anal,* and *phallic*) of Sigmund Freud's stages of *psychosexual* development.

pregroup preparation   AKA *pregroup training.* Preparing group members, especially those in *therapy* groups, ahead of time for how the group will function as well as how a group member's needs may be met. Such a process promotes the development of *group cohesiveness.*

pregroup training   See *pregroup preparation.*

prejudice   Preconceived opinions or judgment about someone or something formed without just grounds or sufficient knowledge. Prejudiced *thinking* is often adversarial, demeaning, and degrading.

Premack principle   David Premack's behavioral *intervention.* The principle states that *behavior* that occurs at a naturally high rate of frequency may be used to reinforce behavior that occurs at a naturally low rate. Thus, a *client* may be assigned *homework* in which he or she must first do less pleasant tasks, such as study, before being allowed to engage in *leisure* activities, such as *play.*

premature termination   *Termination* that occurs when individual *client*s, couples, or families abruptly quit *counseling* without having achieved preset *goals* or when *counselors* must end the experience because of unexpected *situations* (e.g., illness, extended and unexpected *family* emergencies). Premature termination makes it difficult for clients and counselors to reach *closure* in regard to clinical concerns or *relationships.*

preoperational stage   The second *stage* of development in Jean Piaget's four-stage *theory* of *cognitive development.* The preoperational stage (lasting from age 2 to age 7 or 8) is marked by a huge increase in a child's vocabulary and creative imagination and consists of two substages: intuitive *thinking* and preconceptual *thinking.*

preschool- and early school-aged children Children between the ages of 5 and 9.

prescribing the symptom   A type of *paradox* in which *client*s are asked to continue doing as they have done. This *technique* often leads to clients either admitting they have control over a *symptom* or giving it up.

prescriptive norms   *Norms* that describe the kinds of *behavior*s that should be performed. See also *norms.*

presenting problem   The initial concern a *client* presents as a reason for coming to *counseling.*

pretend technique A *technique* originated by Cloe Madanes in which the *counselor* asks *client*s to pretend to enact a troublesome *behavior* (e.g., a fight with one's spouse). By acting as if they were so engaged, clients learn to control a once involuntary action.

pretest A *test* administered to a *client* before *treatment* to establish a *baseline*. Pretest results are compared to *posttest* results.

prevention The use by *counselor*s of educational or behavioral means (e.g., instruction or *rehearsal*) to help *client*s avoid or minimize potential *problem*s.

prevention groups A type of *counseling* using a *group* format in which people meet face-to-face with a trained group leader who assists them in gaining knowledge, attitudes, and *behavior*s that empower them to live their lives more fully and more meaningfully.

primacy effect The idea that all things being equal, those things that are learned first in a sequence are remembered best. It is the opposite of, but complementary to, the *recency effect*.

primal horde Sigmund Freud's conceptualization of a *group*. Freud thought leaders within the group function as parental figures.

primal scream therapy Arthur Janov's therapeutic approach that focuses on the recognition and expression of *affect*. Janov first makes *client*s miserable and then encourages them to relive miserable *feeling*s of their *childhoods*. The culmination of the approach is a primal scream that supposedly rids the client of negative *emotion*s and sets the *stage* for his or her healthy development.

primary affiliation group A *group* that people most identify as belonging to (e.g., a *family* or *peer group*).

primary empathy A *process* in which the *counselor* listens for basic *client* messages and responds to them through *paraphrasing* and *reflection* of *feeling*s so that the client begins to feel understood. See also *empathy*.

primary prevention The attempt to stop *problem*s or *disorders* before they occur or develop.

primary process A term in *psychoanalysis* for the *id*'s means of reducing tension by imagining what it desires.

primary reinforcer A *reinforcer* that people will naturally work for (e.g., food).

principle of awareness A *Gestalt therapy* assumption that people are free to choose only when they are *self-aware*, that is, in touch with their existence and what it means to be alive. *Awareness* includes all sensations, *thought*s, and *behavior*s of the individual.

principle of holism A *Gestalt therapy* term for *integration*.

principle of polarities A *Gestalt therapy* belief that if people are to meet their *need*s, they must first differentiate their perceptual field into opposite poles (e.g., active/passive, good/bad). According to the polarity principle, people fail to resolve *conflict*s because they are not in contact with the opposite of the *situation*.

private logic An *Adlerian counseling* term for an individual's unique pattern of *thought*s, *feeling*s, and attitudes that predict and manage life experiences.

private practice A practice in which a *clinician* assumes total responsibility for the nature and quality of the *treatment* provided and collects fees directly or indirectly in turn for such services.

private self One of the four quadrants in the *Johari Awareness Model*. The private self is known to *self* but not to others.

privilege The benefits of having access to services, advantages, and rewards in a society because of membership in a particular *group*, regardless of one's merit.

privileged communication A *client*'s *legal* right that guarantees confidences originating in a therapeutic *relationship* will be safeguarded and not disclosed to others.

proactive A type of *intervention* by *counselor*s acting as *change agents*, who attempt to improve conditions for *client*s through actions that foster changes in society.

probability A statistical term for how often something is likely to happen outside chance.

probe A *question* that usually begins with "who," "what," "where," or "how" and that requires more than a one- or two-word answer (e.g., the question: "How do you plan on getting a job?"). A probe is used in *counseling* to gather information from a *client*.

problem A matter over which the *client* thinks or feels he or she does not have the ability to solve. A problem may result from a deficit of behavioral skills or from a novel and sometimes overwhelming event.

problem-centered group A small *group* set up to focus on one particular concern (e.g., coping with *stress*).

process **1.** A series of operations performed in the making of a product or the completion of an outcome. **2.** The way in which information and the resulting *emotions, thoughts*, and *behaviors* are handled (e.g., the *techniques* and *methods* used) in *interpersonal relationships*. **3.** The integration of thoughts, feelings, and behaviors over time into a unified whole.

process commentary When a group leader brings up *conscious* and *unconscious* concerns to the group's attention and discusses how *behavior* around these concerns is affecting the *group*.

process evaluation AKA *formative evaluation*, an evaluation that provides information about how well a program is being implemented (i.e., whether programs are operating in accordance with stated plans, objectives, and expectations). Process evaluation also involves monitoring of what services are being provided by whom, for whom, to how many, when, and at what cost.

process observer A professional human services person who is neutral in regard to a *group*'s agenda and personalities and who can observe the group and offer *feedback* with regard to what and how they are functioning.

process research *Research* that focuses on the dynamics of *counseling*. Attention is directed to the mechanisms by which *counselors* help bring about improvements in *clients*. Process research is intense and demands a concentrated amount of time and energy. The emphasis on how something is done is as important as what is done.

processing The act of dealing in the present with significant issues, *behaviors, thoughts*, and *feelings* that may be occurring within an individual or in a *group* to deepen understanding of what is happening and *generalize* learning to life outside the group.

profession A discipline that has its own unique body of literature, prescribed course of study, membership organization, standards of conduct, and *ethics*.

professional association A membership organization of qualified individuals who voluntarily join together to educate the public about issues, *advocate* for *clients* and agendas, maintain ethical standards, and promote the generation of a body of literature on subjects pertinent to their discipline.

professional liability insurance Insurance designed specifically to protect a *counselor* or other *helping professional* from financial loss in case of a civil suit.

professional networking Associating with colleagues to receive support and to gain additional perspectives on *problems* or *research* encountered in professional practice.

professional self-disclosure statement A statement given to the *client* by the *counselor* that outlines the counselor's professional qualifications, the conditions that will be adhered to in *treatment*, the fee, if any, that will be charged, and the rights and recourses open to the client.

profile A *graph* that depicts a person's *scores* on a *test* or a series of tests.

prognosis A prediction about the *outcome* of a *disorder* or the outcome of a *counseling intervention*.

program evaluation The process by which program decision makers, recipients, and other key stakeholders determine whether a program is effective, to what degree, under what conditions, at what costs, and with what *outcomes*. In *counseling*, program evaluations of *counselor education* departments are often conducted in concert with *CACREP* or *CORE* during national accreditation.

program planning   The process by which services provided by a program are designed and assessed for appropriateness and effectiveness.

programmed workbooks for parents   Instrumental behavioral books parents may employ to help their children and, ultimately, their families modify *behaviors*.

progress notes   Written documentation that shows how well a *client* is progressing on the *treatment plan*.

projection   **1.** A *defense mechanism* in which an unwanted *emotion* or characteristic is attributed to someone else in an effort to deny that the emotion or characteristic is part of oneself. For example, people may say that their bosses are angry at them instead of saying that they are angry at their bosses. **2.** Attributing a quality or characteristic onto someone or something without considering consciously whether one has that quality of characteristic (e.g., seeing a person in a picture as angry or happy).

projective tests   *Personality tests* that are usually unstructured and require *client*s to respond to figural or pictorial stimuli. These tests yield measures that, in varying degrees, depend on the judgments and interpretations of administrators/scorers. They are meant to tap into the *unconscious*. Projective tests include the *Rorschach Inkblot Test*, the *Thematic Apperception Test (TAT)*, and *the House-Tree-Person (HTP) Test*.

promoting hope   One of the basic *curative factor*s described by Irvin Yalom. If *client*s believe that their *situation*s can be different and better, they are likely to work harder.

pro   A *self-help group leader* who gains his or her *position* from experience and longevity.

propoxyphene   A *narcotic* that goes under the trade name Darvon.

proscriptive norms   *Norms* that describe the kinds of *behaviors* that are to be avoided. See also *norms*.

prosocial behavior   *Behavior* that is *altruistic* in nature and that is undertaken to benefit society at large.

protagonist   The person who is the subject of a *psychodrama* enactment. He or she may play many parts.

protected health information   A *HIPAA* term for individually identifiable health information that is explicitly linked to a particular individual or health information data that could allow individual identification.

protection   Care, on the part of a *group leader*, that keeps members of a *group* safe from psychological or physical harm.

provider   The term used by *third-party* payment organizations to describe a *clinician* who is offering services.

provider contract   A written agreement between a licensed health care provider, such as a physician, *counselor*, facility, and a health plan.

proxemics   The study of how people use the space around them.

proximate self   That which a person considers to be *self* in contrast to the rest of the world.

Prozac   The trade name for one of the world's most widely prescribed antidepressants (i.e., fluoxetine).

pseudo-individuation   A pretend *self*. This concept involves the attempt by young people who lack an *identity* and basic coping skills to act as if they had both.

pseudomutuality   The facade of *family* harmony that many *dysfunctional* families display that is a masquerade for serious internal conflicts.

psyche   **1.** Carl Jung's term for the totality of one's *personality*. **2.** A synonym for the mind.

psychiatric nurse   A nurse who has advanced training and specializes in working with the mentally disturbed.

psychiatric social worker A *social worker* who has advanced training and specializes in working with the mentally disturbed.

psychiatrist A physician who has had specialized postdoctoral training in the *diagnosis, treatment,* and *prevention* of mental and emotional *disorder*s. A psychiatrist is permitted by *law* to prescribe the use of *drugs* as well. A psychiatrist will also use other physical and psychological means for the *treatment* of *mental disorder*s.

psychiatry A medical specialty that focuses on the *diagnosis, treatment,* and *prevention* of *mental disorder*s.

psychic energy Energy that emanates from the *id*. According to *psychoanalytic theory*, this energy is converted by the *ego* and *superego* into actions.

psychoactive drugs A group of *drugs* that induce *changes* in a person's *mood, cognition*s, or *perception*.

psychoanalysis A *theory* of *psychotherapy* that originated from the writings and work of Sigmund Freud. One's *personality* consists of three dynamically interrelated parts: *id, superego,* and *ego*. Children go through and must resolve tasks associated with *psychosexual stage*s of development. Much of the emphasis in this *theory* is on the importance of the *unconscious* and sexuality in human *behavior*. *Treatment* focuses on the release of *anxiety* and repressed memories through such *techniqu*es as *free association, dream analysis, transference,* and *interpretation*.

psychoanalyst A professional who has been educated in and uses the *theory* of Sigmund Freud (i.e., *psychoanalysis*) as the basis for his or her *treatment* of *client*s. Professionals who are psychoanalysts are primarily those holding degrees in *psychiatry* and *clinical psychology*.

psychoanalytic A descriptor for the use of some form of *psychoanalysis* in a treatment situation, for example, using the psychoanalytic method in working with a client.

psychodrama Jacob L. Moreno's *interpersonal* group approach to exploring the human *psyche*. In psychodrama, participants act out their *emotion*s and attempt to clarify *conflict*s. See also *American Society of Group Psychotherapy and Psychodrama* (ASGPP).

psychodrama process The three phases of *psychodrama: warm-up* (preaction), *action,* and *integration*.

psychodynamic theories Theories of *treatment* that include Sigmund Freud's *psychoanalytic theory* and other closely related theories that are neopsychoanalytic (e.g., the theories of Anna Freud, Karen Horney, and Otto Rank).

psychoeducation Helpful strategies regarding areas of emotional and *relationship* functioning that are taught to *client*s so that they can prevent dysfunction from occurring and cope with life events.

psychoeducational group A *group* whose primary purpose is to educate or instruct *client*s in regard to certain subjects or areas pertinent to their lives (e.g., a *parent education group*).

psychohistory The study of historical events and people in light of modern psychologically based theories. Psychobiographies are often an *outcome* of this process (e.g., Erik Erikson's *Young Man Luther*). Prominent practitioners of psychohistory include Erik Erikson, Kenneth Keniston, and Robert Coles.

Psychological Abstracts A reference to the international literature in *psychology* and related disciplines (e.g., *counseling*) that has been published by the *American Psychological Association (APA)* since 1927. Monthly issues, organized by subject area, contain summaries of English-language *journal* articles, technical reports, book chapters, and books. Cumulative author and subject indexes are published annually. For more information, visit the Web site at http://www.apg.org/psycinfo/.

psychological first aid (PFA) A systematic and initial set of helping actions, which are a part of a comprehensive disaster response effort, aimed

Psychosexual Stages of Development

Stage	Age	Emphasis
Oral	Birth to 1 year	Gratification through sucking, biting; chief zone of pleasure is the mouth.
Anal	1st to 2nd year	Gratification through the withholding or eliminating of feces; chief zone of pleasure is the anus.
Phallic	3rd to 5th year	Gratification through stimulation of the genital area, sexual fantasy; resolution comes in giving up wish to possess opposite-sex parent and identifying with same-sex parent.
Latency	6th to 11th year	A period devoted to activity and achievement with peers; it is a quiet time sexually.
Genital	12th year on	This is the time of relating to persons of the opposite gender in an appropriate manner if previous stages have been resolved successfully.

at reducing initial posttrauma distress and supporting short- and long-term adaptive functioning for people who have been in natural or man-made disasters. PFA is constructed around eight core actions: contact and engagement, safety and comfort, stabilization, information gathering, practical assistance, connection with social supports, information on coping support, and linkage with collaborative services. PFA is sometimes known as *crisis counseling.*

psychological test A standardized measure of an individual's *behavior.* See also *standardized test; test.*

psychologist A *helping professional* who has earned an advanced degree in *psychology* and whose coursework and *internships* are concentrated in clinical, counseling, or school-related areas. All states license *psychologists,* but the requirements for *licensure* differ from state to state.

psychometrics The discipline of testing.

psychometrist A testing and appraisal specialist whose primary *job* is the administration and interpretation of *psychological tests* and instruments.

psychomotor test A *test* that measures a person's fine or gross motor skills.

psychopath A lay term for someone with a serious *mental disorder,* often a person with what is considered to be an *antisocial personality disorder.*

psychopathology The study of *disorders* and *dysfunctional behavior.*

psychopharmacology The study of the effects of *drugs* in the *treatment* of *disorders.*

psychosexual/psychosexual stages of development Psychosexual is a term used to describe psychological phenomena based on sexuality. From a psychosexual point of view, sexually based forces and motives drive *development.* In *psychoanalytic theory,* each *stage* of development is characterized by the body area providing maximal erotic gratification. The four stages of psychosexual development according to Sigmund Freud are *oral, anal, phallic,* and *genital.* There is a *latency* period between the phallic and *genital stage.*

psychosis A term used to describe serious *mental disorders* such as *schizophrenia.*

psychosocial development A term that underlies Erik Erikson's *theory* of human development, which deals with the resolution of social crises and the development of social competencies. The term refers to events or *behaviors* that relate to social aspects of life. Erikson's eight *stages* of psychosocial development are *trust* versus *mistrust* (0 to 1 year), *autonomy* versus *shame* and doubt (1 to 2 years), *initiative* versus *guilt* (3 to 5 years), *industry* versus *inferiority* (6 to 11 years), *identity* versus *role confusion* (12 to 14 years), *intimacy* versus *isolation* (20s to 30s), *generativity* versus *stagnation* (40s to 50s), and *integrity* versus *despair* (60 years and over).

psychosomatic   Psychological *symptoms*, such as *anxiety,* that are manifested in physical ways.

psychosurgery   Surgery employed in the *treatment* of *disorder*s. Usually such surgery involves an operation on the brain.

psychotherapist   A general term used to describe a *helping professional* who provides *mental health treatment* to *client*s. Many professionals can be described as psychotherapists. The *legal* qualifications for such a title vary from state to state.

psychotherapy   Cognitive, affective, and behavioral means of *helping* troubled individuals *change* their *thoughts, feelings,* and *behavior*s so that they reduce their *stress* and achieve greater life satisfaction. See also *therapy*.

psychotic   A term used to describe someone with a serious *mental disorder*.

PTSD   See *posttraumatic stress disorder.*

Public Law 94-142   The *Education of All Handicapped Children Act,* which was passed by Congress in 1975. The *law* requires that schools make provisions for the free, appropriate public education of all children in the *least restrictive environment* possible. Part of this *process* is the development of an *individual education plan (IEP)* for each child as well as the provision for due-process procedures and for identifying and keeping *records* on every child with a *disability*.

Public Offender Counselor Association   The former name of the *International Association of Addictions and Offender Counseling (IAAOC)*.

public self   One of the four quadrants in the *Johari Awareness Model*. The public self is known to *self* and others.

publication bias   The bias against publishing studies with nonsignificant results.

Publication Manual of the American Psychological Association   The official resource and guide for *counselors* and other helping professionals who write for academic publications.

punishment   **1.** The presentation of an aversive *stimulus* or the removal of a pleasant stimulus. Punishment decreases the frequency of the occurrence of some undesirable *behavior*. **2.** A penalty imposed for an *illegal* act.

Purpose in Life   **1.** A *test* developed by Everett Shostrom that is based on *logotherapy* and attempts to measure meaningfulness and meaninglessness in a person's life. **2.** The *meaning* a person derives from participating in some activity or event such as *work, family,* accomplishment, or *spirituality*.

PWP   See *Parents Without Partners*.

pyromania   The deliberate setting of fires to decrease tension and experience pleasure.

q

Q   A symbol in statistics that stands for *quartile*. A number after Q represents which quartile is being discussed (e.g., Q2 is the second quartile; 26%–50%).

Q sort   A three-step *evaluation* procedure based on Rogerian *theory*. First, the *client* is given one hundred cards, each of which contains a self-descriptive sentence, such as "I am intelligent" or "I despise myself." Next, the client is asked to place the cards in nine piles, from "most like me" to "least like me." After this self-sort, the client sorts the cards again by placing them according to how he or she would ideally like to be. Finally, the counselor correlates the degree of similarity between the two sorts, before, during, and after *counseling*.

quack   An untrained *helper* who uses unproven therapeutic *techniques* and practices.

qualitative growth   See *discontinuous development.*

qualitative research   *Research* that is characterized by an emphasis on *open-ended questions* and the collection of narrative *data* on many *variables* over an extended period of time. This approach is often utilized in *theory* building.

quality circles   See *quality groups.*

quality groups   Also known as *quality circles; work groups* or *task groups* first set up and utilized by the Japanese after World War II under the direction of W. Edwards Deming to ensure *work* was done correctly and efficiently the first time.

quantitative growth   See *continuous development.*

quantitative research   *Research* that is characterized by an emphasis on *closed-ended questions* and the utilization of large *sample* sizes to gather information. *Data* is gathered in a precise form, frequently using standardized instruments, and reported in a statistical format. Analyzed and deductive *conclusions* are made that tend to "prove" or "disprove" theories and assertions.

quartile   A *score distribution* segment that has been divided into fourths or quarters.

quasi-experimental design   A *research* design in which the conditions of *treatment* are controlled by the experimenter (e.g., assigning specific subjects to certain groups in a nonrandom way).

quasi-kin   A formerly married person's ex-spouse, the ex-spouse's new husband or wife, and his or her blood kin.

questioning   A query that is used to gather information, increase clarity, stimulate *thinking,* or elicit further discussion. See also *closed-ended questions; open-ended questions.*

questionnaire   A *survey* instrument, similar to a structured *interview,* used to gather information or opinions on specific topics.

quid pro quo   A something for something *relationship.* In social economic *theory,* married partners will stay in a relationship because it is quid pro quo (i.e., spouses are both giving and receiving). If the relationship ceases to be quid pro quo, it is likely to dissolve.

r

r   A symbol in *statistics* for *correlation coefficient.*

race   An anthropological concept that classifies people according to their biological and physiological characteristics, such as skin color, hair texture, and facial features. Race contributes virtually nothing to cultural understanding.

racial identity development   A complex *psychosocial process* that encompasses *race* or ethnic-related attitudes, beliefs, and *behaviors* and entails understanding oneself in light of these *factors* and the *environment* in which one lives.

racism   *Prejudice* displayed in blatant or subtle ways due to recognized or perceived differences in the physical and psychological backgrounds of people. It is a form of *projection* usually displayed out of fear or ignorance.

racket   A *transactional analysis* term for one's self-indulgence in negative or nongenuine *feeling*s (e.g., *guilt,* inadequacy, hurt, fear, or resentment).

radical behaviorists   Behaviorists who avoid any mentalistic concepts and concentrate exclusively on observable actions.

rainbows   See *barbiturates.*

random sample   A *sample* drawn from a *population* in such a way that each member of the population has an equal chance of being selected.

randomization Both the random selection and random assignment of participants in a *research* study.

rank-order To arrange *data* or *scores* from the lowest to the highest (e.g., 1, 7, 15) or from the highest to the lowest (22, 18, 9).

range A statistical measure of variability that encompasses the width or spread of *scores* in a *distribution*. The range is calculated by subtracting the lowest from the highest score in the distribution (e.g., 85 − 40 = 45 point range).

rape Forced sexual intercourse without *consent,* usually with a girl or woman by a man.

rape myth *Stereotypes* and myths that are prejudicial ways of *thinking* about *rape* and that lead to the victimization of women (e.g., "Only bad girls or women get raped"; "Anyone can resist rape").

rapport The establishment of a warm, personal, and trusting *relationship* with a *client* by a *counselor*. Rapport is the foundation on which *counseling* is built.

rating scale A subjective observational estimate of *behaviors* or *attitudes* where the rater indicates the degree of severity of the characteristics being measured (e.g., level of energy).

ratio IQ score An *intelligence quotient* derived by dividing a person's *mental age score* on an *intelligence test* by the person's *chronological age* and multiplying by one hundred. See also *intelligence quotient (IQ)*.

ratio scale A scale with a true zero point and equal units of *measurement*. Height and weight are examples of measurements on a ratio scale, but most *test scores* are not on such a scale.

rational behavior therapy (RBT) An approach to *counseling* formulated by Maxie Maultsby. RBT emphasizes cognitive *change* in a way more behavioral than Albert Ellis originally conceptualized. It involves checking activating events as if one had a camera to be sure of objectivity. Disputation of a person's *self-talk* takes the form of a debate based on five *rules* for rational *behavior*.

rational emotive behavior therapy (REBT) The *theory* of *counseling* established by Albert Ellis in the late 1950s and originally called *rational emotive therapy*. The emphasis of the approach is that it is people's *thoughts* about events, rather than the events, that are the source of emotional and behavioral difficulties. REBT focuses on *helping clients change* or modify their *negative thoughts* to neutral, positive, or *mixed thoughts* and thus think more rationally and behave more responsibly and with less *interpersonal* and *intrapersonal* difficulty.

rational emotive behavior therapy (REBT) types of thoughts The four types of *thoughts* in REBT *theory:* negative, positive, neutral, and mixed. The theory proposes that individuals can choose to think in one of these four ways. See also *thoughts*.

rational emotive imagery (REI) A *rational emotive behavior therapy* (REBT) *technique* for disputing *irrational beliefs* (IBs). REI may be used in one of two ways. First, the *client* is asked to imagine a *situation* in which he or she is likely to become upset. The client examines his or her *self-talk* during that imagined situation. Then the client is asked to envision the same situation but this time to be more moderate in his or her self-talk. In the second way, the client is asked to imagine a situation in which he or she feels or behaves differently from some real instance. Then the client is asked to examine the self-talk used in this imagined situation.

rational emotive therapy (RET) The original name Albert Ellis gave to his theory before he changed it to rational emotive behavior therapy. See *rational emotive behavior therapy (REBT)*.

rational self-analysis (RSA) A *technique* devised by Maxie Maultsby in which *clients* are instructed to write down significant events in their lives and their *thoughts* and *feelings* associated with the events. The beliefs of the persons are then evaluated for their degree of rationality and *changed* in accordance with the *rules* of rational *behavior*. This *method* of assessing clients' thoughts is useful in maintaining a record of therapeutic progress. The standard RSA format consists of six steps.

rationalization A *defense mechanism* in which a person finds reasonable explanations for unreasonable or unacceptable *behavior*s to make them sound logical and acceptable (e.g., "I did it because everyone else was"; "I really didn't think it was going to be worth the time I'd have to spend, so I didn't do it").

raw score A *score* that has not been converted into a *derived score* such as a *standard score*.

RBT See *rational behavior therapy*.

reaction formation A *defense mechanism* in which *anxiety*-producing *thought*s, *feeling*s, or impulses are repressed and their opposites expressed. For example, a host at a party may shower a disliked guest with attention. A reaction formation is often detected because of the intensity with which the opposite *emotion* is expressed.

real self The essence of a person (i.e., the person's true *thought*s, *feeling*s). In an *incongruent* person, the real self is in sharp contrast to the *ideal self*.

realistic people Individuals, according to Holland's *career* typology, who enjoy working in practical environments that they can build or make better. They like to work with machines, tools, animals, and plants (e.g., construction workers, farmers). See *RIASEC*.

reality principle The principle by which the *ego* operates in Sigmund Freud's schema of the *personality*. Under this principle, reality is seen as that which exists in the outside *environment*. To deal with reality, the ego must sometimes delay immediate gratification. It is the opposite of the *pleasure principle*.

reality therapy A *counseling* theory originated by William Glasser in the 1960s that focuses on the present and seeks to help *client*s *change* by evaluating what they are doing, making new plans, and then implementing

them. Reality therapy is pragmatic and has behavioral overtones. See *choice theory*.

reality-oriented groups *Groups* that are set up for older individuals who have become disoriented with regard to their surroundings. These groups, although educationally focused, are therapeutically based in that their emphasis is on *helping* group members become more attuned to where they are with respect to time, place, and people.

reassuring/supportive response A *low facilitative response* in which the *counselor*'s intent is to encourage someone, yet the response itself dismisses the person's real *feeling*s.

reauthoring An aspect of *narrative therapy* that encourages individuals and families to *change* the emphases in their stories and focus on aspects of their lives that have not been previously emphasized.

REBT See *rational emotive behavior therapy*.

recall **1.** A *psychoanalysis* term for reviving or reinstating a past experience from memory. **2.** To remember or recollect.

recency effect The idea that all things being equal, those things that are learned last in a sequence are remembered best. It is the opposite of, but complementary to, the *primacy effect*.

recidivism The *relapse* of treated *client*s into *behavior*s they were displaying before *counseling*.

reciprocal inhibition A *behavior therapy* approach created by Joseph Wolpe based on the idea that an individual cannot feel anxious and relaxed at the same time. Thus, *client*s are taught to relax before they deal with *anxiety*-producing *situation*s. The most classic example of reciprocal inhibition is *systematic desensitization*. See also *systematic desensitization*.

reciprocity The likelihood that two people will reinforce each other at approximately equitable rates over time. Many marital *behavior* counselors view marriage as based on this principle.

records **1.** Written summaries of *counseling* sessions. Records of *client*s are legally protected except under special circumstances. Records allow *counselors* an opportunity to document their work with clients and afford counselors *legal* protection against suits if they show that they followed a *treatment plan* based on an appropriate *diagnosis*. **2.** To set down in writing or in any other permanent way accounts of events (e.g., personal *reflections* or impressions).

recycling   A *process* in which individuals who have not benefited from a *counseling* experience go through a similar experience again and learn lessons missed the first time.

red birds   See *barbiturates*.

redecision school of transactional analysis   An approach to *transactional analysis* in which the emphasis is on *intrapsychic processes*. Individuals are encouraged to *change* their *life scripts*. Redecision is based on the premise that early life decisions are reversible if *clients* reexperience their decisions both intellectually and emotionally.

redefining   Attributing *positive connotations* to symptomatic or troublesome actions. The idea is that *symptoms* have *meaning* for those who display them, whether such meaning is logical or not. Redefining is one way of lowering *resistance* to counseling.

redundancy principle   The fact that a *family* interacts within a limited *range* of repetitive behavioral sequences.

referral   The transfer of a *client* to another *counselor*. The referral *process* itself involves four steps: **1.** identifying the need to refer; **2.** evaluating potential referral sources; **3.** preparing the client for the referral; and **4.** coordinating the transfer.

reflection   A *counseling technique* similar to a restatement but dealing with *verbal* and *nonverbal* expression. Reflections may be on several levels; some convey more *empathy* than others. Some are based on rephrasing a *client's feeling*; others are based on rephrasing the client's *content*. An example of a feeling-based reflection would be a *counselor* responding to a client's silently sobbing over the *loss* of a parent by saying, "You're still really feeling the pain."

reflecting skills   The use of *reflection* in *paraphrasing* clients' statements and underlying *feelings*.

reframing   A *process* in which a *perception* is *changed* by explaining a *situation* from a different and more positive context. For instance, a misbehaving child may be said to be "behaving younger than his years" rather than being "incorrigible." Reframing allows people to make new *responses* because the situation is now seen in a new way.

registration   The lowest level of credentialing. It requires a practitioner to submit information to the state concerning the nature of his or her practice. Usually a professional organization, such as a state *counseling* association, assumes the responsibility for setting standards necessary to qualify as a registrant and maintains a list of names of those who voluntarily meet those standards.

registry   A voluntary listing of persons who use a title and/or provide a service. Registry is the simplest and least restrictive form of credentialing.

regression   **1.** A *defense mechanism* in which a person returns to an earlier *stage* of *development*. For example, a child under *stress* may begin to wet the bed during early adolescence after suffering a *trauma*. Virtually all people regress if placed under enough pressure or *stress*. **2.** A statistical *technique* used to predict *scores* when the value of one set of *scores* is known and correlates highly with the other. Regression may be simple or multiple (using more than one predictor variable).

regression toward the mean   The tendency of an extreme value when it is remeasured to be closer to the *mean*. For example, on a retest a very high or low score will probably be closer to the mean than before.

rehab   An abbreviated form of the word *rehabilitation*.

rehabilitation   The reeducation or restoring to healthy conditions of individuals who have *handicap*s and who have previously lived independent lives.

Rehabilitation Act of 1973   Federal legislation that broadened the interpretation of those eligible for *rehabilitation* services.

rehabilitation counseling   A *counseling* specialty that focuses on serving individuals with *disabilities* and *handicap*s. The practice of rehabilitation counseling requires knowledge in areas of medical terminology, *diagnosis, prognosis,* vocational *evaluation* of disability-related limitations, and *job* placement in the context of a socioeconomic *system*. See *postvention*.

rehearsal   A *process* in which individuals practice *behavior*s or repeat materials so that the action or information becomes permanently encoded and stored in their memories.

REI   See *rational emotive imagery*.

reinforcement   Any *stimulus* that increases the *probability* of a *response*.

reinforcer   A *stimulus* event that increases the *probability* that the *response* that immediately preceded it will occur again.

relabeling   A *technique* utilized in *counseling*, especially with families, to bring about *change* by giving a different perspective to a *behavior*.

relapse   The reoccurrence of *dysfunctional behavior*s once they have been treated.

relationship   The degree of psychological and emotional closeness, connection, and/or association between two or more entities, for example, a *counselor* and *client* or *family* members. The nature of a relationship often determines the *outcome* of *situation*s in *counseling*.

reliability   The consistency, dependability, or repeatability of a person achieving similar results from a *test, measurement,* or appraisal instrument given under comparable conditions.

religion .   The institutionalized and codified expression of one's beliefs in the transcendent in an integrated *system* that is oriented toward *helping* people find *meaning,* purpose, and spiritual connectedness in life. Major world religions include Judaism, Christianity, Islam, Hinduism, Buddhism, Confucianism, and Taoism. See also *spirituality*.

reluctant client   A *client* who has been referred by a *third party* and is frequently unmotivated to seek help (e.g., many schoolchildren and court-referred clients). Such individuals do not wish to be in *counseling,* let alone talk about themselves. Many reluctant clients terminate *counseling* prematurely and report dissatisfaction with the *process*.

remarried families   Also referred to as *stepfamilies,* reconstituted families, recoupled families, merged families, and *blended families*. Regardless of terminology, these families consist of two adults and stepchildren, adoptive children, or foster children.

remediation   The *process* by which *counseling* procedures are implemented with the goal of correcting a *situation*.

reminiscing therapy   A *therapy,* originating in the 1960s, that is based on the importance of *life review*. Reminiscing therapy helps individuals who have not yet fully realized their own older life *stage* to comprehend and appreciate more fully who they are and where they have been. In this approach, persons share memories, increase personal *integration,* and become more aware of their lives and the lives of those their age. *Insight* gained from this *process* helps these persons to realize more deeply their finiteness and to prepare for death.

remotivation therapy groups   *Groups* aimed at *helping* older *client*s become more invested in the present and future. Group membership is composed of individuals who have "lost interest" in any time frame of life except the past.

reorientation   An *Adlerian counseling technique* in which *client*s are encouraged to act differently and take more control of their lives. Such a procedure means taking risks, *acting "as if"* they were the persons they wished to be, and *"catching oneself"* in old, ineffective patterns and correcting them.

reparation therapy AKA *conversion therapy,* involves methods intended to convert *bisexual, lesbian,* and *gay* people to *heterosexuality* (i.e., change their sexual orientation).

REPLAN An atheoretical model of *helping* developed by Mark Young. "R" stands for *relationship,* "E" for efficacy and *self-esteem,* "P" for practicing new *behaviors,* "L" for lowering or raising emotional arousal, "A" for activating experiences and changing *perceptions,* and "N" for providing new *learning* and experiences in changing perceptions.

replication study The repeating of an *experimental research* study in the exact same way as a means of verifying the findings.

repression The *defense mechanism* on which others are built. Using this most basic mechanism, the *ego* involuntarily excludes from *consciousness* any unwanted or painful *thoughts, feelings,* memories, or impulses. The ego must use energy to keep excluded areas from *consciousness,* but sometimes the repressed *thoughts* slip out in dreams or *verbal* expressions. Repression is considered the cornerstone or foundation stone of *psychoanalysis.*

rescuer A person in a *transactional analysis* game who is seen as a *problem* solver or hero to the victim.

research A systematic procedure for investigating facts and observations. Research in *counseling* is for the most part *applied research* that links basic science and *theory* to issues of counseling practice.

research design The way a research study is set up. Five commonly used categories are exploratory, descriptive, developmental, experimental, and correlational.

research question A query that explores the relationship between two *variables* but does not state any specific expectation about the findings that may emerge from the study.

resilience The *power* to recover readily or spring back from *stress, trauma,* or other negative conditions in life.

resistance Any *behavior* that moves a *client* away from areas of discomfort or *conflict* and prevents the client from developing or changing (e.g., getting bogged down in details and becoming preoccupied with the unimportant compared to focusing on growth).

resistant client A *client* who is unwilling or opposed to *change.* Such an individual may actively seek *counseling* but does not wish to go through the pain that change demands. Instead, the client clings to the certainty of present *behavior,* even when such action is counterproductive and *dysfunctional.* Some resistant clients refuse to make decisions, are superficial in dealing with *problems,* and do not take any action to resolve their difficulties. One of the most common forms of *resistance* is the simple statement "I don't know."

respondent conditioning A behavioral view that human *responses* are learned through association. See also *classical conditioning.*

responding Use of *open-ended questions* and *closed-ended questions* to acknowledge a *client.*

response The reaction of the mind and/or body to a *stimulus.*

response set The tendency for a person to respond in a relatively fixed or stereotyped way to a *situation* in which there are at least two *choices* on a *test.* For example, a response set on a true/false test might be to answer all questions true.

responsive listening An empathetic *verbal response* by the *counselor* that communicates acceptance and concern.

restatement Saying in slightly different words what a *client* has said to clarify a statement's *meaning.* Restating helps provide support and *clarification* within the *counseling process.*

restraining A *paradoxical technique* of telling a *client* that he or she is incapable of doing anything other than what he or she is presently doing. The intent is to get the client to show he or she can behave differently.

restructuring **1.** To make a basic change in the *structure* of something, such as *cognitions,* to modify or improve *thinking* and reasoning processes. See *cognitive restructuring*. **2.** Changing the *structure* of the *family*. The rationale behind restructuring is to make the family more functional by altering the existing hierarchy and interaction patterns.

retardation **1.** A delay in *development*. **2.** A term used to describe significantly lower than average intellectual ability or significantly slower than average psychomotor reaction. Intellectual retardation is classified as: mild (IQ level 50–55 to 70), moderate (IQ level 35–40 to 50–55), severe (IQ level 20–25 to 35–40), and profound (IQ level below 20–25).

retirement counseling Interventions undertaken to assist individuals in preparing for and adjusting to the transitions they experience when they enter retirement.

Revolution in Counseling A landmark book written by John Krumboltz in 1966 that promoted *learning* beyond *insight* as the root of *change*.

revolving door A descriptive term for *clients* who *relapse* and reenter *therapy* after a brief period of time.

reward An object, event, *stimulus,* or *outcome* that is perceived as being pleasant or needed and is therefore used as a *reinforcer*.

RIASEC An acronym for John Holland's *career typology theory*. The letters stand for the six types of personalities and environments in the *theory:* realistic, investigative, artistic, social, enterprising, and conventional. See also *Self-Directed Search (SDS)* and *career typology*.

rigid boundaries Inflexible *rules* and habits that keep *family* members separated from each other.

risk management documentation A document of what the *client* did or said that implied what he or she was engaging in or considering engaging in. This document includes the severity level of any threat, recorded clinical options considered, an explanation of clinical decision making involving this client, documentation of *consultation,*

rational for options chosen, and what occurred after clinical action was taken.

risk-taking New *behavior*s that generate some *anxiety* but are taken by a *client* to *change* behaviors and reach therapeutic *goals*.

rituals **1.** A *family counseling* term for specialized types of *directive*s that are meant to dramatize significant and positive *family relationship*s or aspects of *problem situation*s. **2.** A *transactional analysis* term for simple and *stereotyped complementary transaction*s like hellos and good-byes.

role A dynamic *structure* within an individual (based on *need*s, *cognition*s, and *value*s) that usually comes to life under the influence of social stimuli or defined *position*s (i.e., status). The manifestation of a role is based on the individual's expectation of *self* and others and the interactions he or she has in particular *situation*s.

role collision A *situation* in which there is a *conflict* between the *role* an individual plays in the outside world (e.g., that of a passive observer) and the role expected within the *group* (e.g., that of an active participant).

role confusion **1.** The opposite of *identity* in Erik Erikson's fifth *stage* of *psychosocial* development. Role confusion is a lack of clarity about one's identity. **2.** A *situation* that occurs when a member of a group does not know what *role* to perform. This often happens in *leaderless group*s; members do not know whether to be assertive and help to establish an agenda or passive and allow the leadership to emerge.

role incompatibility A *situation* that occurs when a person in a *group* is given a *role* (such as that of *group leader*) that he or she does not want, is unprepared for, or is uncomfortable exercising.

role induction Explaining before the fact what one's *role* will be in a *situation*. *Client*s benefit from role induction in *counseling* because they find out what their roles are at the beginning of the *process,* before mistakes are made.

role model A person who is exemplary and a standard of emulation.

role overload A *situation* that occurs when a person tries to fulfill a greater variety of *role*s than he or she has energy or time for. Role overload is a common *phenomenon* of newly divorced single parents.

role playing A procedure in which *client*s are asked to *act "as if"* they are the persons they ideally want to be. *Client*s practice a number of *behavior*s to see which work best. *Feedback* is given, and ideally, *insight* and *empathy* emerge from the *process*.

role reversal The taking on of a *role* opposite of what one normally assumes (e.g., becoming assertive if one is usually passive). Through role reversal, *client*s experience new *thought*s, *feeling*s, and *behavior*s and expand their abilities to switch roles as well as *empathize* more with individuals who tend to be different from themselves.

role transition When an individual gives up one *role* to take on another role. A role transition may be stressful, for example, transitioning from a follower to a leader.

S

SAD PERSONS scale A scale used to assess the risk of *suicide*. The acronym describes persons at risk. The letter "S" stands for sex (male), "A" for age (older *client*s), "D" for *depression*, "P" for previous attempt, "E" for ethanol (alcohol) *abuse*, "R" for rational *thinking* loss, "S" for social support *system* lacking (lonely, isolated), "O" for organized plan, "N" for no spouse, and "S" for sickness (particularly chronic or terminal illness).

sadist A person who derives pleasure from inflicting pain on someone else.

sadistic personality disorder A *personality disorder* in which a person seeks to impose mental or physical cruelty on someone else.

Rorschach Inkblot Test A projective *personality test* developed in the 1920s by Hermann Rorschach. The test consists of 10 standardized inkblot cards.

rounds Also known as *go-rounds*; the *process* of giving members of a *group* an equal chance to participate in the group by going around the circle in which they are sitting and asking each person to make a comment on a subject that is presently before the group. Sometimes rounds are used to ensure group member participation. They are less confrontational than the *Gestalt therapy group process* of *making the rounds*.

rules **1.** Prescribed guidelines for conduct with others. **2.** The guidelines under which *counseling* is conducted and that are a part of the *structure* of counseling that *counselor*s must establish early in a therapeutic *relationship*. **3.** A *structural family therapy* term for the explicit or implicit guidelines that govern a family's interaction.

rumination A condition in which a person has the same *thought* continuously and dwells on it. Rumination is one of the signs of an *obsessive-compulsive disorder*.

sadomasochism A simultaneous tendency toward *sadist* and *masochist behavior*s.

salad bowl A term used to describe assimilation of immigrants in American life in which each *culture* keeps its own distinct qualities and does not merge into a single homogeneous culture.

Salvation Army An international, evangelical Christian, faith-based organization founded in England by William Booth in 1852. Among services offered by the Salvation Army is a disaster relief operation; the first aim is to meet the basic needs of those who have been affected, both survivors and first responders (such as firefighters) (http://www.salvationarmyusa.org/usn/www_usn_2.nsf).

sample   1. The number of people involved in a *research* study. **2.** A *subset* of a *population*.

sampling   The process of selecting individuals who are members of the *population* that the researcher wishes to study.

sand play   A nondirective, projective *treatment* procedure, based on Jungian *theory,* that offers *client*s an opportunity to project internal and external troubling and traumatic experiences metaphorically with figures in a container of sand.

sandwich generation   Couples who have adolescents and their aging parents to take care of and are squeezed psychologically and physically between these two responsibilities.

SAT   See *Scholastic Aptitude Test.*

satiation   See *habituation.*

SAWV   See *Scale to Assess World Views.*

scaffolding   Lev Vygotsky's term for help from others in learning, understanding, and *problem* solving that could not be achieved independently.

Scale to Assess World Views (SAWV)   A scale that measures a *client*'s *worldview* using the following categories: human nature, social *relationship*s, nature, time orientation, and activity orientation.

scaled score   A *score* that has been converted from a *raw score* to a standardized number. Raw scores on many *test*s must be converted to scaled scores before test results can be tabulated and reported.

scaling   A *technique* of turning a dichotomy into a continuum, so that individuals do not see things as "all or nothing." It is used in *solution-focused therapy* and in other therapeutic approaches for challenging *dichotomous thinking.*

scapegoat   A person who is designated or blamed by a *group* or a *family* as the cause of its difficulties or *problems.* See also *identified patient (IP).*

scattergram   A two-dimensional *graph* that plots pairs of *score*s on two *variables* and visually depicts the relationship between them. A scattergram is also known as a *scatterplot.*

scatterplot   See *scattergram.*

schedule of reinforcement   A way of initiating or maintaining *behavior.* To initiate a behavior, a schedule of reinforcement should be continuous (i.e., every *response* to a *stimulus* should be rewarded). To maintain a behavior, schedules of reinforcement operate on either a *ratio* (number of responses) or *interval* (length of time between *reward*s) basis. Both ratio and interval schedules are either *fixed* (occurring after a definite number of responses or a set period of time) or *variable* (occurring randomly).

schema   See *schemata.*

schemata   Jean Piaget's *cognitive development* term for a way of *thinking*; a unit of cognitive *structure.* A schemata is comprised of core beliefs and basic assumptions about how things operate.

schism   The division of the *family* into two antagonistic and competing groups.

schizophrenia   A *mental disorder* characterized by a *loss* of contact with reality, *withdrawal* from others, and a loss of interest in external activities. In addition, there is a breakdown of personal habits and an inability to deal with daily events. *Delusion*s, *hallucination*s, and *thought* abnormalities are also usually present. Subtypes of schizophrenia include paranoid, catatonic, disorganized, undifferentiated, and residual.

schizophrenia and other psychotic disorders   A diagnostic category found in the *DSM* that include *disorder*s characterized by *symptom*s that reveal a *loss* of contact with reality.

Scholastic Aptitude Test (SAT)   A standardized *aptitude test* published by the College Board that measures a student's ability to do college-level work. SATs have two sections, one in math and one in English; *score*s for the two sections are added to give an overall score. Most colleges and universities require students to submit either SAT or *ACT (American College Testing)* scores as a part of the admissions process. The College Board address is 45 Columbus Avenue, New York, NY 10023-6917 (212-713-8000; http://www.collegeboard .com/splash).

school boy A street name for *codeine*.

school counseling Services that are systematically provided by professional *school counselors* and that are specifically designed for elementary, middle, and secondary school environments. These services include such activities as classroom *guidance, career* decision making, teacher and parental *consultation,* personal *counseling,* and *group work*. See also *American School Counselor Association (ASCA)*.

school counselor A professional *counselor* who has had specialized training in working with children and adolescents and who is employed in a school setting. See also *American School Counselor Association (ASCA)*.

school phobia A fear of going to school. School phobia is often attributable to unresolved *dependency* issues or *separation anxiety*.

school psychologist A *psychologist* specifically educated to work in school settings with students experiencing academic, behavioral, and emotional *problems*. The services of most school psychologists are tied to state and federal mandates for the comprehensive *evaluation* of students who may qualify for programs, such as special education. Three of the primary duties of school psychologists are *assessment, consultation,* and *intervention*. See also *National Association of School Psychologists (NASP)*.

School-to-Work-Opportunities Act (STWOA) An act passed by Congress in 1994 that offered community funding of comprehensive programs that provided a wide *range* of *career* and employability skills information for secondary school students entering the *job* market after graduation. STWOA was not refunded in 1998.

score **1.** Also known as a *test score,* a number on a test that when compared to other numbers takes on a *meaning* as to where a person stands in *relationship* to others on a *measurement* instrument. See also *derived score; raw score; scaled score*. **2.** To assign a numerical value to a response made on a *test* or task.

screening **1.** A *process* in which potential *clients* are interviewed prior to their entering *counseling* to see whether they are suitable for *treatment*. **2.** A *process* for selecting members of a *group*.

script/script analysis A procedure in *transactional analysis* for understanding the life plan that an individual is following.

scriptotherapy The use of writing as a primary or adjunct therapeutic tool in *counseling*.

scripts A *transactional analysis* term for the habitual patterns of *behavior* that influence how people spend their time. Most people initially script their lives as a *child* in the "I'm not OK"/"You're OK" stance (characterized by powerlessness), but *change* to an *adult* stance in later life as they affirm an "I'm OK"/"You're OK" *position* (characterized by *trust* and openness). Other options open are "I'm OK"/"You're not OK" (characterized by a *projection* of blame onto others) and "I'm not OK"/"You're not OK" (characterized by hopelessness and self-destructiveness). See also *OK positions*.

sculpting An experiential *exercise,* usually found in *family counseling* or *group counseling,* in which individuals use *nonverbal methods* to arrange others (e.g., office personnel, *family* members, or social *peers*) into a configuration like that of significant persons with whom they regularly deal. The *positioning* involves body posturing and assists *clients* in seeing and experiencing their *perceptions* of *significant other*s in a more dynamic way.

SDS   See *Self-Directed Search.*

secondary affiliation groups   Those groups with which people least identify (e.g., as a member of a club that one never attends).

secondary gains   Extra attention or other benefits a person gets from having a *disorder.*

secondary prevention   Raising *awareness* to address *problem*s already in existence.

secondary process   A *psychoanalysis theory* term for the reality-based decision-making and *problem*-solving activities of the *ego.*

secondary reinforcer   A *reinforcer* that acquires its value by being associated with a *primary reinforcer* (e.g., money and what it can buy).

secondary school counseling   *Counseling* in schools that occurs in grades 9 through 12 or 10 through 12 by *counselors* specially educated to deal with developmental and situational concerns of *adolescents* in educational settings. See also *American School Counselor Association (ASCA).*

secondary traumatization   See *compassion fatigue.*

second-degree games   A term in *transactional analysis* for the more serious *games,* compared with those of the *first-degree games.* The interactive *process* in second-degree games leaves those involved feeling negative. See also *games.*

second-order change   A qualitatively different way of doing something; a basic *change* in function and/or *structure.*

second-order cybernetics   The *cybernetics* of *cybernetics.*

sedative   A *drug* that tends to calm, moderate, or tranquilize nervousness or excitement (e.g., *barbiturates*).

self   The concept a person has of himself or herself in a *cognitive, emotional,* or *behavioral* way.

self theory   Another name for the theoretical ideas of Carl Rogers. For Rogers, the *self* is an

outgrowth of what a person experiences; an awareness of the self helps a person *differentiate* himself or herself from others.

self-actualization   A constant striving and *need* on the part of human beings to grow and realize their full potential; to be autonomous and healthy, according to Abraham Maslow. Self-actualizing persons are motivated by enduring and universal *values* such as truth, beauty, *wisdom,* and peace.

self-assessment   The use of written and reflective activities, such as *questionnaires* and self-monitoring, that help individuals discover their interests, *values,* achievements, and *aptitudes.*

self-awareness   An ongoing *process* in life of recognizing *thought*s, *emotions, senses,* and *behavior*s that influence a person on multiple levels.

self-care   A lifestyle that promotes *wellness* in the physical, mental, emotional, and spiritual side of life.

self-concept   The way one thinks of oneself in regard to qualities and competencies based on information from *significant other*s and experiences; an overall assessment of the self. Self-concept includes *self-image.*

self-defeating behavior   Any action that a person takes to prevent himself or herself from achieving success.

Self-Directed Search (SDS)   A popular *career assessment* instrument based on the *trait-and-factor (RIASEC) theory* of John Holland in regard to *personality* and *environment* fit. The SDS is self-administered, self-scored, and self-interpreted. *Score*s are linked with the *Dictionary of Occupational Titles (DOT)* codes through the Holland codes. The SDS is applicable for persons ages 15 to 70 who are in *need* of *career guidance.*

self-disclosure   A *conscious,* intentional *technique* in which clinicians share information about their lives outside the *counseling relationship.* The original work in this area was done by Sidney Jourard. For him, self-disclosure referred to making oneself known to another person by revealing personal information. Jourard discovered that self-disclosure helped to establish *trust* and facilitated the counseling relationship. He labeled reciprocal self-disclosure the *dyadic effect*.

self-efficacy An individual's beliefs about his or her ability to successfully perform a particular task. Self-efficacy beliefs and outcome expectations may influence the development of *career*-related interests and influence the development of career-related aspirations and goals.

self-esteem The evaluative, attitudinal component of the *self*; the affective judgments placed on the *self-concept*. Self-esteem consists of *feelings* of worth and acceptance and develops as a consequence of a sense of *identity,* awareness of competence, and *feedback* from the external world.

self-exploration A *client's exploration* of his or her *thoughts, feelings,* and *behaviors* and their usefulness or *consequences*.

self-fulfilling prophecy A prediction by persons that something will happen to them whether there is factual evidence supporting such an assumption or not. Often a self-fulfilling prophecy will come true because of the way people live their lives or shape their *environment*. For instance, a person may state that he or she will not be able to hold a *job* and will act in such a way, such as getting drunk, that he or she will be dismissed from *work*.

self-help group A *mutual-help group* that does not include professional leaders but is led instead by *group* members. An example of such a group is *Alcoholics Anonymous (AA)*.

self-hypnosis To hypnotize oneself. See *autohypnosis*.

self image See *self-concept*.

self-instructional training A *technique* originated by Donald Meichenbaum for teaching *clients* to become aware of their internally generated *maladaptive thoughts* and

to replace such *self-talk* with self-enhancing *cognitions*.

self-monitoring The keeping by a *client* of detailed, daily *records* of particular events or psychological reactions to evaluate what he or she is doing.

self-report inventory A *test* in which persons check off statements that are characteristic or not characteristic of themselves.

self-report research format A *research method* in which participants write out or check off ways that they are different as a result of an experience such as *counseling*.

self-talk The internal messages people give themselves. Self-talk is sometimes known as *self-verbalization*.

self-theory Another name for Carl Rogers's *person-centered* approach.

self-verbalization See *self-talk*.

sensate focus A *sex therapy* procedure devised by Masters and Johnson to eliminate performance *anxiety* by instructing a couple to engage in noneoretic *touching*.

senility/senile A term to denote the deterioration of mental and physical capacities in *old age*.

senses Any of the faculties by which a person obtains information about the physical world, such as thought sight, sound, touch, and taste.

sensitivity group See *basic encounter group*.

sensorimotor stage The first *stage* in Jean Piaget's *theory* on the development of human *intelligence*. During this stage (which lasts from birth to about age 2), *children* understand their world primarily through their senses and activities. An important milestone in this stage is the development of *object permanence*.

sentence completion test A *personality test* that is composed of a number of incomplete sentences that a person is asked to finish as soon as possible.

separation anxiety *Anxiety* experienced by children when they are separated from *caregivers* (e.g., their mothers) to whom they are emotionally attached.

serendipity The discovery of something unexpected in the process of searching for something else.

serial art therapy A *creative arts therapy* procedure based on Jungian *theory* in which young *clients* are requested to draw a picture at each *counseling* session. Pictures are not analyzed, but clients are encouraged to draw images that help them heal. Serial drawings may be structured or unstructured.

service delivery The providing of particular *counseling* or supportive services to *clients* or agencies in a community.

Servicemen's Readjustment Act See *G. I. Bill.*

session A term used to describe a meeting between a *counselor* and a *client.*

setting a tone Overtly setting a *norm* in a *group* for others to follow and putting a climate in place, for example, serious or humorous. The group leader usually sets the tone.

sex Biological categories (i.e., male vs. female).

sex differences The naturally occurring differences in males and females. According to *research* by Eleanor Maccoby and Carol Jacklin and their associates, four basic differences appear to be present from birth on. Boys excel in visual-spatial and mathematical tasks and are more aggressive; girls have greater *verbal* ability.

sex discrimination Treating individuals differently, often in a biased fashion, based on their *sex.* Women have most often been the *victims* of sex discrimination.

sex roles Cultural *roles* assigned to males and females based on their gender.

sex therapy A specialized type of *treatment* that is aimed at *helping* couples overcome sexual difficulties in their *relationships.*

sexual harassment Any type of sexual solicitation, physical advances or *verbal* or *nonverbal* conduct that is sexual in nature that is deemed *unprofessional* or unwanted.

sexism The belief (and the *behavior* resulting from that belief) that persons should be treated on the basis of their *sex* without regard to other criteria, such as interests and abilities. Such *treatment* is arbitrary, illogical, biased, counterproductive, and self-serving.

sexual and gender identity disorders A *DSM* diagnostic category of three very different *disorders: paraphilias, sexual dysfunctions,* and *gender identity disorders.*

sexual dysfunctions A category under *sexual and gender identity disorders* in the *DSM* that involves *problems* in the expression of one's sexuality (e.g., arousal disorder, premature ejaculation). Sexual dysfunctions are usually straightforward problems that respond well to behavioral *interventions.*

sexual identity A dynamic *process* influenced by personal and cultural experiences that involves the affectional and sexual dimensions of the *self* connected to *thoughts, feelings,* and *behaviors.* Sexual identity is based on attraction, interests, and self-identification and can be viewed across a *life span* of development.

sexual orientation The orientation people have toward being *heterosexual, homosexual, bisexual,* or *transsexual.*

shadow A Jungian concept for the *unconscious,* unaccepted, and unrecognized parts of an individual's *personality* that are often negative, such as acting nice to a person while simultaneously *thinking* of harming them.

shadowing See *career shadowing.*

shame **1.** Dishonor, disgrace, or other painful *emotions* one feels for having failed. **2.** The opposite of *autonomy* in Erik Erikson's *psychosocial* development *theory.*

shame attack A *rational emotive behavior therapy (REBT) technique,* often in the form of *homework,* in which a person actually does what he or she dreads and then finds the world does not fall apart regardless of the *outcome.* For example, a man might go into a restaurant and ask for a drink of water without ordering food. Whether he receives the water or not is irrelevant. He finds through the experience that he can actually do something he fears.

shaping An *operant conditioning* procedure that involves reinforcing *responses* that come successively closer to the desired response; the *process* of *learning* in small gradual steps. Shaping is often referred to as *successive approximation*.

shaping competence The procedure in which *structural family therapy counselors* help families and family members become more functional by highlighting positive *behaviors*.

shifting the focus The *technique* of turning a *client's* attention to a different topic. This procedure is employed when a client seems to be rambling or otherwise avoiding an important area that needs addressing.

Short Michigan Alcoholism Screening Test (SMAST) A shortened version of the *Michigan Alcoholism Screening Test (MAST)*. It consists of 13 questions and can identify over 90% of alcoholics who take it.

short-term counseling *Counseling* that is set up to last a specific number of *sessions* and whose emphasis is usually limited. See also *brief therapy*.

siblings A person's brothers and sisters.

sibling position The position a child occupies in a family. See *birth order*.

sibling rivalry The competition between siblings within a *family* unit, usually for attention.

SIGI See *System of Interactive Guidance and Information*.

side effect The unexpected and unintended effect of a *treatment*, especially medications.

sidetracked When a *counselor* and *client* stray from an intended course of *treatment*.

significant difference/level A statistical term for a difference or result that is unlikely due to chance or randomness in regard to the effect of the *independent variable*. In *counseling* and social science *research* a significance level is set at.05 or lower (e.g., .01).

significant other A term coined by George H. Mead that refers to a parent, teacher, relative, or other person in one's life who is important and meaningful to that individual. Significant others influence a person's *thoughts*, *feelings*, and *behaviors*.

SII See *Strong Interest Inventory*.

silence A passive form of a lead in which the *counselor* pauses and allows the *client* to speak or elaborate on a topic. Silence encourages clients to talk or reflect.

singlehood A lifestyle that may be permanent or transitional where an *adult* functions independently disconnecting and reconnecting with family and friends and establishing an *identity*.

single blind A *research* procedure in which participants are unaware of which *experimental group* they are in until after the *experiment* is complete. See *double blind*.

single parent A person of either *sex* who has complete responsibility for the raising of his or her *children*. Single-parent *situations* are usually created by *divorce* or the death of a spouse but may occur through *choice,* such as in adoption.

single-parent family A *family* that includes one parent, either biological or adoptive, who is solely responsible for care of *self* and *child/children*. Single-parent families are created as a result of *divorce,* death, abandonment, unwed pregnancy, or adoption.

single-subject research design A procedure in which *counselors* follow one of two *methods* in *evaluation*. In the first method they follow an *ABAB research design* to evaluate the *relationship* of an *intervention* on *changes* that may have occurred. In the other method, counselors employ a *multiple baseline design* that more randomly measures change across subject, *variables,* or *situations*.

SIT See *stress inoculation training*.

situation **1.** A *psychodrama* concept in which the emphasis is on the present, and natural barriers of time, space, and states of existence are obliterated. Under these circumstances, *clients* are able to work on past *problems*, future fears, and current difficulties in a here-and-now atmosphere. **2.** A person's position or status in regard to such factors as location, context, conditions and circumstances. A person may be in a favorable situation if s/he has health, wealth, and happiness; however, in *counseling* most clients' situations are of some concern.

situational crises   Times of *change* in the *life span* that are unexpected but significant and affect a person for better or worse such as winning the lottery or being in an accident.

situational interpretation   A level of *interpretation* that is context centered and emphasizes the immediate interactions of the *client*.

situational therapy   Activity groups for children ages 8 to 15 based on *psychoanalytic* principles first created by Samuel Slavson.

six-step model of crisis intervention   An organized framework to guide *counselors* in dealing with crises. Developed by James and Gilliland, the steps are (1) define the problem, (2) ensure *client* safety, (3) provide support, (4) examine alternatives, (5) make plans, and (6) obtain commitment.

Sixteen Personality Factor (16 PF) Questionnaire   A *personality inventory* based on the *trait theory* of Raymond B. Cattell. The *questionnaire* measures self-reported opposite characteristics of individuals (e.g., reserved versus outgoing) on 16 different dimensions.

skeleton keys   A concept in Steve deShazer's *brief therapy* approach. Skeleton keys are *interventions* that have worked before and that have a universal application.

skewness   The degree of asymmetry in a *frequency distribution*. Skewness is positive if more *scores* are to the left of the *mean* and negative if more scores are to the right of the mean.

slander   Injury to a person's character or reputation through *verbal* means.

sleep disorders   A *DSM* category of *disorders* that can be either primary (not caused by other medical conditions) or secondary (related to other specific disorders) in nature. There are multiple *factors* involved in sleep disorders, for example, *emotions*, *environment*, and *lifestyle*. Sleep disorders include *insomnia, hypersomnia, narcolepsy,* nightmares, night terror, and sleepwalking.

sliding fee scale   The practice of charging *clients* a fee based on their ability to pay (i.e., on their income).

Slosson Intelligence Test (SIT)   A quick (10 to 30 minute) individual screening *test* of crystallized *verbal intelligence* normed for ages 4 years through 65.

SMAST   See *Short Michigan Alcoholism Screening Test.*

snorting   The ingestion of powdered *drugs* through rapid inhalation through the nostril.

snow   See *cocaine.*

social action   *Behaviors* designed to promote *social justice* and eradicate social inequities.

social construction   An idea about the way things are or should be that is built more on the shared *perceptions* of members of a society than on objective reality. According to the social construction point of view, there is no objective reality and no universal human nature.

social desirability   A *response* set in which a person tends to give answers that are more socially desirable than accurate.

social ecology   The social context of a *group.*

social exchange theory   An approach that stresses the *rewards* and costs of *interpersonal relationships* according to a behavioral economy. If individuals give more than they receive, they may well withdraw from a relationship; if the exchange is even or in their favor, they will continue in the relationship.

social influence model   In research conducted by Stanley Strong, he found that *counselors* have maximum influence with *clients* when they are seen as strong on two dimensions: *credibility* and *interpersonal attractiveness.*

social interest An *Adlerian counseling* term that describes not only a person's interest in others but also that person's interest in the interests of others. Individuals with social interest have a *need* to and are willing to contribute to the general social good of others.

social justice A belief system that values fair and equal treatment for all members of society.

social learning theory A *theory* developed by Albert Bandura that stresses the importance of *modeling* and *learning* through observation as a primary way of acquiring new *behavior*s and developing.

social modeling See *imitation.*

social people Individuals, according to Holland's *career* typology, who enjoy working in people oriented environments where they can help others and serve, such as teaching, advising, and serving. See *RIASEC.*

social reinforcement Attention given to an individual either verbally or nonverbally by a *significant other* that reinforces a *behavior* and makes it more likely to reoccur.

social science The study of people. Social science subjects include anthropology, history, psychology, and sociology.

Social Sciences Citation Index An index published by the Institute for Scientific Information (ISI). The multidisciplinary database contains searchable author abstracts covering the *journal* literature of the *social sciences.* It indexes 1,700 journals spanning 50 disciplines and covers individually selected, relevant topics from over 3,300 of the world's leading scientific and technical *journals.* Their Web site address is http://thomsonreuters .com/products_services/science/science_ products/a-z/social_sciences_citation_index

social time Time characterized by landmark social events in one's life such as marriage, parenthood, and retirement.

social work A *helping profession* that focuses on individual well-being in a social context and the well-being of society. Fundamental to social work is attention to the environmental forces that create, contribute to, and address *problem*s in living.

social workers *Mental health* professionals who are trained in case work, *group work,* and community organization approaches. They provide social services and *counseling* to individuals and families with medical, *legal,* economic, or social *problem*s.

social-cognitive theory A form of *learning* in which people acquire new knowledge and *behavior* by observing other people and events without engaging in the behavior themselves and without any direct *consequences* to themselves. Social-cognitive *theory* is also referred to as *observational learning, imitation, social modeling,* and *vicarious learning.*

socialization The *processes* through which a child learns the *rules* and *norms* of a society.

societal regression The idea that if a society is under too much *stress* (e.g., population growth, economic decline); it will regress because of too many toxic forces countering the tendency to achieve differentiation.

Society of Counseling Psychology See *Division 17 of the American Psychological Association.* See *Counseling Psychology, Division 17 of the American Psychological Association.*

sociocultural theory A theory that focuses on the *zone of proximal development,* which emphasizes a range of tasks too difficult for a child to complete alone but is possible with the help of others. The implication for *counseling* is to use *groups* to facilitate *learning* and accomplishment.

sociodrama A *group technique* devised by Jacob L. Moreno that uses *role playing* to help persons learn about and understand social *factor*s that influence human interactions.

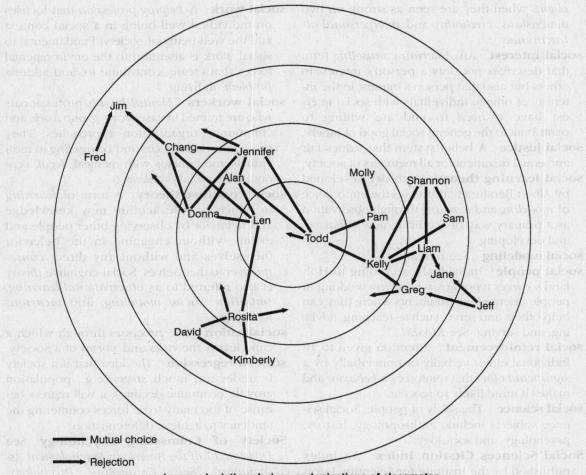

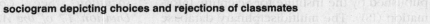

sociogram depicting choices and rejections of classmates

sociogram A tool of *sociometry* that plots group members' interactions with lines. In a sociogram, circles represent members in a *group,* and lines indicate persons closest to each other.

sociometry A phenomenological *method* for investigating and describing *interpersonal relationship*s within a *group.* In sociometry, members of a group provide *feedback* about their interpersonal preferences (i.e., what attracts or repulses them).

sociopath A term used in relation to a *psychopath* that implies the *pathology* of the person is not an isolated, *intrapsychic phenomenon* but rather a complicated *problem* between the individual and society.

SOICC See *State Occupational Information Coordinating Committee*

SOLER An acronym devised by Gerald Egan (1998) that summarizes five *nonverbal* skills involved in initial attending. The "S" is a reminder to face the *client* squarely, which can be understood literally or metaphorically, depending on the *situation*. The "O" is a reminder to adopt an open posture, free from crossed arms and legs, and showing nondefensiveness. The "L" reminds the *counselor* to lean toward the *client*. Leaning too far forward and being too close may be frightening, but leaning too far away indicates disinterest. The "E" represents eye contact. Good eye contact with most clients is a sign that the counselor is attuned to the client. The "R" is a reminder to the counselor to relax. A counselor needs to be comfortable.

soliloquy technique A *psychodrama technique* that involves the *protagonist* (i.e., the *client*) giving a monologue about his or her *situation* as he or she is acting it out. A variation on this activity is the therapeutic soliloquy *technique*.

solution-focused family therapy An approach to working with families, originated by Steve deShazer, Insoo Kim Berg, and Bill O'Hanlon, that is systemic, brief, present oriented, focused on small *changes,* and geared to having *client* families examine exceptions to their typical ways of interacting. The approach emphasizes *solutions* (as opposed to *problems*) and *family* resources, including those that are both unique and universal.

somatoform disorders *Mental disorder*s that take the form of physical illnesses. The *DSM* classifies *conversion reaction, hypochondriasis,* and *body dysmorphic disorder* under somatoform disorders.

specialist A professional who has a high level of education and experience in a given discipline or area of expertise (e.g., a *clinical mental health counselor*, a *school counselor*).

specification A *transactional analysis* term for the *identification* of the *ego state* that initiated a *transaction*. Specification takes place from the *adult ego state* of both *client* and *counselor.*

speed A lay term for *amphetamines.*

speed test A *test* with a large number of *items* of the same or equal difficulty but having a short time for completion. Speed tests are often used in assessing clerical or mechanical skills.

spillover effect The impact on others who are *helping* or watching a main character in *psychodrama* reach resolution on important issues. These "others" see themselves as interacting in a new and better way.

spiritual bypass The unhealthy misuse of the spiritual life to avoid dealing with psychological difficulties.

spirituality A word that comes from the Latin "spiritus," meaning "breath of life." Spirituality refers to a unique, personally meaningful experience of a transcendent dimension that is associated with wholeness and *wellness*. It is an active *process* that involves a quest for meaningfulness in one's life. It is not the same as *religion*. See religion.

spitting in the client's soup An *Adlerian counseling technique* in which the *counselor* points out certain *behavior*s to *client*s and thus ruins the payoff for the behavior. For example, a mother who always acts superior to her daughter by showing her up may continue to do so after the behavior has been pointed out, but the *reward* for doing so is now gone.

split-half reliability A *method* of computing *test reliability* in which one half of the *test* is correlated with the other half.

splitting A *psychoanalytic* term for object representations being viewed dichotomously as either all good or all bad. The result is a *projection* of good and bad qualities onto persons within one's *environment*. Through splitting, people are able to control their *anxiety* and even the objects (i.e., persons) within their environment by making them predictable. However, those who engage in splitting pay a high price because of the misrepresentation of the person in question.

spontaneous recovery The sudden reappearance of a *behavior* after it has been extinguished.

S

sports counseling   A type of *counseling* that focuses on an athlete's psychoemotional needs and difficulties as well as the athlete's development as a person.

squeeze technique   An approach used in sexual *therapy* in which a woman learns to stimulate and stop the ejaculation urge in a man through physically stroking and firmly grasping his penis.

stability   See *test-retest reliability*.

stable coalition   A fixed and inflexible union (such as that of a mother and son) that becomes a dominant part of the *family*'s everyday functioning. See also *coalition*.

staff notes   AKA *case notes*. See *case notes*.

stage   **1.** An identifiable period in a person's life such as childhood or old age. **2.** The area in *psychodrama* in which the action takes place.

stage theories   Theories that propose human *development* goes through *stages*, psychological as well as physical, each building on the other. Examples of stage theories are those proposed by Sigmund Freud, Erik Erikson, Jean Piaget, and Lawrence Kohlberg.

stagnation   A part of Erik Erikson's seventh *stage* of *psychosocial development* where a person becomes self-centered and stagnant. It is the opposite of *generativity*.

stamps   See *trading stamps*.

standard deviation   The square root of the *variance* and the most widely used measure of *variability*. The wider the spread of *scores* from the *mean,* the larger the standard deviation.

standard error of the mean   The *standard deviation* of the *sampling distribution*.

standard error of measurement   A *statistic* that indicates what a person's *score* would likely be should they take the same *test* over and over.

standard of care   Professional conduct as practiced by reasonable and prudent practitioners who have specialized knowledge and ability in the *diagnosis* and treatment of clinical conditions.

standard score   A *score* that is used in a *norm-referenced* context and describes the location of a person's score within a set of scores.

standardization   **1.** Uniformity and consistency in the way a *process* is implemented. **2.** The administration of a *test* to a large number of people under standard conditions for the purpose of determining *norms*.

standardized test   A *test* that is composed of empirically selected materials and administered under standard conditions with definite directions. In addition, a standardized test contains *data* on its *reliability* and *validity,* has information on scoring and appropriate use, and has adequately determined *norms*.

Standards for Educational and Psychological Testing   A document recognized as the criteria against which *tests,* test procedures, test manuals, and other test information should be evaluated. The document was developed through the collaboration of the *American Psychological Association (APA),* American Educational Research Association, and National Council on Measurement in Education.

Standards for the Ethical Practice of Internet Counseling   A set of guidelines developed by the *National Board for Certified Counselors (NBCC)* that address practices unique to *Internet counseling* and are based on the principles of ethical practice that embody the NBCC Code of Ethics. Specific areas addressed include the counseling relationship, *confidentiality*, data security, *licensure*, and *certification*   (http://www.nbcc.org/ethics/Default.aspx).

Stanford Achievement Tests   A major *achievement test battery* that is used in grades 1.5 through 9.9. The Stanford Achievement Tests are updated and revised periodically.

Stanford-Binet Intelligence Scale   A popular individually administered *intelligence test*. *Items* on the Stanford-Binet are categorized according to age, with items at increased age levels being more difficult than items at early age levels. The Stanford-Binet is updated and revised periodically.

stanine A *standard score* scale consisting of the numbers 1 through 9 with a *mean* of 5 and a *standard deviation* of 2.

star Also known as *explorer*, Virginia Satir's term for the central character in the *family reconstruction process*.

State Occupational Information Coordinating Committee (SOICC) The state branch of *National Occupational Information Coordinating Committee (NOICC)* that works in conjunction with NOICC to accomplish overarching national goals. See *NOICC*.

statistical significant A difference in the *means* of *samples* that is not attributable to chance.

statistics The mathematical means researchers use in analyzing and interpreting *data*. Communication of these findings to others is done through numbers that describe a quality being measured.

statutory law *Law* passed by legislative bodies, such as state and national legislatures, and signed by an authorized source, such as a governor or the president.

STEP See *Systematic Training for Effective Parenting*.

stepfamily A *family* created when two people marry and at least one of them has been married previously and has a child. See also *blended family*.

stereotype A fixed image or *thought* of people, things, and places that is oversimplified, rigid, and often *prejudiced*. A stereotype allows no room for individual judgment. For example, some people hold a stereotype that like Napoleon, all short men have a desire for *power* or that all people who seek *counseling* are mentally ill.

stigma A *prejudice, stereotype,* or discrimination against a service such as *mental health treatment.* A stigma may be public or self-imposed. Either way, it sets up a negative reaction and/or avoidance of the service *provider*.

stimulant A *drug* of arousal including all forms of *cocaine, amphetamines,* and some prescription (as well as some over-the-counter weight-reducing) products.

stimulus Something that stirs people to action or effort and/or that excites them (e.g., a *change* in people's physical *environment* that introduces them to new individuals is a stimulus).

stimulus control Arranging the *environment* in such a way that a person can better control it in a desirable manner (e.g., if persons are tempted to overeat, they can make sure there is a limited quantity of snacks available to them).

storming The second *stage* of *group development,* in which there is *conflict* and turmoil as group members attempt to deal with issues. The *group* moves from *primary tension* (awkwardness about being in a strange *situation*) to *secondary tension* (intragroup conflict). During storming, group members and leaders struggle with issues related to *structure,* direction, control, *catharsis,* and *interpersonal relationships*.

storytelling A *counselor*'s use of others' experiences in the form of *metaphors*, analogies, or even fairy tales to illustrate how they overcame *problems* similar to the *client*'s. Stories suggest to clients, either indirectly or directly, ways to deal with their *situations*.

stranger anxiety A fear of new and unfamiliar people usually found in young children. See also *separation anxiety*.

strategic family therapy A systemic view of *problem behaviors* that focuses on the *process* rather than the *content* of *dysfunctional* interactions. Strategic family therapy strives to resolve *presenting problems* and pays little attention to instilling *insight*. This *therapy* is brief and limits the number of times a *family* can be seen.

strategic therapy/strategic family therapy A term coined by Jay Haley to describe the therapeutic work of Milton Erickson in which extreme attention was paid to details of *client* *symptom*s and the focus was to *change* behavior by manipulating it and not instilling *insight*.

stress   A state of tension in a person accompanied by physiological arousal and strain. Stress interferes with coping and functioning; if it does not abate after a period of time, *distress* may set in, causing a person mental or physical incapacitation.

stress inoculation training (SIT)   A *process* in which *client*s break down potentially stressful events into manageable units that they can think about and handle through *problem*-solving *technique*s. Units are then linked together so that possible events can be envisioned and handled appropriately.

stress management   Specific strategies of a physical, mental, or an environmental nature that a person uses to keep his or her *stress* low. For example, mental stress management might involve evoking relaxing images in one's mind before, during, or after a stressful *situation*; environmental stress management might take the form of avoiding whenever possible *situation*s that produce high stress.

stressors   Particular stimuli that produce *stress,* for example, working under a time restraint.

striving for perfection   **1.** An *Adlerian counseling theory* term for people's tendency to try to fulfill their own unique potential. **2.** A term in *psychoanalysis* for the *superego*'s attempt to live up to standards set by one's parents or society and to make life perfect as a result.

strokes   A *transactional analysis* concept for *verbal,* psychological, or *nonverbal* recognition of one person by another.

Strong Interest Inventory (SII)   An expansion of previous editions of the original Strong Vocational Interest Blank published in 1927. The SII is a pencil-and-paper self-administered career *interest inventory* that yields six general occupational themes and *personality* types (based on the acronym *RIASEC*: realistic, investigative, artistic, social, enterprising, and conventional). Results are displayed in basic interest scales, occupational scales, and professional scales.

structural analysis   An approach undertaken to understand what is happening within the individual through assessing how the three *ego states* (i.e., the *parent, adult,* and *child*) in *transactional analysis* interact and express themselves.

structured exercise   A specific exercise or technique, such as *role playing*.

structural family therapy   An approach, based on *general systems theory,* that advocates structural *changes* in the organization of the *family* unit. Particular attention is paid in this approach on changing interactional patterns in *subsystems* of the family, such as in the marital *dyad,* and establishing clear *boundaries* between family members.

structure   **1.** To set up *boundaries* in *counseling* (e.g., the length of the *sessions*, when they will occur, and where). **2.** A term in *structural family therapy* for an invisible set of functional demands by which *family* members relate to each other. **3.** To organize in a certain way, such as in logical *thinking* where one *thought* is premised on the preceding one.

structured activities   See *exercise*s.

structured life review   A procedure to help older people review their lives and become more integrated. Structured life reviews can take numerous forms, from individually telling one's story to someone else to a *reminiscing therapy* group experience.

student personnel point of view   See *Minnesota Point of View*.

student personnel work   A variety of services (e.g., *counseling,* financial aid, placement, student center, admission) in higher education that are provided by professionals who interact with students to help them make the most of their college experience.

student services   A theoretical model for working with students in a college *environment* that emphasizes the student as consumer and mandates services that *facilitate* development. This approach stresses a cafeteria-style manner of program offerings that students select according to what they think they *need*.

study groups A type of *task group,* typically involving three to four individuals who meet at least weekly to share information, knowledge, and expertise about a course in which they are all enrolled. The idea is that each group member will support and encourage the others and will obtain *insight* and knowledge through the group effort.

style of life An *Adlerian counseling* concept for describing the way one prefers to live and relate to others. Adlerians stress that a faulty *lifestyle* is based on competitiveness and a striving to be superior to others.

style-shift counseling A *method* of *counseling* in which as *need*s change, *counselors* depart from the *theory* they are using to another approach that is a better fit for the *client*.

subconscious A *psychoanalytic* concept that includes aspects of the *conscious* and *unconscious*.

subgroup **1.** A clique of group members who band together, often to the detriment of the *group* as a whole. **2.** A small group within a group.

subject **1.** A course of study such as *counseling*. **2.** A term that is sometimes used in *research* studies to describe a *participant*.

subjective reasoning A type of reasoning that places *feelings* on the same level as facts.

sublimation A positive form of *displacement* in which a drive that cannot be expressed directly is channeled into constructive activities. For example, those who are unable to express themselves sexually may take care of *children*. Sigmund Freud thought sublimation was not only a *defense mechanism* but a major means of building civilization.

subpoena A *legal* document ordering a person to appear in court at a certain time.

subproblems Smaller, more manageable *problem*s broken down from larger, more complicated problems to provide leverage and focus.

subset A set within a set, such as the number of *ADHD* children within a school setting.

substance A *drug* of *abuse,* a medication, or a toxin.

substance abuse The habitual and often addictive use of *alcohol, drug*s, and tobacco. *Drug*s are any *substance* other than food that can affect the way a person's mind and body works. Drugs include *stimulants, depressant*s, and *hallucinogen*s. A person who abuses substances is known as a *substance abuser*.

Substance Abuse and Mental Health Services Administration (SAMHSA) A division of the Department of Health and Human Services. Its mission is on building *resilience* and facilitating recovery for people with or at risk for mental or *substance* use disorders (www.samhsa.gov).

substance dependence People who use *substances,* such as *alcohol* or drugs, in a self-damaging way, usually with the knowledge that what they are doing is harmful.

substance-related disorders A category in the *DSM* that includes psychological and behavioral disorders associated with *substance abuse* (e.g., abuse of *alcohol, amphetamine*s, *caffeine, cannabis, cocaine, hallucinogen*s, *inhalant*s, *nicotine, opiates, phencyclidine hydrochloric, sedatives,* or *polysubstances*) as well as induced *disorder*s resulting from the *abuse*.

subsystems Smaller units of the *system* as a whole. In *counseling,* a subsystem is usually composed of members of a *family* who, because of age or function, are logically grouped together (e.g., such as parents). They exist to carry out various family tasks.

subtest A subset of *item*s on a *test* or a distinct portion of a test.

success identity The development of a psychologically healthy sense of *self* by being accepted as a person by others. Especially important in this *process* is experiencing love and worth.

successive approximation   The *process* of *learning* in small gradual steps; a procedure used in *shaping*.

suicidal ideation   Thoughts associated with killing oneself.

suicide   The intentional taking of one's life.

summarize/summarization   *Reflections* by a *counselor* or *client* that recall significant events or *learning* experiences in a *counseling* session. Summarization prevents fragmentation and provides continuity and *meaning*. As a *technique,* summarization is best used at the beginning or end of a counseling session or after a lengthy dialogue in which several points were made.

superego   A *psychoanalytic* concept for that part of the *psyche* that contains the *values* of parents and parental figures. The superego operates according to the *moral principle* by punishing the person through the *conscience* when he or she disobeys parental messages and by rewarding the person through the *ego ideal* when parental teachings are followed. The superego strives for perfection.

superiority complex   A term in *Adlerian counseling theory* for the *overcompensation* by a person for *feelings* of *inferiority.*

supervision   An intensive, *interpersonally* focused, individual or *group relationship* in which a more experienced *helping professional* is designated to *facilitate* the development of therapeutic competence in less-experienced professionals.

support group   A type of *self-help group* in which members share a common concern but in which there is a professional *group leader.*

supporting   Providing encouragement and *reinforcement* for a *client* to create *trust* or encourage desired *behaviors.*

suppression   The *conscious* mechanism of putting unwanted or unpleasant *thoughts* out of one's mind. Suppression is the opposite of *repression,* which is an *unconscious process.*

suppression of the conflict   A strategy that consists of playing down *conflict*. It is often used when issues are minor. It keeps *emotions* under control and helps *group leaders* build a supportive climate.

surplus reality   A *psychodrama* concept for psychological experiences that transcends the *boundaries* of physical reality. These experiences include *relationships* with those who have died, with those who have not been born, and with God and are often as important to people as their actual physical experiences.

survey/survey research   A form of *research* that involves soliciting information from people using a series of questions. Survey *data* can be collected in four ways: through personal *interviews*, mailed *questionnaires*, telephone interviews, and nonreactive measures such as existing *records* or archives. Data are gathered in either a structured or nonstructured way with either a *cross-section* of people (many people at one point in time) or *longitudinally* (the same people at two or more points in time).

symbiosis   An intertwined *relationship* between two people that is so fused that it is difficult if not impossible to distinguish a boundary between the two. This type of relationship is most often found in *dysfunctional* parent/child relationships.

symbol   Something that stands for or represents something else by reason of association. Symbols play an important part in the theories of Sigmund Freud and Carl Jung. See also *mandala*.

symbolic drawing of family life space   A projective *technique* in which the *counselor* draws a large circle and instructs family members to include within the circle drawings that represent the *family* and to place outside the circle drawings of those people and institutions that are not a part of the family. Then the family is asked to symbolically arrange themselves, again through a drawing within a large circle, according to how they relate to one another.

SYMLOG An acronym for System for the Multiple Level Observation of Groups, a *research* instrument used in *group work* for examining *personality* and *group relationship*s. The SYMLOG model yields a field diagram that pictures how members of a group are rated on three dimensions and how often members engage in any of 26 *role*s found in groups.

symmetrical relationship A couple relationship in which each partner tries to become competent in doing necessary or needed tasks. Members within these units are versatile. For example, a man or a woman can either work outside the home or care for children.

sympathy A *feeling* for someone (e.g., feeling sorry for a person who has experienced a significant *loss*). Sympathy is not the same as *empathy*.

symptom The manifestation of a *problem* or *disorder* by a *client* on either a physical or psychological level.

Symptom Checklist-90-Revised A standardized *checklist*, usually used during intake sessions in *mental health* settings, where clients or observers simply mark words or phrases that apply to them or their situation.

synchronous counseling Interaction that takes place between the *client* and the *counselor* during the moment of connection in *Internet counseling*. The opposite of *asynchronous counseling*.

syncretism A sloppy, unsystematic *process* of putting unrelated clinical concepts together; a crude but first step in the *process* of *learning eclectic counseling*.

system A set of elements standing in interaction with each other. Each element in the system is affected by whatever happens to any other element. Thus, the system is only as strong as its weakest part. Likewise, the system is greater than the sum of its parts.

System of Interactive Guidance and Information (SIGI) A computer-assisted *career guidance system* that contains five components: self-assessment (evaluate), identification of occupational alternatives (locate), review of occupational information (compare), review of information on preparation programs (plan), and the making of tentative occupational choices (strategize).

systematic desensitization A *counterconditioning process* in which a person's *dysfunctional anxiety* is reduced or eliminated through pairing it with incompatible *behavior,* such as muscular or mental relaxation. This is a step-by-step gradual procedure in which events that produce increasingly higher levels of *anxiety* are treated by pairing them with relaxation procedures and positive imagery one at a time.

Systematic Training for Effective Parenting (STEP) An *Adlerian counseling*-based *parent education group* program.

systemic family therapy Also known as the *Milan family therapy*; an approach that stresses the interconnectedness of *family* members while emphasizing the importance of *second-order change* in families.

systems theory Also known as *general systems theory*; a *theory* that focuses on the interconnectedness of elements within all living organisms, including the *family*. Based on the work of Ludwig von Bertalanffy, systems *theory* proposes that any living organism, including a family, is composed of interacting components, that is, people who mutually affect one another. Three basic assumptions distinguish systems theory from other counseling approaches: (1) the idea that causality is *interpersonal*, (2) the basic assumption that *psychosocial system*s are best understood as repeated patterns of interpersonal interaction, and (3) the idea that symptomatic *behavior*s should be understood from an interactional viewpoint. Much of *family counseling* is based on *systems theory*.

t

T score   A *derived score* on a *test* with a fixed *mean* of 50 and a fixed *standard deviation* of 10.

TA   See *transactional analysis*.

target population   The *population* a *consultant* or *counselor* specifically wishes to help.

Tarasoff v. Board of Regents of the University of California   A landmark *legal* case in *counseling* and *psychotherapy* in which the University of California was found liable for the murder of Tatiana Tarasoff by her boyfriend, Prosenjit Poddar, because the university had failed to warn Tarasoff and her *family* that Poddar had threatened to kill her. Although Poddar retracted his threat after he made it to a *psychologist* in the student health services, the California Supreme Court ruled that the failure of university officials to warn Tarasoff and her family was irresponsible. From this court decision came the principle of a *duty to warn* and the implication that *confidentiality* must be broken in counseling if a *client* is considered dangerous either to *self* or others.

task-approach skills   Work habits, expectations of performance, cognitive process, and emotional response patterns.

task group   A *group* in which there is an emphasis on accomplishment and efficiency in completing identified work *goals*. Task groups are united in their emphasis on achieving a successful *performance* or a finished product through collaborative efforts and take the form of task forces, committees, planning groups, community organizations, discussion groups, and *learning* groups. Task groups are also known as *work group*s.

task setting   A procedure in *Adlerian counseling* in which *client*s initially set short-range, attainable *goals* and eventually work up to long-term, realistic *objective*s. Once clients

make behavioral *changes* and realize some control over their lives, counseling ends.

TAP   See *Three Approaches to Psychotherapy*

TAT   See *Thematic Apperception Test*.

Tavistock Institute   A British psychoanalytic institute located in London whose present staff and past practitioners, such as *Wilfred Bion*, are (and were) concerned with *group* behavior and organizational behavior (http://www.tavinstitute.org/).

teachable moment   A time when people are ready and able to learn.

teaching to the test   See *coaching*.

team   A number of persons associated together in work or an activity, such as in athletic or artistic competition, who act and perform in a coordinated way to achieve a goal. Teams differ from basic *groups* in four main ways: They (1) have shared *goals* (as opposed to individual goals), (2) stress more interdependency, (3) require more of a commitment by members to a team effort, and (4) are by design accountable to a higher level within the organization.

team building   The effective development of a *team* through managing *conflict,* promoting *interpersonal* relationships, and achieving consensus.

teamwork   Work performed cooperatively by all members of a *group*.

teasing technique   A sexual *therapy* approach in which a woman learns to start and stop sexually stimulating a man.

technical eclecticism   An approach to integrating *counseling* theories that is best exemplified in the work of Arnold Lazarus. In this approach, procedures from different theories are selected and used in *treatment* without necessarily subscribing to the theories that spawned them. The idea is that *technique*s, not theories, are used in treating *client*s. Therefore, after properly assessing clients, *counselors* may use behavioral techniques (such as *assertiveness training*) with existential techniques (such as confronting persons about the *meaning* in their lives), if warranted by the *situation*.

technique   **1.** A discipline-specific procedure in *research*. **2.** A specific way, in *counseling*, of implementing part of a *theory*. For instance, *free association* is a technique in *psychoanalysis*.

teleological   Purposeful and goal directed *behavior*.

temperament   The overall *mood* or disposition of an individual.

tentative interpretation   A hunch about a *client*'s *situation* that is open to discussion. This type of *interpretation* is the opposite of absolute interpretation, where the client feels that the *counselor* is the expert and is more resistant or uncooperative.

Tennessee Self-Concept Scale (TSCS)   A self-administered instrument consisting of 100 questions on a *Likert scale*, ranging from "completely true" to "completely false," meant to measure different aspects of the *self* (e.g., self-satisfaction, personal self). The TSCS is updated and revised periodically.

terminal program outcomes   The most recognizable *goals* and *performance objectives* in *evaluation*.

termination   **1.** A transition event that ends one set of conditions so that other experiences can begin. Termination provides *client*s with an opportunity to clarify the *meaning* of their experiences, to consolidate the gains they have made, and to make decisions about the new *behavior*s they want. The decision to stop *counseling* should be made mutually whenever possible and should occur over a period of time rather than abruptly. Termination usually involves a four-step *process:* orientation, *summarization*, discussion of *goals, follow-up*. **2.** Another name for the final step in *group development*. See also *adjourning*.

tertiary prevention   Efforts, equivalent to *therapy*, to reduce the long-term *consequences* of a *disorder*.

test   Also known as a *psychological test*. A test is an *objective* or *projective* instrument that measures *behavior*(s) or reported behaviors and characteristics.

test adaptation   The *process* through which a *test* originally developed for one population is altered for another population that may have a different *culture*, language, or both.

test anxiety   Considerable concern over taking a *test* because of the fear that one might fail. High test anxiety is crippling; moderate test anxiety can be helpful and can increase a person's *performance*.

test battery   A group of *test*s utilized in the *evaluation* of a person or *group*. See also *battery*.

test bias   A *test* that discriminates against individuals or *groups* because of their backgrounds.

test interpretation   The *interpretation* of a *test* as to the *meaning* of its *score*s.

test score   *Test* results, usually reported in a quantifiable way.

test wiseness   A person's capacity to receive a high *score* on a *test* by *learning* how to utilize the characteristics of the test or the testing *situation* (e.g., *learning* to avoid making errors, using time effectively, and devising strategies for effective guessing).

test-retest reliability   The degree to which *score*s on a *test* are consistent, or stable, over time. Test-retest reliability is also known as *stability*.

testing effects   The tendency for most people to perform better on a *test* or task after having taken the same or a similar test or experienced a similar task. See *test wiseness*.

Tests in Print (TIP)   A comprehensive bibliography to all known commercially available *test*s that are currently in print. TIP is published by the *Buros Institute of Mental Measurements*.

Tetrahydrocannabinol (THC)   The active ingredient in *marijuana* and similar *substance*s, such as *hashish*.

T-group   1. An approach to *groups* developed at the *National Training Laboratories (NTL)* in the 1940s in which primary attention is devoted to *theory, group dynamics,* and social material involving groups. **2.** A small group of people who spend a period of time together both for *counseling* and educational purposes. Participants are encouraged to examine their *interpersonal* functioning.

thanatos   A term used in *psychoanalysis* for an *unconscious* drive toward ending life, i.e. the *death instinct*. It is one of the two basic *instinct*s within the *id*, the other being *eros,* the *life instinct*. See *life instinct*.

The Counseling Psychologist   The professional journal of APA's Division 17—*Society of Counseling Psychology*.

Thematic Apperception Test (TAT)   A projective *personality test* that is individually administrated. The TAT is made up of 20 cards with ambiguous pictures on them that the test taker is instructed to tell a story about.

thematical   interpretation   A   level   of *interpretation* that is broad based and covers the whole pattern of a person's existence, including *behavior*s that are self-defeating.

themes   Specific topics or subjects related to the genuine interests of *clients* or *group* participants, thereby holding their interest and inviting their participation. Many adolescent *groups* work best when they are *structure*d around themes.

theoretical   integrationism   A   form   of *eclecticism* that requires *counselor*s to master at least two *theories* before trying to combine them in an eclectic approach. The weakness of this approach is that it assumes some equality in *counseling* theories.

theory   A formally stated and coherent set of propositions that purports to explain a *range* of phenomena, order them in a logical way, and suggest what additional information might be gleaned under certain conditions. A theory guides empirical inquiry and is useful in testing *hypotheses*.

Theory X group leadership   An *authoritarian leader* who takes complete control and responsibility for a group, such as setting an agenda, making rules, and establishing *goals*.

Theory Y group leadership   A *democratic leader* who is a *facilitator* rather than a director and who encourages *group* interaction.

Theory Z group leadership   A *laissez-faire leader* who takes little or no responsibility for a *group* and assumes group members will take care of themselves.

therap-e-mail   See *Internet counseling*.

therapeutic alliance   Two people in therapeutic contact. There are three common factors to an effective therapeutic alliance: a collaborative relationship, an *affective* bond, and an agreement on *goals* and tasks.

therapeutic contracts   Specific, measurable, concrete statements of what *client*s intend to accomplish. Therapeutic contracts place responsibility on clients for clearly defining what, how, and when they want to *change*.

therapeutic factors   See *curative factors*.

therapeutic neutrality   Accepting and nonjudgmental *behavior* by *counselors,* especially when working with families. Neutrality keeps counselors from being drawn into *coalition*s and disputes and gives them time to assess the dynamics within the *family*. Neutrality also encourages family members to generate solutions to their own concerns. However, therapeutic neutrality may work against ethical decision making.

therapeutic professionals   *Mental health* professionals who have been educated to help people with *cognitive, affective, behavioral* and other *disorders* that have their origins in physical, psychological, or spiritual dimensions.

therapeutic   soliloquy   technique   A *psychodrama technique* in which private reactions to events in the life of a *protagonist* (i.e., a *client*) are verbalized and acted out, usually by other actors (i.e., *auxiliary egos*). See also *soliloquy technique*.

therapist A synonym, in *mental health* circles, for the word *psychotherapist*. A therapist is a trained health *provider*. Because there are a number of different types of therapists (e.g., physical, occupational, etc.), professionals who work with the mentally distressed are wise to use a prefix such as psycho- before the word *therapist*.

therapy A term sometimes used interchangeably with *psychotherapy* and *counseling*. Traditionally, therapy and psychotherapy have been used to describe psychological *interventions* with *clients* who have serious (as opposed to mild) disturbances and *disorders*. Therapy and psychotherapy are also traditionally associated with long-term *treatment*, although this distinction has become blurred in recent years with the onset of *brief therapy*.

thinking The *conscious* generation of ideas, *thoughts,* and *cognitions*.

third ear The idea set forth by Theodor Reik that *counselors* can often help best when they go beyond what the *client* has literally communicated and use their clinical *intuition* and hunches.

third force A term used by Abraham Maslow to describe *humanistic* approaches to *counseling* and *psychology*. The first and second forces are *psychoanalysis* and *behaviorism*.

third party An entity, such as a person or an organization, that is neutral and not connected or affiliated with parties that are engaged in an enterprise or activity, such as *counseling* or *mediation*. *HMOs* and *PPOs* are examples of third-party entities in *counseling* because they are not connected with the *process* itself but with reimbursement for the services.

third-degree games The deadly *games,* often played for keeps, in *transactional analysis*. There is nothing socially redeemable about third-degree games. See also *games*.

Thorazine A prescription medication known as an antipsychotic.

thought The intellectual *process* of representing ideas, beliefs, and images in one's mind in an organized manner. The process of thought is developmental and individually manifested in reason and expression. Thought is an underlying base on which the *theories* of *cognitive counseling* and *cognitive behavioral counseling* have been built. See also *cognition*.

thought stopping A cognitive behavioral *theory technique* in which *clients* are taught how to stop unproductive *obsession* about an event or person through overt and mental procedures.

Theory of Vocational Choice John Holland's theory that stresses the *interpersonal* nature of *careers* and associated lifestyles and the performance requirements of a *work* position. Individuals of a particular type are attracted to environments of similar types and achieve the most work satisfaction when their work environment matches their personality type. See *RIASEC*.

Three Approaches to Psychotherapy A film produced by Everett Shostrom in 1964 featuring a *client* named Gloria being counseled in individual sessions by Carl Rogers, Fritz Perls, and Albert Ellis.

tics Rapid, sudden, repetitive motor or vocal movements of an involuntary nature.

time-limited therapy An approach to *counseling* that limits the number of sessions (such as 10 in *strategic family therapy*) that *clients* may be seen in *treatment*. The idea is that a limited number of sessions will motivate clients to work harder on their specific issues.

time-out A *process* that involves the removal of persons (most often children) from an *environment* in which they have been reinforced for certain actions. *Isolation,* or "time-out," from *reinforcement* for a limited amount of time (approximately 5 minutes) results in the cessation of the targeted *behavior*.

time sampling A *research method* in which *behavior* is observed during specific times with the aim of recording the frequency of a specific behavior.

time tripping   A technique used in *multimodal therapy* where the client moves forward or backward in time to experience an event or resolve a problem.

TIP   See *Tests in Print*.

title law   Legislation requiring that *counselors* in *private practice* hold a state license or *certification* to use a professional title, such as "certified practicing counselor." A title *law* sometimes comes before more complete *licensure* legislation. In title law states, counselors may practice privately without the credential if they do not use the *legal* title.

token economy   A *system* of *reinforcement* used in *behavior modification* in which students or *clients contract* to earn token points of varying amounts in exchange for fulfilling specific *behavioral objectives*. They may then "cash" their tokens in for a *reward*.

tolerance   **1.** The decreasing effectiveness of a *drug* after repeated use. **2.** The capacity for and/or practice of respecting the beliefs and practices of others.

top-dog/underdog dialogue   A *technique* in *Gestalt therapy* in which *clients* are asked to examine the top-dog *introjections* they have learned from parents (usually represented by "shoulds" and "you" statements) and their own real *feelings* about *situations* (usually represented by "I" statements).

topic-specific groups   *Groups* that are centered around a particular topic (e.g., widowhood, sexuality, health, or the arts). They are designed ultimately to improve the quality of daily living for older people. They also assist the aged to find more *meaning* in their lives and to establish a group of like-minded people.

tort   A wrongful act that *legal* action is designed to set right; the concept on which civil *liability* rests. The legal wrong can be against a person, property, or even someone's reputation and may be unintentional or direct.

touching   A *nonverbal counseling response* usually meant to comfort or support. Touching is usually physical. It can be controversial if not done judiciously and correctly.

toxic   *Substances* or *thoughts* that can harm the body or the mind.

tracking   A way of *joining* in which the *counselor* follows the *content* (i.e., the facts) of the *client*.

trading stamps   A *transactional analysis* term for particular *feelings* the *child ego state* collects.

traditional college student   A student between the ages of 18 and 22 whose background and circumstances are similar to the majority of students found on a college campus.

traditional eclecticism   A form of *eclecticism* in which compatible features from diverse *counseling* sources are combined into a harmonious whole.

training-group   See *T-group*.

trait   An enduring characteristic of a person.

trait-and-factor theory   A *theory* that stresses that the *traits* of *clients* should first be assessed and then systematically matched with *factors* inherent in various *occupations*. Its most widespread influence occurred during the Great Depression, when E. G. Williamson championed its use. It has resurfaced in a more modern form, best reflected in the work of researchers such as John Holland. The trait-and-factor approach has always stressed the uniqueness of persons.

tranquilizer   A *drug* used to reduce mental disturbance, such as *anxiety* and tension. Examples of major tranquilizers are Thorazine, Stelazine, and Mellaril. Examples of minor tranquilizers are Valium and Librium.

transactional analysis   **1.** The name of the *theory* developed by Eric Berne. **2.** The analysis of what people do and say to one another. Transactional analysis often involves diagramming *ego state* (i.e., *parent, adult, child*) *transactions*. The diagramming of transactional analysis is *interpersonal*, in contrast to the *intrapersonal* diagramming of *structural analysis*. Transactions may occur on one of three levels: *complementary, crossed, or ulterior*.

transactions Social action between two or more people, manifested on social (*overt*) and psychological (*covert*) levels.

Transcendental Meditation A relaxation *technique* in which a person is given a *mantra* (a sound or word without any real meaning) to repeat silently again and again.

transescents Early *adolescents*; *children* in middle school.

transcultural counseling See *multicultural counseling*.

transferable skills Those skills that *clients* possess in life that may be applicable or useful in a number of settings, such as social skills. This term was first made popular in *career counseling* by Richard Bolles (1996) in *What Color Is Your Parachute?*, where he divided basic units of *occupations* into three families: things; people; and information, *data,* and ideas.

transference The *displacement* of *affect* from one person to another; the *projection* of inappropriate *emotions* onto someone else. Transference occurs when a person unconsciously reenacts a latter-day version of forgotten *childhood* memories and repressed *unconscious* fantasies in the *counseling* session. For example, a *client* might say to a *counselor* "You sound just like my mother" and start behaving as if the counselor were the client's mother.

transference pull A *client's* reaction to the image of the *counselor* in terms of the client's personal background and current conditions. The way the counselor sits, speaks, gestures, or looks may trigger a client reaction.

transgender A broad term used to describe the continuum of individuals whose *gender identity* and expression, to varying degrees, does not correspond with the social or cultural *norms* or expectation of their genetic *sex*.

transient children *Children* who have moved to a new community and a new school.

transients Individuals who move frequently and have no permanent home address.

transition An event or *nonevent* that results in changes to a person's roles, routines, or assumptions. For example, losing a job, not getting a job, getting married, moving, having a child.

transparent self The *self* as revealed to another in an open and honest way. Such a *process* invites disclosure on the part of the listener and helps to build a *relationship*. This idea and *research* supporting it were the result of clinical work by Sidney Jourard.

transpersonal theories/counseling *Theories* and *counseling* emphases that propose humans possess the potential to ascend beyond their ordinary limits and attain higher levels of *consciousness,* including transcendence of *self,* cosmic awareness, ecstasy, wonder, and *altruism*.

transsexual An individual who presents him/herself and lives as a *gender* different to his/her genetic sex at birth.

Transtheoretical model of change A model developed by Prochaska and associates that provides a way to conceptualize different levels of readiness for *change*: precontemplation, contemplation, preparation, action, and maintenance. Assessing a client's readiness for change according to these levels informs decisions regarding *treatment* and *interventions*.

transvestism Sexual gratification through dressing in the clothes of the opposite sex.

trauma An injury or nervous shock that is usually intense and unpleasant.

trauma counseling A three-stage process of helping after a *trauma*: establishment of safety; remembrance and mourning; and reconnection with ordinary life.

treatment Planned *interventions* to alleviate or modify a *disorder* or *change* a *dysfunctional* condition.

treatment contract A specific, concrete *contract* that emphasizes agreed-on responsibilities for both *counselors* and *clients*. The contract lets each know when *counseling goals* have been reached. *Behavioral therapy* approaches to *counseling* often make use of a treatment contract.

treatment plan   A plan a *counselor* makes in regard to a *client* that includes information such as the theoretical approach to use, frequency of *sessions*, length of sessions, and so on.

triadic questioning   The *process* of asking a third person how two other people in a *family* or *group* relate.

triage   The process of prioritizing sick or injured people for *treatment* according to the seriousness of their condition.

triangle   The basic building block of any emotional *system* and the smallest stable *relationship* system in a *family*, according to Murray Bowen.

triangulate   To focus on a *third party*. When people have *stress* within their marriages, they tend to turn their attention to and project on a third party such as a child, a church, a school, or even a physical ailment.

triangulation   The *process* in which dyadic *interpersonal relationship* difficulties are projected onto a third person or object (i.e., a *scapegoat*) thus relieving the tension in the *dyad*.

tricyclics   A popular class of *drugs* used to treat *depression* (e.g., imipramine).

tripartite model of multicultural counseling competencies   A model of *counseling* whose three components are the competencies necessary for effective work with *clients* from various cultures: skills, knowledge, and *awareness*.

trust   **1.** The first of Erik Erikson's virtues in his *psychosocial* model of *development*. *Trust* is developed in an infant when his or her *needs* are met consistently. It is the opposite of *mistrust*. **2.** The placing of confidence or faith in someone or something. If therapeutic progress is to be made, a *client* must develop trust in the *counselor*. Trust is

gained through the counselor's display of his or her credentials and over a period of time as the client realizes the counselor understands him or her, wants to be genuinely helpful, and will not betray *confidentiality* matters.

trustworthiness   The qualities of sincerity and consistency, in *counseling*. The *counselor* shows genuine concern about the *client* over time through patterns of *behavior* that demonstrate care. Many clients *test* the trustworthiness of the counselor by requesting information, telling a secret, asking a favor, inconveniencing the *counselor*, deprecating themselves, or *questioning* the motives and dedication of the counselor. Therefore, in order to *facilitate* the counseling *relationship*, it is essential that the counselor respond to the question of *trust* rather than the *verbal content* of the client.

T-score   A transformed standard *score* using 50 as the *mean* and 10 as the *standard deviation*. T-scores eliminate negative integers and are therefore desirable.

t-test   A commonly used statistical *test* that establishes whether a *significant difference* exists between two *sample means*. It is derived through a *ratio:* the difference between two sample means divided by an estimate of the *standard deviation* of the distribution of the differences.

Type A behavior   *Behavior* that is characterized by time-urgent, competitive, and hostile nature.

Type A stress   *Stress* associated with a *situation* that is foreseeable and avoidable, such as not walking in a dangerous area at night.

Type B behavior   *Behavior* that is characterized by patience, noncompetitiveness, and a relaxed attitude about time.

Type B stress   *Stress* associated with a *situation* that is neither foreseeable nor avoidable, such as an unexpected death.

Type C stress   *Stress* associated with a *situation* that is foreseeable but not avoidable, such as going to the dentist.

Type I error   Rejecting the *null hypothesis* when it should be accepted; to claim there is a real difference in *data* when there is not. Type I error is also known as an *alpha error*.

Type II error   Accepting the *null hypothesis* when it should be rejected; to claim there is not a real difference in *data* when there is. A Type II error is also known as a *beta error*.

u

UCR   See *unconditioned response*.

UCS   See *unconditioned stimulus*.

ulterior transaction   A *transaction* in *transactional analysis* in which two *ego states* operate simultaneously and one message disguises the other. Ulterior transactions appear to be complementary and socially acceptable even though they are not. For example, at the end of a date, one person may say to the other, "Do you want to come in and see my etchings?" On the surface this question might seem to be coming from the *adult ego state*. In reality it is coming from the *child ego state:* "Want to come in and have some fun together?"

unbalancing   When a *counselor* therapeutically allies with a *subsystem* in a *family*. In this procedure, the counselor supports an individual or subsystem against the rest of the family.

unconditional positive regard   Total acceptance of the experiences of a *client* without conditions; a nonpossessive caring and acceptance. According to Carl Rogers, unconditional positive regard is a *necessary and sufficient condition for change* to occur.

unconditioned response (UCR)   A *response* elicited automatically by an *unconditioned stimulus* (e.g., salivating at the sight of food).

unconditioned stimulus (UCS)   A *stimulus* (e.g., food) that automatically elicits an *unconditioned response* (e.g. salivating) prior to *learning*.

unconscious   The most powerful and least understood part of the *personality*. According to Freudian *theory*, the instinctual, repressed, and powerful forces of the personality exist in the unconscious.

undifferentiated family ego mass   Murray Bowen's term for excessive emotional togetherness or *fusion* within a *family*.

understanding   Accurately comprehending the meaning of a *client's verbal* and *nonverbal behavior*.

undoing   A *defense mechanism* in *psychoanalysis theory* in which a person engages in repetitive *rituals* to abolish the results of actions previously taken. For example, Lady Macbeth's action of repetitively washing her hands after urging her husband to commit murder is an attempt to "wash away" or undo what she has done.

unfinished business   Emotional debris from one's past that interferes with present functioning. For example, if someone hurts another and fails to resolve the *conflict* with that person, he or she may avoid that person.

unimodal   A *frequency distribution* in which there is a single *score* class that has the highest frequency (i.e., a single peak).

unintentional civil liability   A lack of intent to cause injury.

unipolar   A major *depression mood disorder*, opposite of *bipolar disorder* in which there are two poles.

univariate   The study of a single *variable*.

universal approach to multicultural counseling   An approach to *multiculturalism* that includes *ethnicity, gender, lifestyle,* age, *religion, disability,* and so forth. It is a more inclusive approach than the *focused approach to multicultural counseling*.

universal culture The commonality shared by all cultures and people that transcend cultural boundaries, for example, bodily needs, feelings, cognitions.

universalization A *client*'s realization that he or she is not unique in regard to his or her concern.

unknown self One of the four quadrants in the *Johari Awareness Model*. The unknown *self* is not known to self or to others.

unlearned behavior Innate, reflex, and instinctive *behavior* that occurs without training, conditioning, learning or instruction. It is *unconditioned behavior*.

unlearning Eliminating previously learned *behavior*, often through *counterconditioning* and *extinction*.

unprofessional Outside of or in violation of the conduct expected and required of a person in a *profession*.

unrealistic aspirations *Goals* beyond a person's capabilities.

uppers A lay term for *amphetamines*.

utilitarian marriage A couple that gets or stays married for practical rather than emotional purposes.

utilization principle A foundation of *solution-focused family therapy* originated by Milton Erickson that states *counselors* should use whatever *client*s present in *counseling* as a basis and means for client solutions and *change*. Erickson believed that people have within themselves the resources and abilities to solve their own *problems*.

utilization review The process where a *managed care organization* (MCO) reviews the *diagnosis, treatment plan*, and response to treatment before authorizing the use or extension of a client's benefit plan.

v

V codes Conditions for which *mental health* services are sought, such as bereavement or an *identity problem*, but which are not considered *disorders*. These codes are listed in the back of the *DSM*. Most third-party payers do not reimburse mental health professionals if V codes are the only reason given for seeking *treatment*.

validity The extent to which a *test* measures what it purports to measure, for example, certain *traits*, characteristics, *behaviors*, or constructs. Validity makes a test useful and meaningful.

Valium A prescriptive *drug* utilized as a tranquilizer for *anxiety* and *panic attacks*.

values Principles or qualities that are desirable. Basically, there are four domains of values: personal, *family,* political/social, and ultimate. Each has an impact on the other. *Ethics* are based on values.

variable A property, *measurement,* factor, or characteristic that varies and can be measured.

variability The amount of spread in a distribution of *scores*.

variance A statistical *measurement* of how widely spread *scores* are from the *mean*.

venereal diseases Sexually transmitted diseases such as syphilis, gonorrhea, and genital herpes.

verbal Expression through the use of either oral or written language.

verbal test A *test* that requires an oral or written *response*. It is the opposite of a *performance test*.

verbalizing presuppositions An experiential *technique* in which the *counselor* helps families take the first step toward *change* by talking of *hope* or dreams that the *family* has.

verbatim account A word-by-word transcript of a *counseling* session including *nonverbal* factors such as *silence* and *body language*.

vertical stressors   Events dealing with *family* patterns, myths, secrets, and legacies. Vertical stressors are historical phenomena that families and their members inherit from previous generations.

Veterans Administration (VA)   A federal government agency that provides patient care and federal benefits to veterans and their dependents, including *mental health* services (http://www.va.gov/).

vicarious   The act of substituting observation and imagination for one's own *behavior* and thus receiving pleasure or pain from the behaviors of others, such as one's children or partner.

vicarious learning/conditioning   Learning through observing others. See *imitation*.

victim   1. A *position* in a *transactional analysis game* in which the person assumes a stance of appearing to be innocent. 2. A person who is *abused, neglected,* or *maltreated* by another.

violence   *Aggression* with extreme harm as its intent.

visitors   A type of *client,* classified by Steve deShazer, characterized by no overt complaints and whose rationale for being in *counseling* comes from an exterior source, such as a court order. See also *complainants; customers*.

vocation   The *work* in which one is regularly employed. A vocation usually is composed of a number of *jobs*.

vocational counseling   See *career counseling*.

vocational maturity   See *career maturity*.

Vocational Preference Inventory (VPI)   A pencil-and-paper *personality test* composed of 160 *items* in which individuals are asked to circle *occupations* they like or might consider. The VPI is based on *RIASEC,* John Holland's *theory* of vocational adjustment.

vocational rehabilitation   A *counseling* specialty that focuses on serving individuals with physical, emotional, intellectual, and behavioral disabilities. Vocational rehabilitation counseling practice requires knowledge in areas of medical terminology, *diagnosis, prognosis,* vocational *evaluation* of *disability*-related limitations, and *job* placement in the context of a socioeconomic *system*.

voice   Carol Gilligan's term for moral language. Accordingly, men's voice is based on individual *justice* and independence; women's voice is based on *care,* connectedness, and concern for others.

voyeurism   Sexual gratification through clandestine observations of other people's sexual activities or sexual anatomy.

VPI   See *Vocational Preference Inventory*.

vulnerable populations   Individuals who experience a similar kind of *stress* for an extended time such as the poor, homeless, unemployed, pregnant teens, people with chronic disease, *victims* of *discrimination,* and those undergoing *divorce* and marital *distress*.

w

WAIS   See *Wechsler Adult Intelligence Scale*.

warmth   A positive *feeling* as well as the ability to demonstrate genuine caring, concern, and *acceptance* of others.

warm-up   An activity staged at the beginning of a *group* experience to help group members become better acquainted or to prepare them to become more relaxed or focus on areas they wish to explore.

washout period   The period of time in *research* when there is no *treatment* given to a *client*.

WDEP system An acronym device created by Robert Wubbolding as a way of *helping counselors* and *clients* make progress in *reality therapy.* In this *system* the "W" stands for wants; at the beginning of the *counseling process,* counselors find out what clients want and in turn share their wants for and *perceptions* of clients' *situations.* The "D" stands for the direction of clients' lives and exploring that direction. The "E" stands for *evaluation* and is the cornerstone of reality therapy. Clients are helped to evaluate their *behaviors* to determine how responsible their personal behaviors are. The "P" stands for plan. A client focuses on making a plan for changing *behaviors.* The plan stresses actions that the client will take, not behaviors that he or she will eliminate. The best plans are simple, attainable, measurable, immediate, and consistent. Clients are requested to make a commitment to the plan of action. If the client fails to accomplish the plan, the client suffers the natural or reasonable *consequences* of that failure.

web counseling See *Internet counseling.*

Wechsler Adult Intelligence Scale (WAIS) A popular individually administered *intelligence test* for individuals ages 16 and up. The WAIS is revised periodically and yields *verbal, performance,* and overall *intelligence quotient (IQ) scores.*

Wechsler Intelligence Scale for Children (WISC) A popular individually administered *intelligence test* for children ages 6 to 16 years. The WISC is revised periodically and yields *verbal, performance,* and overall IQ *scores.* The six *verbal subtests* on the WISC are general information, general comprehension, arithmetic, similarities, vocabulary, and digit span. The six performance *subtests* on the WISC are picture completion, picture arrangement, block design, object assembly, coding, and mazes.

Wechsler Preschool and Primary Scale of Intelligence (WPPSI) A popular individually administered *intelligence test* designed for children ages 4 years to 6 years, 6 months. The WPPSI is revised periodically and yields *verbal, performance,* and overall *intelligence quotient (IQ)* scores.

Wechsler scale A *standard score* scale with a *mean* of 10 and a *standard deviation* of 3, used with the *Wechsler intelligence tests.*

Wechsler-Bellevue Scale The predecessor of all the Wechsler series of *intelligence tests* developed by David Wechsler. The Wechsler-Bellevue Scale Form I, published in 1939 at Bellevue Hospital in New York, was strictly for adults; it was followed by the Wechsler-Bellevue Scale Form 2, published in 1947. The Form I version of the test was completely revised again in 1955 and became the *Wechsler Adult Intelligence Scale (WAIS).*

Weldon v. Virginia State Board of Psychologists Examiners A 1974 decision by the Virginia Supreme Court that stated that *counseling* was a *profession* distinct from *psychology.*

wellness A state of being that emphasizes good health, a positive *lifestyle,* and *prevention.* See also *positive wellness.*

weltanschauung A German word for *worldview.* See also *worldview.*

we/they mentality An overidentification with a particular *group* that tends to develop into an antagonism toward other groups. Other points of view are seen as "uninformed," "naive," or "heretical."

Wickline v. State of California A 1987 landmark medical case about the issue of responsible treatment of *clients* where the service provider was held liable for the *HMO's* decision to limit hospitalization, even though the provider had recommended additional treatment. The court maintained that the provider did not protest the HMO's decision aggressively enough.

wheel A *group* formation in which only the leader, or center spoke, has face-to-face interactions with others in the group.

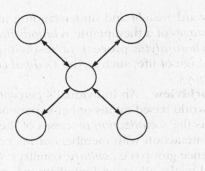

wheel

wheel or circle of influence People who have been important to the *star,* or *explorer,* in Virginia Satir's *family reconstruction* model.

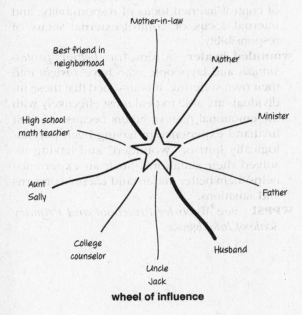

wheel of influence

why questions A focused query intended to elicit information about the reason, purpose, or cause of a *behavior.* However, many individuals do not know "why" and are put on the defensive when asked.

Wide Range Achievement Test (WRAT) A frequently used and easily administered

achievement test designed for a wide *range* of ages, kindergartners through adults. The WRAT is periodically revised and covers reading, spelling, and arithmetic.

will to power An *Adlerian counseling* concept for a person's striving for superiority and dominance in order to overcome *feelings* of *inferiority.*

William Glasser Institute See *Institute for Reality Therapy.*

wired A lay term for someone who is under the influence of *drugs.*

WISC See *Wechsler Intelligence Scale for Children.*

wisdom The ability to make effective *choices* among alternatives.

withdrawal 1. Removing oneself physically or psychologically from people or events that are disturbing. 2. The physical and psychological *symptoms* that occur in an addicted person when their use of *drugs* is discontinued. The severity of withdrawal is dependent on what *drug* was being taken and the abruptness of the cessation. See also *detoxification.*

withdrawal from the conflict A strategy that involves *group leaders* distancing themselves from *conflict* and postponing *interventions.*

word association test A *personality test* in which a person responds with the first word that comes to mind after another word is read by the examiner (e.g., a *response* to the word "mother" might be the word "warm").

work Activities that are engaged in for gain or *reward* rather than for the pleasure that might be derived from them.

Workforce Investment Act Federal legislation passed in 1998 intended to guide the implementation of *One-Stop Career Centers.*

work group See *task groups.*

Work of the Counselor One of the early and influential texts in the *counseling profession* written by Leona Tyler.

work sample See *performance test.*

work up The use of *tests* and *interviews* to acquire information to *diagnose* a *client.*

workaholic   A person with *Type A behavior* who is a hard-driving perfectionist and in a hurry most of the time. Workaholics often prefer to act alone and have a hard time delegating authority. People with Type A behavior may be at higher risk than others of developing heart attacks and other *stress*-related conditions. Type A people can benefit from training in how to relax, how to manage their anger, and how to manage their time.

working alliance   An agreement between a *counselor* and a *client* on the *goals* and tasks on which they will focus. They form an emotional bond in this mutual act of *counseling*.

working out a compromise   A *process* in which each party involved gives up a little to obtain a part of what they want to avoid *conflict*. The result is a win–win *situation* in which cooperative *behavior* and collaborative efforts are encouraged. This approach is effective in *groups* in which there are limited resources.

working stage   The most unified and productive stage in individual, *group,* or *family counseling*. It focuses on the *achievement* of individual and group *goals* and/or the movement of a family or group as a *system* into new ways of functioning. The working stage is sometimes known as the *action stage*.

working through   **1.** A *psychoanalytic technique* that refers to the *client's* movement toward *insight* and understanding in the latter *stages* of a therapeutic *relationship*. **2.** A *psychoanalytic* process of resolving a critical stage of life, such as the *Oedipal complex* for boys.

worldview   An individual's *perception* of the world based on his or her experiences as well as the *socialization processes* of the person in interaction with members of his or her reference group (i.e., *culture,* country). Worldviews directly affect and mediate people's belief *systems*, assumptions, modes of *problem* solving, decision making, and conflict resolution styles. The four most prevalent worldviews as proposed by Derald Wing Sue are internal *locus of control* and responsibility, external locus of control and responsibility, external locus of control/internal locus of responsibility, and internal locus of control/external locus of responsibility.

wounded healer   A term for *helping professionals* and laypeople who have *insight* into their own suffering. It is assumed that these individuals are able to deal most effectively with the emotional pain of others because of their firsthand experience in having been psychologically hurt or "wounded" and having resolved their situations. Such an experience helps them better understand *clients'* concerns and situations.

WPPSI   See *Wechsler Preschool and Primary Scale of Intelligence*.

X

xenophobia   An intense and persistent fear of strangers or foreigners.

y

Y A *group* formation that combines the structural elements of a *wheel* and *chain* group arrangement and has a perceived leader. The Y arrangement is similar to the chain in that group members may become frustrated in not having direct contact with each other and that information may not be equally shared.

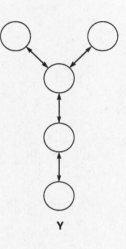

Y

YAVIS An acronym for young, attractive, *verbal*, intelligent, and successful. The acronym is used to describe the most successful candidates for traditional *counseling*.

yellow jackets See *barbiturates*.

yoga A form of *meditation* that involves a number of *techniques* such as breathing *exercises*, body postures, and focused concentration. Yoga is sometimes employed in *counseling* settings to help *clients* relax or gain *insight*.

young adult/adulthood The *stage* of *maturation* between 20 to 40 years old. The primary concerns of young adults, according to Erik Erikson, are establishing an *identity* and finding *intimacy*.

young-old Individuals between ages 65 and 74.

z

z score A number that results from the transformation of a *raw score* into units of *standard deviation*. A z score indicates how far above or below the *mean* a given *score* is.

zeitgeist A German word that means "spirit of the times." Understanding the zeitgeist, or cultural climate, of an era gives one *insight* into the *thoughts* and actions of people of that period.

zero-sum game A *game* in which there is a winner and loser. In marriages, some couples argue with the assumption that one must win and be correct and the other must lose and be incorrect. Zero-sum games produce *feelings* of resentment and revenge from losers and lead to more intensified arguments and *behaviors*. Zero-sum games are the opposite of *non-zero-sum games*.

Zoloft A popular antidepressant medicine.

zombie A street term for a person who uses a lot of *drugs*.

zone of proximal development Part of Lev Vygotsky's sociocultural theory that emphasizes a range of tasks too difficult to complete alone but possible with the help of others, which he called "*scaffolding*".

Z-score A *standard score* that expresses the number of *standard deviations* a *raw score* is from the *mean*. Numerically, Z-scores are the same as standard deviations (e.g., a 2 standard deviation above the mean is a Z-score of +2). Z-scores always have a mean of 0 and a standard deviation of 1 that can be positive or negative. A Z-score is also known as a sigma score as well as a standard score.

y

z

zombie A street term for a person who is a bit offensive.

Appendix A: Prominent Names in the Counseling Profession

a

Ackerman, Nathan (1908–1971) A pioneer in family counseling who helped focus the attention of psychoanalysis and the profession of psychiatry on the treatment of family units. Ackerman was cofounder of *Family Process*.

Adler, Alfred (1870–1937) A Vienna theorist who formulated a theory of counseling that focused on social interests as being the main motivators of human interactions.

Altekruse, Michael A past president of ACES and North Central ACES, Altekruse has been influential in working with CACREP and in the governance of counselor education.

Arbuckle, Dugald A former president of the American Counseling Association in 1959–1960. Arbuckle is a leading writer and advocate of existential and humanistic counseling.

Arnold, Mary Smith (1946–2003) An active advocate for social justice causes in counseling.

Arredondo, Patricia One of the authors of the *Multicultural Counseling Competencies and Standards* and the first Latina to be president of the American Counseling Association.

Aubrey, Roger (1929–1997) A leading writer in the field of counseling and the 28th president of the Association for Counselor Education and Supervision.

b

Baker, Stan A leading author in the field of school counseling.

Bandura, Albert The founder of social learning theory (SLT), a theory related to behaviorism. Bandura is best known for his emphasis on modeling as a way of learning. He contends that most people learn by imitating others, through observation.

Barret, Bob A leader in the fight for the rights of gays, lesbians, bisexuals, and transgender people within the counseling profession.

Beck, Aaron A Philadelphia psychiatrist and director of the Center for Cognitive Therapy at the University of Pennsylvania's Department of Psychiatry, Beck developed a cognitive approach to mental disorders at about the same time that Albert Ellis developed his ideas about rational emotive behavior therapy (in the late 1950s).

Bedell, Ralph C. (1904–1991) The director of the National Defense Education Administration (NDEA) Counseling and Guidance Institute Program from 1958 to 1966. Bedell insisted that these institutes incorporate practicum into their training. Under his direction the number of counselors in the United States grew substantially.

167

Beers, Clifford (1876–1943) An early leader in the mental hygiene movement in the United States. Beers was hospitalized for mental illness several times and found conditions in mental institutions deplorable and exposed them in his book, *A Mind That Found Itself* (1908), which became a popular best seller.

Bemak, Fred A leading scholar in prevention, multicultural counseling, and social justice.

Berg, Insoo Kim (1935–2007) A primary developer of solution-focused brief therapy along with her husband, Steve deShazer.

Bernard, Janie A leading scholar in counselor education on supervision.

Berne, Eric (1910–1970) The founder of transactional analysis. Berne's theory conceptualized the human personality as composed of three ego states—Parent, Adult, and Child—that are in continuous interaction with each other and with other people.

Binet, Alfred (1857–1911) The founder of the first intelligence tests initially involving his own children. With Théodore Simon, he expanded the tests (1905) to encompass the measurement of relative intelligence among deprived children.

Birdie, Ralph (1916–1974) The president of American Counseling Association from 1970–1971 and a prolific writer.

Bleuer, Jeanne A cofounder of Counseling Outfitters and a coordinator with Garry Walz of ERIC/CASS and VISTAS to promote research and publications in counseling.

Bobby, Carol The executive director of the Council for Accreditation of Counseling and Related Educational Programs (CACREP).

C

Capuzzi, David A leading writer and editor of counseling texts and a former president of the American Counseling Association.

Borders, DiAnne A leading scholar of supervision in counselor education.

Bowen, Murray (1913–1990) The founder of Bowen Family Therapy, and the originator of the genogram as well as the Georgetown Family Center, and the founder of the American Family Therapy Academy (AFTA).

Boy, Angelo A leading writer on the application of person-centered counseling to school counseling.

Bradley, Loretta A past president of American Counseling Association and a champion for advocacy in counseling.

Brammer, Lawrence A leading author of books on the skills and process of counseling.

Brewer, John (1877–1950) A pioneer in guidance who published a book entitled *Education as Guidance* (1932). Brewer proposed that every teacher be a counselor and that guidance be incorporated into the school curriculum as a subject.

Brooks, David (1944–1997) An advocate for counseling and counseling licensure and a former president of AMHCA. The American Counseling Association has a mentoring award named in his honor.

Brown, Duane A prolific author and leader in the area of career counseling.

Burke, Mary Thomas (1929–2002) A leading proponent and writer on spirituality and counseling and a former president of Chi Sigma Iota and ASERVIC.

Bertram, Burt A private practitioner who is the coauthor with Nancy Wheeler on the book and tape series *The Counselor and the Law: A Guide to Legal and Ethical Practice*.

Carkhuff, Robert A pioneer researcher and writer in the area of helping skills. Carkhuff factored out primary skills as effective in helping clients regardless of the counselor's theoretical orientation.

Carlson, Jon   An innovator in the field of interviewing and videotaping prominent counselors; past editor of *The Family Journal;* a prolific author.

Carroll, Marguerite   One of the first counselors to produce a videotape showing and analyzing an actual group work session; former president of the ASGW.

Cattell, Raymond (1906–1998)   An influential researcher in the study of personality who developed objective measures of personality including the Culture-Free Intelligence Test.

Cecil, Jean (1927–1998)   A pioneer and advocate for the accreditation of counselor education programs; past president of ACES.

Chickering, Arthur   Author of *Education and Identity,* Chickering became a major force in college student affairs by outlining seven critical "vectors" of development in college students and how education practices can be designed to promote student development.

Chope, Robert C.   A leading expert in the field of career counseling.

Chung, Rita Chi-Ying   A leading author in multicultural counseling and social justice.

Clawson, Thomas   The executive director of the National Board for Certified Counselors

and a leader in the field of internationalizing counseling as a profession.

Collison, Brooke   A leader in the counseling profession known for his humor, wisdom, and advocacy for counseling; a past president of the American Counseling Association.

Conyne, Robert   A leading writer in the area of groups, past president of ASGW.

Cooley, Fannie   A humanitarian counselor; a former president of the Association for Specialists in Group Work.

Corey, Gerald   A leading writer and presenter in the area of group work, one of the first fellows of the American Counseling Association.

Corey, Marianne S.   A cowriter with Gerald Corey of group work texts.

Corsini, Raymond (1914–2008)   A leading writer and editor of books on counseling and psychological theories.

Cottingham, Harold F. (1913–1981)   A past president of the American Counseling Association, who was invited by President Lyndon Johnson to witness the signing of the National Defense Education Act's extension in October 1964.

Coy, Doris   A past president of the American Counseling Association and an expert on school counseling.

d

Daley, Thelma   The first woman of color to serve as president of the American Counseling Association (1975–1976), Daley promoted "unity through diversity."

D'Andrea, Michael   A leading author on multicultural counseling.

Davis, Jesse (1871–1955)   A pioneer in school counseling, Davis was the first person to set up a systematized guidance program in the public schools in Grand Rapids, Michigan.

Davis suggested in 1907 that classroom teachers of English composition teach their students a lesson in guidance once a week, with the goal of building character.

deShazer, Steve (1940–2005)   The developer of solution-focused therapy along with his wife, Insoo Kim Berg.

Dingman, Robert L.   A leading counselor educator, author, and director of disaster relief for the American Red Cross.

Donigian, Jeremiah   Past president of ASGW and a leading writer in group work.

Dye, Allan   Past president of ASGW and a major contributor to the field of group work.

Duffey, Thelma   The founder of the Association for Creativity in Counseling and editor of its periodical, *Journal of Creativity in Mental Health.*

Dugan, Willis (1909–2000)   The 20th president of American Personnel and Guidance Association and its executive director from 1966 to 1971.

e

Egan, Gerald   A pioneer in writing helping skills texts that are widely used in instructing counseling graduate students.

Ellis, Albert (1913–2007)   The founder of Rational Emotive Behavior Therapy (REBT), which was originally called Rational-Emotive Therapy (RET). To function in a healthy way Ellis believed it was important to modify thoughts so that they are rational.

Elmore, Patricia   Former editor of *Measurement and Evaluation in Counseling and Development.*

Elmore, Thomas M.   Past president of ACES who transformed the association into a more open and diverse group.

Engels, Dennis W.   A highly involved leader in ACA governance who has written extensively on career counseling and the development of counselors.

Erikson, Erik (1902–1979)   A psychoanalyst and neo-Freudian best known for his eight-stage psychosocial theory of human development set forth in his book, *Childhood and Society.* Erikson was particularly concerned with the issues of identity and personality.

f

Fennel, David   An expert on counseling with military personnel and their families.

Field, Harriet Gardin (1944–2009)   An influential member of the ACA Governing Council who championed professional advocacy and diversity.

Fitzgerald, Paul   A prominent leader in ACES who pioneered multimedia use in counseling.

Fletcher, Frank (1913–1992)   One of the organizers of the American Counseling Association and its president in 1957–1958, Fletcher was also instrumental in the passage of the National Defense Education Act (NDEA).

Footman, Gordon E. (1928–2009)   Past ACA Parliamentarian, Western Region chair, and C-AHEAD president.

Frank, Jerome (1909–2005)   An influential researcher who investigated various dimensions of psychotherapy including the psychology of leadership.

Frankl, Viktor (1905–1997)   The founder of logotherapy and a leading existentialists, Frankl's most influential book is *Man's Search for Meaning.*

Freud, Anna (1895–1982)   An Austrian-British psychoanalyst, noted for her work in the psychoanalysis of children. The daughter of Sigmund Freud, her work stressed the ego in personality development and emphasized the use of defense mechanisms.

Freud, Sigmund (1856–1939) The founder of psychoanalysis and a number of new techniques for treating dysfunctional behaviors (e.g., free association and dream analysis). Freud highlighted the importance of the unconscious and sexuality in human behavior. He developed a theory of personality based on psychosexual development and the resolution of power between the id, ego, and superego.

g

Gazda, George The originator of a developmental education model known as Life Skills Training, Gazda is a past president of the American Counseling Association and an expert on group work.

Gilligan, Carol Author of *In a Different Voice* (1982), a book that describes the ways women form relationships in society. Gilligan challenged Lawrence Kohlberg's stage theory of moral development and its applicability to women

Gladding, Samuel T. A leading writer of counseling texts and a former president of and fellow in the American Counseling Association.

Glosoff, Harriett A leading author in counselor ethics.

Glasser, William The founder of reality therapy/choice theory. Glasser's ideas have been influential in therapeutic environments, especially in educational settings.

Goldman, Leo (1920–1999) A leader in the field of measurement and assessment in counseling, Goldman was editor of the *Journal for Counseling and Development* (then the *Personnel and Guidance Journal*) from 1969 to 1975.

Goodman, Jane A leader in the field of career counseling as well as a past president of the American Counseling Association.

Goodyear, Rodney A leading author in in the area of counseling supervision, and a former editor of the *Journal for Counseling and Development.*

Goud, Nels A leader in the field of humanistic counseling.

Gysbers, Norman A prolific author and the creator of a model school counseling curriculum. Gysbers has served counseling in a variety of ways (e.g. editor of the *Vocational Guidance Quarterly* and president of the American Counseling Association).

h

Hackney, Harold A leading writer of counseling texts and articles, especially related to counseling processes.

Haley, Jay (1923–2007) A pioneer in the field of family therapy, Haley was influenced by Milton Erickson and worked with the Gregory Bateson studying schizophrenia. Haley influenced the development of strategic and structural family therapy.

Hansen, Jo-Ida A former editor of *Measurement and Evaluation in Counseling and Development* and an expert on career development.

Hansen, Sunny   A leading researcher in the field of career counseling; a past president of the American Counseling Association.

Harris-Bowlby, JoAnn   A leading researcher and writer in the field of career counseling and a former president of the National Career Development Association.

Hazler, Richard   A leading author and researcher on counseling and counselor identity.

Hedgeman, Betty S. (1937–2009)   Five-term treasurer of American Counseling Association, past president of the American Rehabilitation Counseling Association, and chair of the Commission on Rehabilitation Counselor Certification.

Helwig, Andrew   A prominent writer of counselor licensure material and a former president of the National Employment Counselors Association.

Henderson, Donna   A past president of ACES and CSI; a leading author in counseling children and school counseling.

Heppner, P. Paul   The author of *Pioneers in Counseling and Development* which includes interviews with some early leaders in the counseling profession.

Herlihy, Barbara   A leading scholar and writer in the field of ethics in counseling.

Herr, Edwin L.   A prolific author; a former president of the American Counseling Association; a former editor of the *Journal of Counseling and Development*.

Hill, George (1907–1977)   A prolific author of counseling texts and articles who was influential in making recommendations for school counseling preparation programs.

Holland, John L. (1920–2008)   A researcher and author in the career development area who identified six categories in which personality types and work environments can be classified: realistic, investigative, artistic, social, enterprising, and conventional.

Hollis, Joseph (1922–2002)   A leading scholar in counseling, Hollis founded his own publishing company, Accelerated Development. He originated the study of counselor education programs and published the results in the classic text, *Counselor Preparation*.

Hood, Albert   A leading author and researcher in counseling assessment.

Hoppock, Robert (1901–1995)   An early leader in the field of occupations, Hoppock developed one of the first job satisfaction scales and published one of the first texts on group guidance.

Horne, Arthur M.   A leading expert in the area of group work and bullying.

Hosie, Thomas Walsh (1945–2008)   The president of ACES, the Louisiana Counseling Association, as well as editor of *Counselor Education and Supervision*.

House, Reese M. (1938–2007)   A leader in the school reform movement and director of the National Center for Transforming School Counseling at the Education Trust.

Hoyt, Kenneth B. (1924–2008)   The president of American Counseling Association, then APGA, in 1966–1967; a strong researcher in career counseling.

Hulse, Diana   A leading writer and scholar in the field of group work; one of the first fellows of the American Counseling Association.

i

Ivey, Alan   A writer and advocate in the field of multicultural counseling and the founder of Microskills Training, a leading producer of videotapes in counseling.

Ivey, Mary B.   A leading writer in developmental and multicultural counseling.

j

Janicke, Mary A secretary in the American Counseling Association from 1952 to 2007 who worked with 55 ACA presidents and seven ACA Executive Directors.

Jepson, David A leading expert in the area of career counseling.

Jourard, Sidney (1926–1974) A pioneer in the research on self-disclosure in counseling. See *self-disclosure*.

Jung, Carl (1875–1961) The founder of the Jungian (analytical) approach to counseling and psychotherapy. Jung stressed the importance of symbols and saw symbols as a link between consciousness and unconsciousness.

k

Kaplan, David A past president of the American Counseling Association, its Chief Professional Officer, and a strong advocate of counselor identity.

Kandor, Joseph Former president of the Association for Assessment in Counseling and the Board of Directors of CACREP.

Kirk, Wyatt D., Jr. (d. 2008) A past president of the Association for Multicultural Counseling and Development and a pioneer in the field of multicultural counseling.

Kohlberg, Lawrence (1927–1987) The originator of a theory of moral development that states children proceed through three stages of moral reasoning—preconventional, conventional, and postconventional.

Kottler, Jeffrey A prolific writer in the field of counseling and an adventurer in exploring

how counseling and healing practices differ in various cultures and countries.

Krumboltz, John A counseling researcher who was instrumental in promoting behaviorism in counseling and who has developed notable career assessment instruments.

Kübler-Ross, Elisabeth (1926–2004) A psychiatrist and pioneer researcher in studying death and dying. Kübler-Ross proposed five stages the terminally ill go through if they successfully face death—denial, anger, bargaining, depression, and acceptance.

Kuder, Frederick (1903–2001) The author of six interest inventories used widely in career assessment; founding editor of the journal *Educational and Psychological Measurement*.

l

Lamdreth, Garry The founder of the Center for Play Therapy at the University of North Texas and a major writer in the field of play therapy.

Lazarus, Arnold The originator of the BASIC ID concept and the originator of multimodal therapy.

Lee, Courtland   A leader in the field of international counselling and a major writer in the field of multicultural counseling; a former president of the American Counseling Association and the International Association of Counselling.

Lewis, Chuck   The American Counseling Association's (then APGA 's) Executive Director from 1972 to 1982.

Lewis, Judith   An originator of the term community counseling, a writer in the field of substance abuse, a past president of American Counseling Association.

Linde, Lynne   An expert in the area of school counseling and a former American Counseling Association president.

Locke, Don C.   A strong advocate for multicultural counseling and the second African American president of the Association for Counselor Education and Supervision.

Locke, Don W.   President of the American Counseling Association (2011–2012).

Loesch, Larry   A prolific author of professional counseling articles and the fifth president of Chi Sigma Iota.

Love, Stan   The founder of Love Publications and the publisher of *Counseling and Human Development*, a popular counseling monograph.

m

Malcolm, David Donald (1916–2008)   Founder of San Diego State University's Department of Counselor Education and the multicultural Community-based Block master's program.

Maples, Mary   A leading counselor educator, in the area of spirituality in counseling and a former president of the American Counseling Association.

Maslow, Abraham (1908–1970)   A founder of the humanistic movement in counseling; Maslow studied healthy people and devised a hierarchy of needs with basic physical and safety needs at the base and psychological needs at the peak.

May, Rollo (1909–1994)   A leader of the existentialist approach to counseling. May was the cofounder of the Association for Humanistic Psychology; his book, *The Meaning of Anxiety*, is influential for its emphasis on the role of anxiety as a motivator.

McDaniel, Carl   A noted, now-retired, leader in the field of career counseling.

McDonough, Patrick J. "Joe" (1932–2008)   The sixth executive director of the American Counseling Association (1983–1990). During his tenure at ACA, 27 states enacted counselor licensure laws, and the association membership grew by 15,000.

McFadden, Johnny   A leading writer in multicultural counseling and a former president of the Association for Multicultural Counseling and Development.

McGowan, Scott   A pioneer in producing public service announcements for counseling and a two-term editor of the *Journal of Counseling and Development*.

Minuchin, Sal   The founder of structural family therapy and the former director of the Philadelphia Child Guidance Clinic.

Miranti, Judith   A leader and writer in the area of spirituality in counseling and a former president of Chi Sigma Iota.

Mitchell, Marianne   A leading writer of texts in counseling and a former president of the American Counseling Association.

Moreno, Jacob (1889–1974)   The founder of psychodrama in the 1920s in Vienna, Austria, Moreno refined his theory in the United States.

The American Society of Group Psychotherapy and Psychodrama was founded in 1942 by Moreno and in 1947, Moreno started *The Journal of Group Psychotherapy, Psychodrama, and Sociometry.*

Muro, James (1934–1996)   A leading writer in the area of school counseling and the 34th

president of the Association for Counselor Education and Supervision.

Myers, Jane   A leading researcher in counseling older adults and a cocreator of the wellness wheel; a former president of the American Counseling Association and Chi Sigma Iota.

n

Niles, Spencer   A leading researcher in career counseling, a past president of the National

Career Development Association, editor of the *Journal of Counseling and Development.*

o

Ohlsen, Merle M. (1914–2008)   A pioneer in the development of group work in counseling and a former president of the American Counseling Association.

Okun, Barbara   The author of books on helping skills and counseling within a broad and process oriented context.

Osborne, Cynthia   A leading counselor educator who publishes in the areas of substance abuse, solution-focused counseling, motivational interviewing, and counselor supervision.

p

Page, Betsy J.   A leading researcher in the area of group work and the use of technology in counseling.

Paisley, Pam   A leading expert on school counseling.

Parham, Thomas   A leader in the field of multicultural counseling.

Parsons, Frank (1854–1908)   Often called the "Father of Guidance," Parsons worked with young people who were in the process of making career decisions and theorized that choosing a vocation was a matter of relating

three factors: a knowledge of work, a knowledge of self, and a matching of the two through "true reasoning." He is best known for founding Boston's Vocational Bureau in 1908, and for his book, *Choosing a Vocation.*

Patterson, C. H. (1912–2006)   One of the leading advocates of person-centered counseling and a prolific author in the field of counseling.

Perls, Fritz (1893–1970)   The founder of the Gestalt therapy approach to counseling. Perls was a colorful character as well as innovative thinker. Perls stressed wholeness.

Perls, Laura (1905–1990)   A Gestalt theorist, married to Fritz Perls, who collaborated with him in developing Gestalt therapy.

Piaget, Jean (1896–1980)   A pioneer in the study of cognitive development. Piaget studied how children learn to know or form concepts. He proposed four stages—sensorimotor, preoperational, concrete operations, and formal operations—through which children sequentially pass in reaching cognitive maturity.

Pope, Mark   The first openly gay and Native American president of the American Counseling Association and a leading scholar in career development.

Purkey, William   The founder of invitational therapy.

r

Rank, Otto (1884–1937)   One of Sigmund Freud's first and most valued pupils. Rank analyzed the underlying significance of myths. He later diverged from Freud and emphasized the birth trauma as the central cause of neurosis.

Remley, Ted   A professional counselor and attorney who has written extensively on ethical and legal aspects of counseling; a former executive director of the American Counseling Association.

Rencken, Robert   A prominent counselor whom ACA has an award named after.

Richardson, Billy Kay "Bill" (1933–2008)   A past president of the American Rehabilitation Counseling Association and prolific contributor to the counseling literature.

Richmond, Lee Joyce   A leading expert in career counseling, a past president of the American Counseling Association.

Robinson, Edward (Mike) H.   A former editor of *Elementary School Guidance and Counseling* and a prolific contributor to the literature and leadership in counseling.

Roe, Anne (1904–1991)   The originator of a theory of career development that proposes the occupations people select are based on the relationships they have with their families.

Rogers, Carl (1902–1987)   The founder of person-centered counseling, Rogers rose to prominence in 1942 with the publication of his book, *Counseling and Psychotherapy,* which challenged the counselor-centered approach of E. G. Williamson, as well as major tenets of Freudian psychoanalysis. He emphasized the importance of the client.

Rosenthal, Howard   A popular writer of counseling texts, especially the *Encyclopedia of Counseling.*

Rothney, John Watson Murray (1906–1987)   One of the early longitudinal researchers in the field of counseling who discovered the positive effectiveness of counseling for adolescents over the short term (i.e., 5 years out).

s

Sampson, James   A leading writer in the area of career counseling.

Sanford, Nevitt (1909–1995)   A pioneer in the area of student development. Sanford's book, *The American College* (1962), asserted, as a result of research, a developmental theory that students either excel or are inhibited in their growth during their college years due to environmental factors, including the curriculum and cocurriculum.

Satir, Virginia (1916–1988) A pioneer in the family counseling, Satir focused on building self-esteem and self-worth in people within families through clear communication.

Savickas, Mark The originator of career construction theory, an American Counseling Association Fellow, editor of *Journal of Vocational Behavior.*

Schmidt, John A leading writer and authority in the area of school counseling.

Schwallie-Giddis, Pat A leader in counselor education and interim executive director of the American Counseling Association in 1993–1994.

Seaborn, Judith A. (1938–2008) President of the Michigan Counseling Association (twice) and a past chair of ACA Midwest Region.

Seligman, Linda (1944–2007) A leading writer and authority in the area of diagnostics and treatment of psychiatric disorders.

Seligman, Martin The originator of the theories of learned helplessness and positive psychology and a researcher and advocate for the concept authentic happiness.

Shaffer, Robert The first president of American Personnel and Guidance Association (1951–1953), which is now the American Counseling Association.

Sheeley, Vernon The official and unofficial historian of the counseling profession, who has written about the development of the American Counseling Association and its divisions.

Shertzer, Bruce A leading author of counseling texts and articles, a former president of the American Counseling Association.

Shostrom, Everett The developer of the *Personal Orientation Inventory (POI)* and the producer of the famous therapy film, *Gloria,* which featured a client named Gloria being counseled in individual sessions by Carl Rogers, Fritz Perls, and Albert Ellis.

Skinner, B. F. (1904–1990) The originator of operant conditioning and a champion of applying the principles of behaviorism to human society. Skinner invented several devices, such as the Skinner Box, and wrote the utopian behavioral novel *Walden II.*

Sklare, Gerald The author of a popular text on solution-focused school counseling.

Smith, Howard A past chair of the American Counseling Association Foundation and a former associate director of the American Counseling Association.

Smith, Robert L. A leading writer in the field of counselor education especially in the areas of family counseling and addiction.

Sparks, Asa (1937–2007) An influential member of the Alabama Counseling Association.

Stockton, Rex A leading researcher and writer in the field of group work and a leader in the Association for Specialists in Group Work.

Stone, Lloyd One of the pioneers behind the development of National Board for Certified Counselors who because of his efforts received the first NCC certificate.

Stripling, Robert (1915–1991) A pioneer in the development of standards for master's and doctoral degrees in counseling, Stripling was the driving force in the accreditation of counseling programs that led to the formation of the Council for the Accreditation of Counseling and Related Educational Programs (CACREP).

Strong, Edward K. Jr. (1884–1963) The originator of the Vocational Interest Blank, which evolved into the Strong Interest Inventory, a widely used career assessment instrument.

Sue, Derald An early proponent of multicultural counseling and first author the Multicultural Counseling Competencies and Standards published in 1992. A former editor of the *Journal for Counseling and Development.*

Super, Donald (1910–1994) The second president of what is now the American Counseling Association (1953–1954) and one of the first theorists to formulate a developmental approach to the study of careers across the life span.

Swanson, Carl D.   A writer on legal issues in counseling such as privileged communication.

Sweeney, Thomas J.   The founder of Chi Sigma Iota (international counseling honor society); a past president of the American Counseling Association; a strong advocate for counselor licensure and the profession of counseling.

t

Terman, L. M. (1877–1956)   A researcher who gained prominence in 1916 with the publication of *The Measurement of Intelligence,* he refined Alfred Binet's work and created the Stanford-Binet Intelligence Scale, an instrument to determine a person's intellectual ability.

Thomas, Carolyn   A past president of the Association for Specialists in Group Work and an influential group worker.

Tiedeman, David V. (1919–2004)   The originator of a career development theory that is based on conscious decision making in life to overcome roles and restrictions, a concept known as lifecareer.

Tyler, Leona (1906–1993)   A pioneer in the development of counseling as a profession. Tyler's most influential book was *The Work of the Counselor.*

v

Vacc, Nicholas (1939–2002)   A leading author in the field of measurement and assessment; a strong advocate for counselor accreditation, and a leader within the American Counseling Association for whom a major award is named.

Vernon, Ann   A noted writer in the area of counseling with children and expert in REBT.

Vontress, Clement   A leading author in existentialism and multicultural counseling.

Vriend, John (1924–2006)   A former president of the Association for Specialists in Group Work and coauthor of audiotapes and books entitled *Counseling Techniques that Work.*

w

Walz, Garry   The founder of ERIC/CASS, VISTAS, and a prolific author of counseling literature; a former president of the American Counseling Association.

Watson, John B. (1878–1958)   Watson is generally credited as being the originator of the school of behaviorism, in which behavior is described in terms of physiological responses to stimuli and the concept of conscious or unconscious mental activity is rejected.

Wechsler, David (1896–1981)   A leading intelligence scale developer in the United

States who, in 1939, published the Wechsler Bellevue Intelligence Scale that was later refined, revised, and published in various forms as the Wechsler Adult Intelligence Scale (WAIS), the Wechsler Intelligence Scale for Children (WISC), and the Wechsler Preschool and Primary Scale of Intelligence (WPPSI).

Weinrach, Stephen (1943–2004) A leading researcher and contributor to the counseling literature.

West, John D. A leading scholar in counseling with a special interest in social construction theory.

West, G. Kenneth A leading author on parenting, family counseling, and human development.

Wheeler, Nancy An attorney who is coauthor with Burt Bertram on a popular and important book and tape series *The Counselor and the Law: A Guide to Legal and Ethical Practice.*

Whitaker, Carl (1912–1995) A pioneer in the family counseling field whose experiential approach challenged families to look at the absurdity of their situations. Whitaker emphasized uncovering and utilizing the unconscious life of families.

Williamson, E. G. (1900–1979) A counseling pioneer who in the 1930s developed an early theory of counseling, the directive counseling approach also known as the counselor-centered approach, the Minnesota point of view, and trait-factor counseling. Williamson also served as president of the American Counseling Association.

Wilson, F. Robert A leading authority in the area of measurement and assessment in counseling.

Winfrey, James K. (1932–2009) A past president of ACES and the ACA Western Region, Winfrey also served as treasurer of the American Counseling Association.

Witmer, Mel An early leading advocate for an emphasis on wellness in counseling.

Wittmer, Joe A prolific writer in the area of school counseling, especially classroom guidance.

Wrenn, C. Gilbert (1902–2001) A pioneer in counseling who was the first editor of *The Counseling Psychologist* and wrote a widely influential book in the counseling profession: *The Counselor in a Changing World* (1962). Wrenn coined the phrase "culturally encapsulated counselor."

Wright, George N. A leader in rehabilitation counseling and one its the most prolific writers.

Wubbolding, Robert One of the leading writers, researchers, and trainers in Reality Therapy/Choice Theory.

y

Yalom, Irvin A psychiatrist whose writings on group work and existentialism have been influential in counseling and whose popular books, such as *Love's Executioner,* have provided the public with insight into the therapeutic process.

Yep, Rich The executive director of the American Counseling Association.

Young, Mark A leading author in the area of helping relationships and wellness.

Appendix B: Self-Help Organizations

Adult Children of Alcoholics (ACoA):   A self-help organization that offers group-based support and information for adults who grew up in homes with alcoholic or otherwise dysfunctional parents. Groups are based on the twelve-step program.

> Address: PO Box 3216; Torrance, CA 90510
> Phone: 310-534-1815
> Web site: http://www.adultchildren.org/

The AGS Foundation for Health in Aging (FHA):   An organization created to bridge the gap between research and aging adults and caregivers. Education, advocacy, and providing referral support for the aging are the primary activities of FHA.

> Address: 350 Fifth Ave., Suite 801; New York, NY 10118
> Phone: 212-755-6810; Fax: 212-832-8646
> Web site: http://www.healthinaging.org/

AIDS.ORG: An organization dedicated to the prevention of the HIV virus and the improvement of life for those affected by HIV and AIDS. The Web site serves as the forum for disseminating information and facilitating discussion to inform the public, professionals, and people with HIV/AIDS.

> Address: 7985 Santa Monica Blvd. #99; West Hollywood, CA 90046
> Phone: 323-656-6036
> Web site: http://www.aids.org

Al-Anon/Alateen: A voluntary mutual-help group based on the 12-step model for relatives and children of alcohol abusers. Members meet regularly to offer support and discuss common problems.

> Address: 1600 Corporate Landing Pkwy.; Virginia Beach, VA 23454
> Phone: 757-563-1600; Fax: 757-563-1655
> Web site: http://www.al-anon.alateen.org/

Alcoholics Anonymous (AA):   An organization that helps alcohol abusers gain and maintain control of their lives by attaining and maintaining sobriety, through total abstinence. The 12-step model of recovery was first developed for AA.

> Address: PO Box 459; New York, NY 10163
> Phone: 212-870-3400
> Web site: http://www.aa.org/

ALS Association: An organization promoting research, education, and public policy to support people with ALS (Lou Gehrig's Disease) and their families. Local chapters also provide support group meetings and clinics to coordinate medical care for ALS patients.

Address: 27001 Agoura Rd., Suite 250; Calabasas Hills, CA 91301-5104
Phone: 818-880-9007; Fax: 818-880-9006
Web site: http://www.alsa.org/

Alzheimer's Association: A national organization with the mission of providing better care for Alzheimer's patients, supporting the advancement of research, and promoting brain health.

Address: 225 N. Michigan Ave., Floor 17; Chicago, IL 60601
Phone: 312-335-8700; Fax: 866-699-1246
Web site: http://www.alz.org/

American Foundation for Suicide Prevention (AFSP):   The leading national organization dedicated to the prevention of suicide. AFSP focus its efforts on research, providing information to the public, and advocacy for social and policy change.

Address: 120 Wall St., 22nd Floor; New York, NY 10005
Phone: 212-363-3500; Fax: 212-363-6237
Web site: http://www.afsp.org/

Anxiety Disorders Association of America (ADAA):   An organization dedicated to furthering prevention and treatment of anxiety disorders, as well as helping better the lives of persons with such disorders.

Address: 8730 Georgia Ave., Suite 600; Silver Springs, MD 20910
Phone: 240-485-1001; Fax: 240-485-1035
Web site: http://www.adaa.org

Autism Society of America (ASA):   The ASA connects parents of children with autism and professionals to improve the quality of life and to provide a representative voice for those with autism.

Address: 7910 Woodmont Ave., Suite 300; Bethesda, MD 20814-3067
Phone: 301-657-0881; Fax: 301-657-0869
Web site: http://www.autism-society.org/

Celebrate Recovery: A Bible-based recovery group for individuals seeking freedom from addictions, hurts, and habits, based on eight principles.

Address: 1 Saddleback Parkway, Lake Forest, CA 92630
Phone: 949-609-8000
Web site: http://www.celebraterecovery.com/

The CFIDS Association of America: A research and education-based organization, whose mission is to promote understanding and prevention of Chronic Fatigue Syndrome and related disorders.

Address: PO Box 220398; Charlotte, NC 2822200398
Phone: 714-365-2343
Web site: http://www.cfids.org/

CFIDS and Fibromyalgia Self-Help: A self-help organization dedicated to providing education and group support for persons dealing with Fibromyalgia and Chronic Fatigue Syndrome. The organization provides online self-help courses and facilitates support group meetings.

Web site: http://www.cfidsselfhelp.org/

Child and Adolescent Bipolar Foundation (CABF):   An organization working to help families with children and teens with bipolar disorder. CABF seeks to educate the public and connect families to resources, primarily using the foundation's Web site.

Address: 1000 Skokie Blvd., Suite 570; Wilmette, IL 60091
Phone: 847-256-8525; Fax: 847-920-9498
Web site: http://www.bpkids.org/

Children and Adults with Attention Deficit/Hyperactivity Disorder (CHADD):   The leading national organization helping those affected by AD/HD, through activities such as education, research, public awareness, and working with government agencies.

Address: 8181 Professional Pl., Suite 150; Landover, MD 20785
Phone: 301-306-7070; Fax: 301-306-7090
Web site: http://www.chadd.org/

Clutterers Anonymous (CLA):   A self-help organization based on the 12-step model for persons suffering from clutter in their lives and personal space.

Address: PO Box 91413; Los Angeles, CA 90009-1413
Phone: 310-281-6064
Web site: http://sites.google.com/site/clutterersanonymous/Home

Co-Anon: Family groups for family members and friends of persons addicted to cocaine, who meet to discuss common problems.

Address: PO Box 12722; Tucson, AZ 85732-2722
Phone: 520-513-5028, 800-898-9985
Web site: http://www.co-anon.org/

Co-Dependents Anonymous (CoDA):   An organization that promotes the development of healthy relationships for persons, using the 12-step model.

Address: PO Box 33577; Phoenix, AZ 85067-3577
Phone: 602-277-7991
Web site: http://www.codependents.org/

Co-Sex and Love Addicts Anonymous (CO-SLAA):   A 12-step support group for family members and friends who are seeking healthy relationships and boundaries with loved ones affected by a sexual addiction.

Phone: 860-456-0032
Web site: http://www.coslaa.org/

Cocaine Anonymous (CA):   A fellowship of individuals seeking recovery and sobriety from addiction to cocaine and other drugs.

> Address: 3740 Overland Avenue, Suite C; Los Angeles, CA 90034
> Phone: 310-559-5833; Fax: 310-559-2554
> Web site: http://www.ca.org/

Codependents of Sex Addicts (COSA):   Self-help groups for those in relationship with a person with a sexual addiction or sexually compulsive behavior.

> Address: PO Box 14537; Minneapolis, MN 55414
> Phone: 763-537-6904
> Web site: http://www.cosa-recovery.org/

Crystal Meth Anonymous (CA):   A fellowship of people recovering from addiction to methamphetamines. The organization operates as independent 12-step meetings, which promote shared understanding, encouragement, and support among members.

> Address: 4470 West Sunset Blvd.; Los Angeles, CA 90027-6302
> Phone: 877-262-6691
> Web site: http://www.crystalmeth.org/

Debtors Anonymous: A self-help group designed to help men and women recover from incurring compulsive, unsecured debt.

> Address: PO Box 920888; Needham, MA 02492-0009
> Phone: 800-421-2383; Fax: 781-453-2745
> Web site: http://www.debtorsanonymous.org/

Depression and Bipolar Support Alliance (DBSA):   Formerly known as the National Depressive and Manic Depressive Association, this organization seeks to educate and provide peer support for people with mood disorders, including depression, bipolar disorder, and anxiety disorders.

> Address: 730 N. Franklin St., Suite 501; Chicago, IL 60654-7225
> Phone: 800-826-3632; Fax: 312-642-7243
> Web site: http://www.dbsalliance.org/

Emotions Anonymous: A supportive fellowship of people working together to recover from emotional difficulties. The issues faced by members may include depression, anger, fears, loneliness, grief, anxiety, and low self-esteem.

> Address: PO Box 4245; St. Paul, MN 55104-0245
> Phone: 651-647-9712; Fax: 651-647-1593
> Web site: http://www.emotionsanonymous.org/

Epilepsy Foundation: An organization dedicated to the welfare of those with epilepsy, working to ensure their ability to participate fully in life experiences and to prevent and treat seizures.

> Address: 8301 Professional Place; Landover, MD 20785
> Phone: 800-332-1000; Fax: 301-577-4941
> Web site: http://www.epilepsyfoundation.org/

Families Anonymous: A support group comprised of people who share concerns with and are affected by friends' and family members' substance addiction.

>   Address: PO Box 3475; Culver, CA 90231-3475
>   Phone: 800-736-9805; Fax: 310-815-9682
>   Web site: http://www.familiesanonymous.org/

Federation of Families for Children's Mental Health (FFCMH):   Provides support services, resources, and leadership for families with children with emotional, behavioral, and mental health challenges.

>   Address: 9605 Medical Center Drive, Suite 280; Rockville, MD 20850
>   Phone: 240-403-1901; Fax: 240-403-1909
>   Web site: http://www.ffcmh.org/

Gam-anon: A support group based on the 12-step model for friends and family members who are affected by the gambling addiction of a loved one.

>   Address: PO Box 157; Whitestone, NY 11357
>   Phone: 718-352-1671; Fax: 718-746-2571
>   Web site: http://www.gam-anon.org/

Gamblers Anonymous (GA):   A mutual help group, based on the 12-step model, composed primarily of compulsive gamblers who have a desire to get help for his/her gambling problem.

>   Address: PO Box 17173; Los Angeles, CA 90017
>   Phone: 213-386-8789
>   Web site: http://www.gamblersanonymous.org/

Marijuana Anonymous (MA):   A self-help group based on the 12-step model designed to help individuals recover together from a marijuana addiction and to bring help to those still struggling with this addiction.

>   Address: PO Box 2912; Van Nuys, CA 91404
>   Phone: 800-766-6779
>   Web site: http://www.marijuana-anonymous.org/

Mental Health America (MHA):   An organization devoted to educating the public about the realities of life with mental illness and to advocate for those with mental health disorders. Founded over 100 years ago by Clifford Beers, MHA was formerly known as the National Mental Health Association.

>   Address: 2000 N. Beauregard St., Floor 6; Alexandria, VA 22311
>   Phone: 703-684-7722; Fax: 703-684-5968
>   Web site: http://www.mentalhealthamerica.net/

Nar-Anon Family Groups: A support group organization that seeks to help people who are affected by an addiction of a family member or close friend. Nar-Anon also has an Internet-based support forum, which can be accessed via the organization's Web site.

>   Address: 22527 Crenshaw Blvd., Suite 200B; Torrance, CA 90505
>   Phone: 310-534-8188; Fax: 310-534-8688
>   Web site: http://nar-anon.org/

Narcotics Anonymous (NA):   An international, community-based fellowship of men and women seeking recovery and sobriety from drug addiction. The NA program is based on the 12 step model of AA.

> Address: PO Box 9999; Van Nuys, CA 91409
> Phone: 818-773-9999; Fax: 818-700-0700
> Web site: http://www.na.org/

National Alliance on Mental Illness (NAMI):   An organization working toward eradicating mental illness, with focused efforts on advocacy, education, research, and support for people with mental illness.

> Address: Colonial Place Three; 2107 Wilson Blvd., Suite 300; Arlington, VA 22201-3042
> Phone: 703-524-7600; Fax: 703-524-9094
> Web site: http://www.nami.org/

National Association of Anorexia Nervosa and Associated Disorders (ANAD):   This organization works to relieve problems associated with eating disorders, raise public awareness, and provide support for those who suffer. Support services include support groups, a telephone hotline, and an e-mail referral service linking individuals with mental and medical professionals.

> Address: PO Box 7; Highland Park, IL 60035
> Phone: 847-831-3438; Fax: 847-433-4632
> Web site: http://www.anad.org/

National Anxiety Foundation (NAF):   An organization focused on educating and providing medical information on anxiety disorders and treatment for individuals suffering from these disorders.

> Address: 3135 Custer Dr.; Lexington, KY 40517-4001
> Web site: http://www.lexington-on-line.com/naf.html

National Coalition of Mental Health Professionals and Consumers, Inc. (NCMHPC):   A foundation providing education and advocacy for mental health care. The organization emphasizes affordable, high-quality, pro-consumer care that is available for all.

> Address: PO Box 438; Commack, NY 11725
> Phone: 866-826-2548; Fax: 631-979-5293
> Web site: http://www.nationalcoalition.org/

National Eating Disorder Association (NEDA):   An organization providing eating disorder information, resources, and support to those struggling with an eating disorder and close friends and family members. NEDA also maintains an information and referral phone service, Helpline (800-931-2237).

> Address: 603 Stewart St., Suite 803; Seattle, WA 98101
> Phone: 206-382-3587; Fax: 206-829-8501
> Web site: http://www.nationaleatingdisorders.org/

The National Family Caregivers Association (NFCA):   A support organization for family care-givers, providing education and empowerment to work for the well-being of themselves and their loved ones.

>   Address: 10400 Connecticut Ave., Suite 500; Kensington, MD 20895-3944
>   Phone: 800-896-3650; Fax: 301-942-2302
>   Web site: http://www.thefamilycaregiver.org/

National Hospice and Palliative Care Organization (NHPCO):   A national organization of Hos-pice providers and volunteers dedicated to improving end-of-life care.

>   Address: 1700 Diagonal Rd., Suite 625; Alexandria, VA 22314
>   Phone: 703-837-1500; Fax: 703-837-1233
>   Web site: http://www.nhpco.org/

National Mental Health Consumers' Self-Help Clearinghouse: An association providing con-sumers updated information and access to mental health issues and service providers.

>   Address: 1211 Chestnut St., Suite 1207; Philadelphia, PA 19107
>   Phone: 800-553-4539
>   Web site: http://www.mhselfhelp.org/

National Parkinson Foundation, Inc. (NPF):   The NPF works to support persons with Parkin-son's disease and caregivers, and to promote research and education for the treatment and cure of the disease. The organization also seeks to meet needs through regional community-based support centers.

>   Address: 1501 NW 9th Ave./Bob Hope Rd.; Miami, FL 33136-1494
>   Phone: 800-327-4545; Fax: 305-243-5595
>   Web site: http://www.parkinson.org/

Neurotics Anonymous/Neuroticos Anonimos (NA):   A 12-step self-help group designed to help persons struggling with mental and emotional illness. The organization defines "neurotics" as anyone whose emotions interfere with his or her ability to function in any way or degree as identi-fied by the individual.

>   Address: PO Box 4866, Cleveland Park Station; Washington, DC 20008
>   Web site: http://www.neuroticosanonimosusa.com/

Nicotine Anonymous (NicA):   A support group based on the 12-step model designed to help all who desire to stop using nicotine. Nicotine Anonymous supports many approaches to stop using to-bacco, including cessation programs and withdrawal aids.

>   Address: 419 Main St., PMB #370; Huntington Beach, CA 92648
>   Phone: 415-750-0328; 877-879-6422
>   Web site: http://www.nicotine-anonymous.org/

North American Council on Adoptable Children (NACAC): An organization that promotes permanent family placements for children, especially those in foster care. NACAC focuses its efforts on advocacy, parent leadership building, education, and support for adoptions.

Address: 970 Raymond Ave., Suite 106; St. Paul, MN 55114
Phone: 651-644-3036; Fax: 651-644-9848
Web site: http://www.nacac.org/

Obsessive Compulsive Foundation, Inc. (OCF): An international organization that supports people with Obsessive Compulsive Disorder and their family and friends, in addition to supporting research and education about the OCD and related disorders.

Address: PO Box 209006 Yale Station; New Haven, CT 06520
Phone: 203-432-2400 Fax: 203-432-7425
Web site: http://www.ocfoundation.org/

Overcomers in Christ: A Christian support group for those struggling with addiction, including substance abuse and sexual addiction.

Address: PO Box 3446; Omaha, NE 68134
Phone: 402-573-0966; Fax: 402-573-0960
Web site: http://www.overcomersinchrist.org/

Online Gamers Anonymous (OLGA): A self-help recovery group, based on the 12-step program, that helps individuals experiencing negative consequences from excessive online and video game playing. OLGA also offers help and support for friends and family members of gamers. Meetings and forums take place in face-to-face settings, as well as by Internet chat rooms and message boards.

Address: 104 Miller Ln., Harrisburg, PA 17110
Phone: 612-245-1115
Web site: http://www.olganon.org/

Overeaters Anonymous (OA): A self-help group offering a 12-step recovery program for people seeking freedom and health from a problem with overeating. OA focuses on physical and emotional wellness, not dieting or weight-loss.

Address: PO Box 44020; Rio Rancho, NM 87174-4020
Phone: 505-891-2664; Fax: 505-891-4320
Web site: http://www.oa.org/

Parents and Friends of Lesbians and Gays (PFLAG): A coalition of family and friends of gay, lesbian, bisexual, and transgendered persons that works to promote diversity and equality for people of all sexual orientations. Primary efforts include advocacy, providing community and support resources, and educating the society.

Address: 1726 M Street, NW; Suite 400; Washington, DC 20036
Phone: 202-467-8180; Fax: 202-467-8194
Web site: http://www.pflag.org/

Parents Anonymous: A child abuse prevention agency that works to strengthen families by providing support and training for parents. The organization also partners with community agencies to promote safe, nurturing home environments.

> Address: 675 W. Foothill Blvd., Suite 220; Claremont, CA 91711-3475
> Phone: 909-621-6184; Fax: 909-625-6304
> Web site: http://www.parentsanonymous.org/

Rape, Abuse & Incest National Network (RAINN):   RAINN works to help prevent sexual assault, provide assistance to victims, and achieve justice for perpetrators. The organization also runs the National Sexual Assault Hotline (800-656-HOPE).

> Address: 2000 L Street NW, Suite 406; Washington, DC 20036
> Phone: 800-656-HOPE; Fax: 202-544-3556
> Web site: http://www.rainn.org/

Rational Recovery: A recovery program providing instruction and materials for individuals to achieve permanent abstinence from any type of addiction. The program is an individual-focused program, and individuals work on their own toward their recovery.

> Address: PO Box 800; Lotus, CA 95651
> Phone: 530-621-2667; Fax: 530-621-4374
> Web site: http://rational.org/

Recoveries Anonymous (RA):   A 12-step solution-focused recovery group for persons with any problem or behavior, as well as family and friends of those seeking recovery.

> Address: PO Box 1212; East Northport, NY 11731
> Web site: http://www.r-a.org/

Recovery International (Recovery, Inc.):   A self-help organization, based on cognitive behavioral techniques, that offers peer-led support groups and a recovery method for those seeking healing from mental and behavioral disorders.

> Address: 802 N. Dearborn St.; Chicago, IL 60610
> Phone: 312-337-5661; Fax: 312-337-5756
> Web site: http://www.recovery-inc.org/

S-Anon: Family support groups for individuals by another person's sexual addiction, based on the 12-step recovery model.

> Address: PO Box 111242, Nashville, TN 37222-1242
> Phone: 800-210-8141, 615-833-3152
> Web site: http://www.sanon.org/

Save Our Selves/Secular Organizations for Sobriety (SOS):   A network of support groups that help individuals work toward sobriety from an addiction. SOS is an alternative to spiritually based and 12-step recovery approaches, respecting unique individual approaches to recovery.

> Address: 4773 Hollywood Blvd.; Hollywood, CA 90027
> Phone: 323-666-4295; Fax: 323-666-4271
> Web site: http://www.sossobriety.org/

Schizophrenia and Related Disorders Alliance of America (SARDAA):   A national organization supporting and offering hope to persons with schizophrenia and related disorders and their families. SARDAA supports Schizophrenics Anonymous, operates a telephone hotline, and provides education to this population and the general public.

> Address: PO Box 941222; Houston, TX 77094-8222
> Phone: 240-423-9432
> Web site: http://www.sardaa.org/

Schizophrenics Anonymous: A support group organization for people with schizophrenia. Meetings use a six-step program and promote professional help and medication use of members.

> Address: 15920 W. Twelve Mile; Southfield, MI 48076
> Phone: 810-557-6777; Fax: 810-557-5995

Sex Addicts Anonymous (SAA):   A 12-step organization helping men and women overcome sexual addiction.

> Address: PO Box 7094; Houston, TX 77270
> Phone: 800-477-8191
> Web site: http://saa-recovery.org/

Sex and Love Addicts Anonymous (SLAA):   A 12-step fellowship for individuals seeking recovery from sexual and love addiction, which can include compulsive sexual activity, overdependence on others, or obsession with romance, fantasy, or relationships.

> Address: 1550 NE Loop 410, Suite 118; San Antonio, TX 78209
> Phone: 210-828-7900; Fax: 210-828-7922
> Web site: http://www.slaafws.org/

Sexaholics Anonymous (SA):   Mutual help group for those who want to cease self-destructive sexual thoughts and behavior.

> Address: PO Box 3565; Brentwood, TN 37024-2565
> Phone: 615-370-6062; Fax: 615-370-0882
> Web site: http://www.sa.org

Sexual Compulsives Anonymous (SCA):   An organization of 12-step recovery groups dedicated to helping people who desire recovery from sexually compulsive behaviors.

> Address: PO Box 1585, Old Chelsea Station; New York, NY 10011
> Phone: 800-977-HEAL (4325)
> Web site: http://www.sca-recovery.org/

SMART Recovery: A self-management and recovery training program that provides recovery materials to help individuals gain freedom from addictions. SMART facilitates group meetings and online forums for the recovery process.

> Address: 7304 Mentor Ave., Suite F; Mentor, OH 44060
> Phone: 866-951-5357; Fax: 440-951-5358
> Web site: http://www.smartrecovery.org/

Suicide Prevention Action Network USA (SPAN USA):   Now part of the American Foundation for Suicide Prevention, SPAN USA is a community-based organization that works to prevent suicide by promoting public policy initiatives and education. The organization is comprised primarily of persons who have survived suicide attempts or are affected by the suicide of a loved one.

> Address: 1010 Vermont Ave., NW, Suite 408; Washington, DC 20005
> Phone: 202-449-3600; Fax: 202-449-3601
> Web site: http://www.spanusa.org/

Survivors of Incest Anonymous (SIA):   A self-help organization based on the 12 steps, providing support for adult survivors of childhood incest. Incest is defined loosely by the organization, including sexual and other unwanted touching activity by family, extended family, or other trusted adults.

> Address: PO Box 190; Benson, MD 21018-9998
> Phone: 410-893-3322
> Web site: http://www.siawso.org/

Tourette Syndrome Association (TSA):   An international group offering resources and referral support for persons with Tourette syndrome and their family members. TSA also works to understand the disorder more fully and to promote accurate public perceptions of the disorder.

> Address: 42-40 Bell Blvd., Suite 205; Bayside, NY 11361-2820
> Phone: 718-224-2999; Fax: 718-279-9596
> Web site: http://www.tsa-usa.org/

Women for Sobriety: A self-help program designed specifically for women with alcohol addiction. The program specifically addresses the unique issues women face in recovery

> Address: PO Box 618; Quakertown, PA 18951-0618
> Phone: 215-536-8026
> Web site: http://www.womenforsobriety.org/

Workaholics Anonymous: A recovery fellowship based on the 12-step group format, designed for men and women who desire to stop compulsive working. Meetings are available in person, online, and over the phone.

> Address: PO Box 289; Menlo Park, CA 94026-0289
> Phone: 510-273-9253
> Web site: http://www.workaholics-anonymous.org/

Appendix C: Marker Events in the History of Counseling and the American Counseling Association

1890s–Early 1900s

The end of the 19th and beginning of the 20th centuries was a time of turmoil and transition in the history of the United States. It was marked by industrialization, massive immigration from southern and eastern Europe, and migration within the country from farms to cities. This period was noted for labor unrest and abuse, mistreatment and exploitation of immigrants, and a good deal of social alienation and despair as the nation and its people went through rapid change. Amid this turbulence, reformers and progressives arose to try to make society more humane and to meet human needs. From their efforts, the seeds were sown that grew into what is now counseling and the American Counseling Association.

1900–1910

Three major figures, basically unknown to one another, begin what is to evolve into the profession of counseling: Frank Parsons, Clifford Beers, and Jesse B. Davis.

Parsons, working at the Vocational Bureau in Boston, devises a three-step process for choosing a vocation: knowledge of self, knowledge of jobs, and "true reasoning" to match oneself with a vocation. He writes a popular book that is published after his death in 1908: *Choosing a Vocation*.

Beers, a Yale student, is hospitalized for mental illness and writes about the deplorable conditions of psychiatric hospitals at the time in *A Mind That Found Itself*. His work is the beginning of the mental health movement.

Davis, the superintendent of schools in Grand Rapids, Michigan, mandates that teachers devote an hour a week to classroom guidance with an emphasis on the teaching of values and behaviors needed to be a good citizen.

1910–1920

The National Vocational Guidance Association is founded in 1913. It is the forerunner of the American Counseling Association.

Passage of the Smith-Hughes Act provides funding for public schools to support vocational education.

Psychometric testing becomes prominent as the United States enters World War I and instruments are needed to help classify recruits for positions in the armed forces.

1920–1930

The Strong Vocational Interest Inventory is published in 1927. It is the first refined, research-based psychometric test of vocational interest.

The certification of counselors begins in Boston and New York.

John and Hannah Stone set up a clinical practice in marriage and family counseling. They are among the early pioneers in couple and family counseling.

1930–1940

E. G. Williamson formulates a directed, counselor-centered approach to counseling known as the Minnesota Point of View. His theory is quite different from psychoanalysis and behavioral theories to counseling and psychotherapy that are popular at the time.

John Brewer advocates that education is guidance, with vocational decision making being a part of that process. He continues and expands on the legacy begun by Jesse B. Davis.

The United States government publishes the first edition of the *Dictionary of Occupational Titles,* a book that classifies and describes all jobs known in the country at the time.

1940–1950

Carl Rogers develops a nondirective, client-centered counseling approach in contrast to E. G. Williamson's counselor-centered approach.

Because of a lack of trained professionals and a need to work with GIs returning from World War II, the Veterans Administration provides grants to train psychologists and counselors through the American Psychological Association.

The American Psychological Association changes the name of its Division of Counseling and Guidance to the Division of Counseling Psychology.

1950–1960

Four independent associations—The National Vocational Guidance Association (NVGA), the National Association of Guidance and Counselor Trainers (NAGCT, now the Association for Counselor Education and Supervision-ACES), the Student Personnel Association for Teacher Education (SPATE, now the Counseling Association for Humanistic Education and Development C-AHEAD), and the American College Personnel Association (ACPA)—convene a joint convention in Los Angeles in 1952 in the hope of providing a larger professional voice. As a result, the American Personnel and Guidance Association (APGA) is established (which eventually evolves into the American Counseling Association).

The American School Counseling Association (ASCA) becomes the fifth division of APGA in 1953.

The American Rehabilitation Counselor Association (ARCA) is chartered as the sixth division of APGA in 1957.

Congress passes the National Defense Education Act (NDEA) in 1958. Title V-B of the act provides money for educating counselors, especially school counselors, and the number of counselors in schools begins to skyrocket.

New theories of counseling emerge: rational emotive therapy (Albert Ellis), transactional analysis (Eric Berne), Gestalt therapy (Fritz and Laura Perls).

1960–1970

The APGA publishes its first code of ethics in 1961.

Gilbert Wrenn writes *The Counselor in a Changing World,* with an emphasis on counseling across cultures and avoiding what he describes as the "culturally encapsulated counselor."

Behaviorism emerges as a prominent counseling approach led by John Krumboltz's book on the subject: *Revolution in Counseling.*

Reality therapy is formulated by William Glasser.

The Community Mental Health Centers Act is passed in 1963, establishing community mental health centers throughout the United States and opening up opportunities for counselors outside of educational settings.

Group work becomes popular as a counseling modality.

The APGA Senate recommends formation of a branch in every state, U.S. territories, and foreign countries.

The Association for Assessment in Counseling and Education (AACE) is chartered as the seventh division of APGA in 1965.

The National Employment Counseling Association (NECA) is chartered as the eighth division of APGA in 1966.

ERIC/CAPS is founded by Garry Walz in 1968 and it begins to build a database of research for counseling.

The Counseling Psychologist begins publication.

Civil rights, the Vietnam War, and the women's movement affect counseling.

1970–1980

Charters are granted to 56 APGA branches and numerous local chapters in 1970.

What are now the Association for Multicultural Counseling and Development (AMCD) and the International Association for Addiction and Offender Counseling (IAAOC) are chartered as the 10th and 11th divisions of APGA in 1972.

The Association for Specialists in Group Work (ASGW) is chartered as the 12th division of APGA in 1973.

What is now the Association for Spiritual, Ethical, and Religious Values in Counseling (ASERVIC) is chartered as the 13th division of APGA in 1974.

The term "community counselor" is coined to describe a counselor who works in multifaceted ways, often outside an educational setting.

The American Mental Health Counseling Association is chartered as the 14th division of APGA in 1978.

APGA relocates its Headquarters from Washington, DC to an interim facility in Falls Church, VA.

Basic helping skills that are atheoretical become popular in counseling circles and eclecticism grows.

Psychology and counseling begin to break into two separate professions over disputes regarding licensure and education (PhD vs. MA).

Virginia becomes the first state to license counselors in 1977.

1980–1990

The Council for Accreditation of Counseling and Related Education Programs (CACREP) is formed in 1981 and begins accrediting counselor education programs.

The National Board of Certified Counselors (NBCC) is established in 1982. It starts a national program of counselor certification.

APGA changes its name to the American Association for Counseling and Development (AACD) in 1984.

Chi Sigma Iota (counseling academic and professional honor society international) is established by Tom Sweeney in 1985.

AACD relocates its headquarters to a new building in Alexandria, VA.

The Association for Counselors and Educators in Government (ACEG) is chartered as the 15th division of AACD.

The American Counseling and Development Association governance (Senate, Board of Directors, and Executive Committee) are combined to form a single governance structure called the Governing Council.

The Association for Adult Development and Aging (AADA) is chartered as the 16th division of AACD in 1986.

The International Association for Marriage and Family Counseling (IAMFC) is chartered as the 17th division of AACD in 1989.

1990–2000

ACPA, one of the founding associations of APGA, disaffiliates as a division.

The American College Counseling Association (ACCA) is chartered as a division in 1991.

AACD changes its name to the American Counseling Association (ACA) in 1992.

The American Counseling Association newspaper, *GUIDEPOST,* changes its name to *Counseling Today.*

First-ever Counseling Awareness Month is celebrated in April.

President Clinton signs into law the American Counseling Association proposed Elementary School Counseling Demonstration Act (ESCDA).

In 1994, the ACA Governing Council creates an identity and vision statements for the association and revitalizes the mission statement. It also creates a Center for Effective Counseling Practice.

The Association of Gay, Lesbian Bisexual Issues in Counseling (AGLBIC) is chartered as a new division of ACA.

ACA files an amicus brief to the U.S. Supreme Court, which is cited along with the ACA *Code of Ethics and Standards of Practice* in the Court's 7–2 ruling in *Jaffee vs. Redmond,* stating that clients have the right to expect confidentiality. The Court rules that communications between psychotherapists and their clients are privileged and protected from forced disclosure.

ACA helps draft and adopt "The Principles for the Provision of Mental Health and Substance Abuse Prevention Treatment Services: A Bill of Rights."

Diversity, multiculturalism, and spirituality receive increased attention in counseling (e.g. the *Multicultural Counseling Competencies and Standards*).

The ACA Governing Council develops a unified definition of professional counseling.

ACAeNews: The electronic news and practice bulletin from the American Counseling Association is launched.

2000–2010

State licensure for counselors is adopted in 50 states, Washington, DC, and Puerto Rico with California being the last state to pass licensure in 2009.

The ACA Governing Council adopts the *Multicultural Counseling Competencies and Standards.*

Dr. Garry Walz initiates the *VISTAS* and *ACA Counseling Digest* projects to encourage more counselors to contribute to the professional literature in the field.

NBCC International is formed and begins supporting counseling efforts in countries outside the United States.

Wellness and technology grow in emphasis within counseling and ACA.

Dealing with managed care and HIPAA regulations becomes more burdensome, but counselors are added to more insurance plans.

A new emphasis on counselors dealing with crises, trauma, and tragedies emerges due to heightened violence in the schools, terrorists' attacks in New York and DC, Hurricane Katrina and its aftermath, the Virginia Tech tragedy, and the wars in Iraq and Afghanistan.

The Association for Creativity in Counseling (ACC) is chartered (2004) as the 19th division of ACA.

ACA publishes a revised code of ethics (2005).

20/20: A Vision for the Future of Counseling begins (2005) in an attempt to unify the profession of counseling. 29 out of 30 associations initially involved in this effort sign on to seven unifying principles to advance the counseling profession.

A new online, open journal, *The Professional Counselor: Research and Practice*, is started by NBCC.

New CACREP Standards on accreditation are formulated and put into effect beginning in 2009.